A TEXT BOOK OF

CONCRETE TECHNOLOGY

FOR

SEMESTER - I

SECOND YEAR DEGREE COURSE IN CIVIL ENGINEERING

ACCORDING TO NEW REVISED SYLLABUS OF

NORTH MAHARASHTRA UNIVERSITY, JALGAON

EFFECTIVE FROM JUNE 2013 - 2014

M. N. Bajad

M.E. (Structural), Research Scholar (NIT), Gold Medalist
Assistant Professor, Dept. of Civil Engg.
Sinhgad College of Engineering,
Vadgaon (Bk.), PUNE - 41

CONCRETE TECHNOLOGY (SE - CIVIL : NMU) ISBN 978-93-83525-53-9

Second Edition : August, 2015
© : Authors

The text of this publication, or any part thereof, should not be reproduced or transmitted in any form or stored in any computer storage system or device for distribution including photocopy, recording, taping or information retrieval system or reproduced on any disc, tape, perforated media or other information storage device etc., without the written permission of Authors with whom the rights are reserved. Breach of this condition is liable for legal action.

Every effort has been made to avoid errors or omissions in this publication. In spite of this, errors may have crept in. Any mistake, error or discrepancy so noted and shall be brought to our notice shall be taken care of in the next edition. It is notified that neither the publisher nor the authors or seller shall be responsible for any damage or loss of action to any one, of any kind, in any manner, therefrom.

Published By : **Printed By :**
NIRALI PRAKASHAN **Repro Knowledgecast Limited**
Abhyudaya Pragati, 1312, Shivaji Nagar **Thane**
Off J.M. Road, Pune – 411005
Tel - (020) 25512336/37/39, Fax - (020) 25511379
Email : niralipune@pragationline.com

☞ **DISTRIBUTION CENTRES**

PUNE
Nirali Prakashan : 119, Budhwar Peth, Jogeshwari Mandir Lane, Pune 411002, Maharashtra
Tel : (020) 2445 2044, 66022708, Fax : (020) 2445 1538
Email : bookorder@pragationline.com, niralilocal@pragationline.com

Nirali Prakashan : S. No. 28/27, Dhyari, Near Pari Company, Pune 411041
Tel : (020) 24690204 Fax : (020) 24690316
Email : dhyari@pragationline.com, bookorder@pragationline.com

MUMBAI
Nirali Prakashan : 385, S.V.P. Road, Rasdhara Co-op. Hsg. Society Ltd.,
Girgaum, Mumbai 400004, Maharashtra
Tel : (022) 2385 6339 / 2386 9976, Fax : (022) 2386 9976
Email : niralimumbai@pragationline.com

☞ **DISTRIBUTION BRANCHES**

JALGAON
Nirali Prakashan : 34, V. V. Golani Market, Navi Peth, Jalgaon 425001,
Maharashtra, Tel : (0257) 222 0395, Mob : 94234 91860

KOLHAPUR
Nirali Prakashan : New Mahadvar Road, Kedar Plaza, 1st Floor Opp. IDBI Bank
Kolhapur 416 012, Maharashtra. Mob : 9850046155

NAGPUR
Pratibha Book Distributors : Above Maratha Mandir, Shop No. 3, First Floor,
Rani Jhanshi Square, Sitabuldi, Nagpur 440012, Maharashtra
Tel : (0712) 254 7129

DELHI
Nirali Prakashan : 4593/21, Basement, Aggarwal Lane 15, Ansari Road, Daryaganj
Near Times of India Building, New Delhi 110002
Mob : 08505972553

BENGALURU
Pragati Book House : House No. 1, Sanjeevappa Lane, Avenue Road Cross,
Opp. Rice Church, Bengaluru – 560002.
Tel : (080) 64513344, 64513355,Mob : 9880582331, 9845021552
Email:bharatsavla@yahoo.com

CHENNAI
Pragati Books : 9/1, Montieth Road, Behind Taas Mahal, Egmore,
Chennai 600008 Tamil Nadu, Tel : (044) 6518 3535,
Mob : 94440 01782 / 98450 21552 / 98805 82331,
Email : bharatsavla@yahoo.com

niralipune@pragationline.com | www.pragationline.com

Also find us on www.facebook.com/niralibooks

PREFACE

I am extremely happy to present this book on **"Concrete Technology"** strictly as per the New Revised Syllabus of North Maharashtra University, Jalgoan.

This book contains simple language to explain fundamentals of this subject. This book provides logical method of explaining various complicated concepts and stepwise methods to explain the important topics. All chapters are arranged in a proper sequence that permits each topic to build upon earlier studies. Each chapter is well supported with necessary illustrations and neat diagrams.

This book covers the entire subject, that makes the understanding of this subject more clear and makes it more interesting. This book will be very useful not only to the students but also to the subject teachers.

I wish to express my thanks to all those who helped us directly, indirectly in making this book in a reality. I wish to thanks the Publisher, Shri. Dineshbhai Furia, Shri. Jignesh Furia and Shri. M. P. Munde who have taken immense effort to get this book in the time with quality printing. I am also thankful to Mr. Akbar Shaikh (for DTP), Mrs. Anjali Mule (for Figures drawn), Mrs. Anagha Kawre (for Proof reading).

I am also thankful to **Mr. Prithviraj More**, Branch Manager, Jalgoan Office for their help and efforts for promotion of this book.

At the last but not the least, we are also thankful to the reader. Any suggestion for the improvement of this book will be acknowledged and well appreciated.

4th September 2013

Pune

Authors

■■■

SYLLABUS

UNIT I [08 Hrs. : 16 Marks]

1. Cement: Manufacture of cement, Chemical composition, Setting and Hydration of Cement. Types of Cement, Properties of Testing of Cement.
2. Aggregates: Classification, Properties, Grading, Impurities in Aggregates and Testing of Aggregates, Its effect of Strength of Concrete, Quantity of water for concrete.

UNIT II [08 Hrs. : 16 Marks]

1. Fresh Concrete: Definition and its Ingredients, Grades of concrete, Concreting process, Significance of water cement ratio, Properties of fresh concrete.
2. Hardened Concrete: Various properties of hardened concrete, Factor affecting various properties, Micro cracking and Stress-strain relation, Testing of hardened concrete, Creep.
3. Shrinkage of concrete, Quality control during concreting.

UNIT III [08 Hrs. : 16 Marks]

1. Admixtures, Classification of their effects on various properties of concrete.
2. Types of concrete: Light weight concrete, Polymer concrete, Fiber reinforced concrete, Ready mixed concrete, Self compacting and High performance concrete, Ferro cement concrete.
3. Special concrete: Transparent concrete, Cellular light weight concrete, Pre-stressed concrete.
4. Under water concreting, Concreting in extreme weather conditions.

UNIT IV [08 Hrs. : 16 Marks]

Concrete Mix Design
1. Introduction, Object of Mix Design, Factors to be considered, Statistical quality control, Introduction to different methods of Mix Design, Scaffolding, Shoring, Under pinning and strutting, Types, Purposes and Precautions.
2. Concrete mix design by I.S. (10262-456) method and IRC method.

UNIT V [07 Hrs. : 16 Marks]

1. Introduction to Non-destructive testing of concrete, Rebound hammer, Ultrasonic pulse velocity, Pull out test, Impact echo test.
2. Deterioration of concrete, Permeability, Durability, Chemical attack, Carbonation of concrete, Corrosion of reinforcement.

■■■

CONTENTS

1. **INTRODUCTION TO CONCRETE AS A CONSTRUCTION MATERIAL**   1.1 – 1.50

2. **FRESH AND HARDENED CONCRETE**   2.1 – 2.36

3. **ADMIXTURES, TYPES OF CONCRETE AND SPECIAL CONCRETE**   3.1 – 3.36

4. **CONCRETE MIX DESIGN**   4.1 – 4.54

5. **NON-DESTRUCTIVE TESTING AND DETERIORATION OF CONCRETE**   5.1 – 5.16

QUESTION PAPER (MARCH 2015)   P.1 – P.2

Unit 1
INTRODUCTION TO CONCRETE AS A CONSTRUCTION MATERIAL

[A] CEMENT

1.1 Introduction

Concrete is a composite material formed by the combination of (a) cement, (b) aggregate and (c) water, in a particular proportion in such a way that concrete produced meets the need of the job on hand, particularly as regards its workability, strength, durability and economy.

Hence, it is necessary to understand the details of the above materials.

1.2 Cement

Cement in general can be defined as a material which possesses very good adhesive and cohesive properties which make it possible to bond with other materials to form a compact mass. That is, cement is a material which possesses cementatious properties. Cement is the most important and costliest ingredient of concrete. It was invented by Joseph Aspdin of U.K. in 1824. He named it Portland Cement because the hardened concrete made out of the cement, fine aggregates, coarse aggregates and water in definite proportions resembled the natural stone occurring at portland in England. The materials which set and harden in the presence of water are said to possess hydraulic properties. As cement gets strength due to the chemical action between cement and water and its ability to harden under water, it is also known as *hydraulic cement*.

1.3 Manufacture of Portland Cement

The manufacture of cement involves three distinct operations as shown in Fig. 1.1.

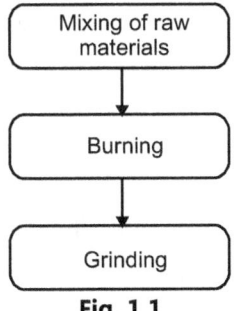

Fig. 1.1

1.3.1 Mixing of Raw Materials

The raw materials used in the manufacture of cement are:

(a) Agrillaceous materials – consisting of silicates of alumina in the form of clays and shales, and

(b) Calcareous materials – in the form of limestone, chalk and marl, which is a mixture of clay and calcium carbonate. These materials are mixed thoroughly. The mixing of raw materials can be done in two ways as shown in Fig. 1.2.

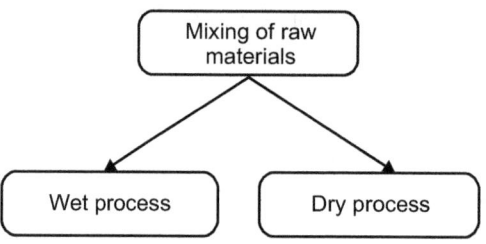

Fig. 1.2

1.3.2 Wet Process

In the earlier part of the century i.e. from 1913 to 1960, the wet process was popular for the manufacture of cement. This was because of the possibility of more accurate control in mixing of the raw materials. The techniques of intimate mixing of raw materials were not available then. Later, with the development of the technique of dry mixing of powdered materials using compressed air, the dry process gained momentum.

The dry process requires much less fuel as the materials are already in a dry state, whereas in the wet process the slurry contains 35% to 50% water. To dry the slurry, more fuel is required. In the wet process, the calcareous materials such as limestone are crushed and stored in silos or storage tanks. The algrillaceous material such as clay is thoroughly mixed with water in a wash mill. The washed clay is then stored in basins. Now, the crushed limestone from the silos and wet clay from basins are mixed together in a wet grinding mill to make slurry. The slurry is led to the correcting basin where it is constantly stirred. At this stage, the chemical composition of the slurry is tested and adjusted as necessary. The corrected slurry is stored in storage tanks and kept ready to serve as feed for a rotary kiln.

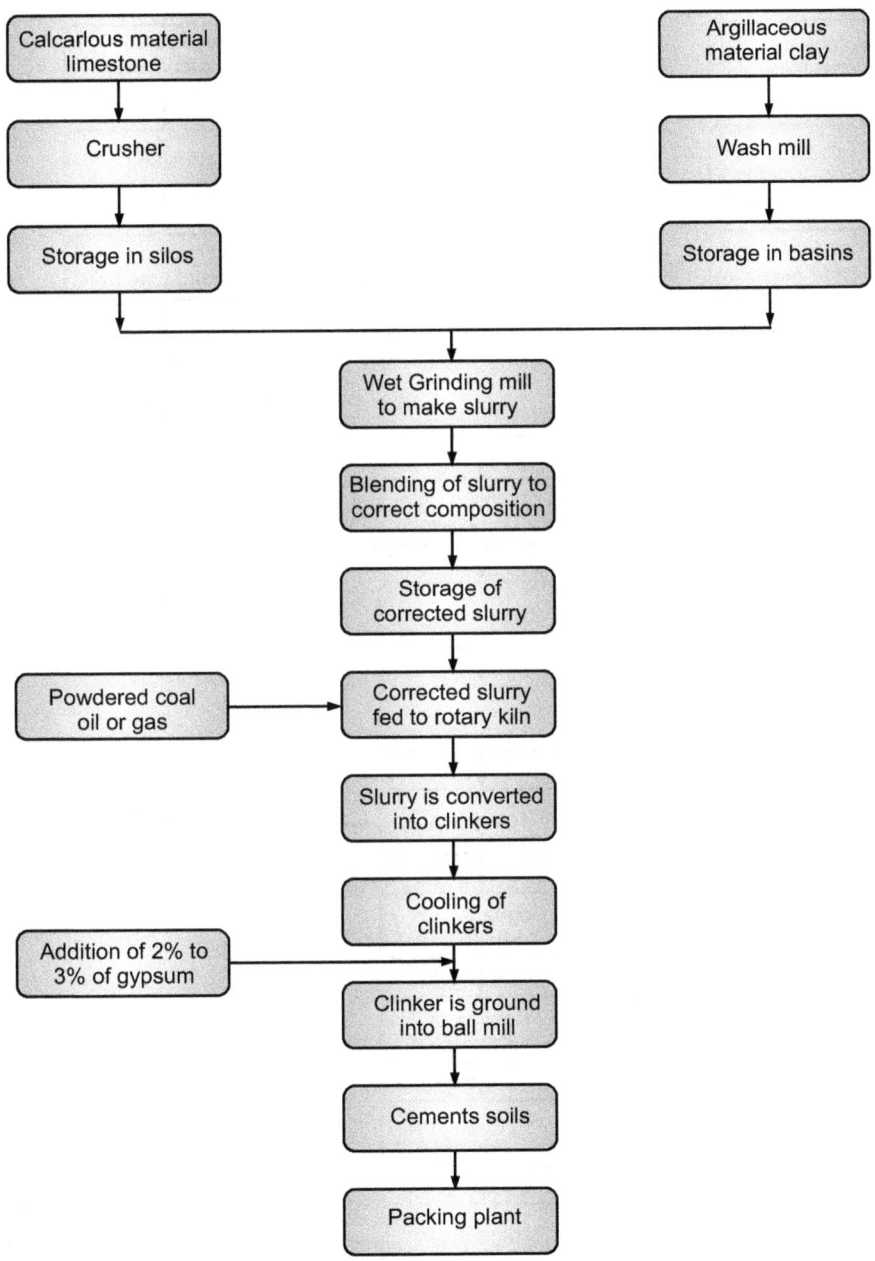

Fig. 1.3: Wet Process of Cement Manufacturing

1.3.3 Dry Process

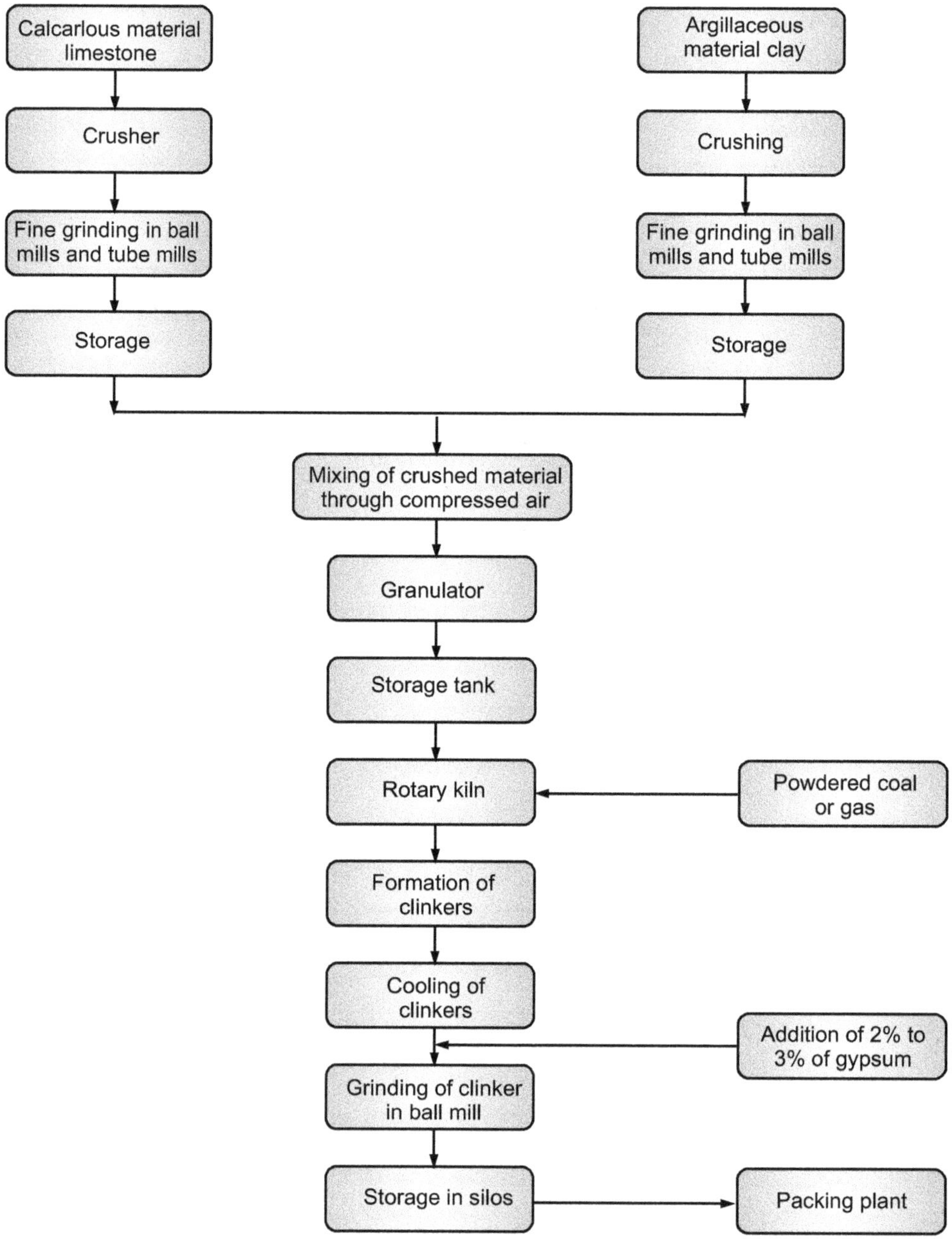

Fig. 1.4: Dry Process of Manufacturing of Cement

The boulders of limestones upto 1.2 m size are transported in huge dumpers and dumped into the hoopers of the crusher. The limestone is now crushed to a size of 75 mm. The crushed limestone is moved from the crusher by a series of conveyors for stacking. The argillaceous material is also crushed and stacked like the limestone. The crushed materials are checked for calcium carbonate, lime, alumina, ferrous oxide and silica contents. Any material found short, is added separately. The materials are then ground to the desired degree of fineness. The dry powder, called the raw meal, is then further blended and corrected for its right composition and mixed by means of compressed air.

The aerated powder tends to behave almost like liquid and in about one hour of aeration, a uniform mixture is obtained. The blended meal is further sieved and feed into a rotating disc called *granulator*. A small quantity of water, about 12% by weight, is added to make the blended meal into pellets. This is done to permit air flow for exchange of heat for further chemical reactions and conversion for the same into clinkers in the rotary kiln.

1.3.4 Burning

Burning is carried out in a rotary kiln. Rotary kiln for a wet process is shown in Fig. 1.5.

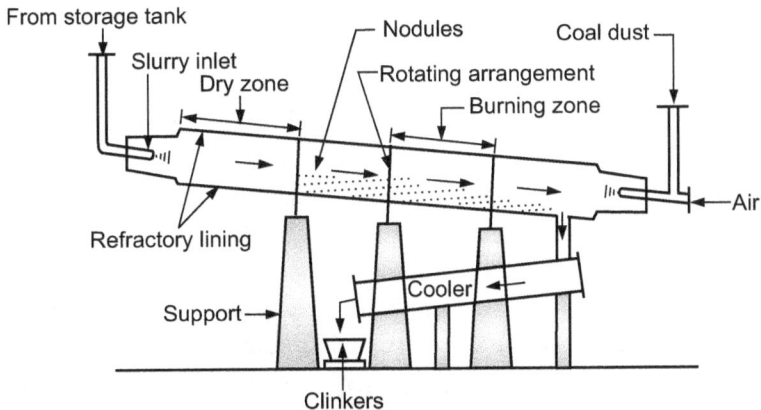

Fig. 1.5: Rotary Kiln for Wet Process

The rotary kiln is so arranged that it rotates at about one to three revolutions per minute, about its longitudinal axis. It is laid at a gradient of about 1 in 25 to 1 in 30. The corrected slurry is injected at the upper end of the kiln and hot gases or flames are forced through the lower end. The portion of the kiln near its upper end is known as the *dry zone*. In this zone, the water of the slurry is evaporated. As the slurry gradually descends, there is an increase in temperature and in the next section of the kiln, carbon-di-oxide from the slurry is evaporated. This leads to the formation of small lumps known as *nodules*. These nodules then gradually roll down to the burning zone, where the temperature is about 1400°C to 1500°C. In the burning zone, the nodules are calcined and formation of small, hard, dark greenish-blue balls known as *clinkers* take place.

In the dry process, coal brought from coal fields is pulverised in vertical coal mill and is stored in silo. It is pumped with required quantity of air through the burners. The preheated raw materials roll down the kiln and get heated to such extent that carbon-dioxide is expelled along with other combustion gases. The material is then heated to a temperature of 1400°C to 1500°C and the formation of clinckers take place.

The size of the clinkers varies from 3 mm to 20 mm. The temperature of the clinkers coming out of the burning zone of the kiln is as high as 1000°C. A rotary kiln of small size is provided to cool down the hot clinkers. Cooled clinkers, having temperature of about 95°C, are collected in containers of suitable sizes.

1.3.5 Grinding

The clinkers, so obtained from the rotary kiln, are ground to the required degree of fineness in a ball mill or a tube mill. During grinding, a small quantity of gypsum (about 3% to 4%) is added. Gypsum controls the initial setting time of cement. If gypsum is not added, the cement would set soon as water is added to it. Thus, gypsum acts as a retarder, and delays the initial setting action of cement.

1.4 Basic Chemistry of Cement

The chief chemical constituents of portland cement are lime, silica, alumina, iron oxide, magnesium oxide and little amount of sulpher trioxide and soda etc. Their chemical composition is as follows:

1. **Lime (CaO):** Lime is the most important ingredient of cement. Its proportion in a good cement is generally in the range of 60% to 67%. However, lime in excess causes the cement to expand and disintegrate. On the other hand, if lime is in deficiency, the strength of cement is decreased and it also causes the cement to set quickly.
2. **Silica (SiO_2):** Silica is also an important ingredient of cement. Its proportion in a good cement is generally in the range of 17% to 25%. It imparts strength of the cement due to the formation of dicalcium and tricalcium silicates. If silica is present in excess, though the strength of the cement increases but at the same time its setting time is also increased.
3. **Alumina (Al_2O_3):** Alumina imparts quick setting property to the cement. It acts as a flux and lower down the clinkering temperature. However, high temperature is essential for the formation of a suitable type of cement and hence, alumina should not be present in excess, as it weakens the cement. In a good cement, the content of alumina is confined to 3% to 8%.
4. **Calcium sulphate ($CaSO_4$):** Calcium sulphate is in the form of gypsum. Its function is to increase the initial setting time of cement. In a good cement, the content of calcium sulphate is confined to 3% to 4%.

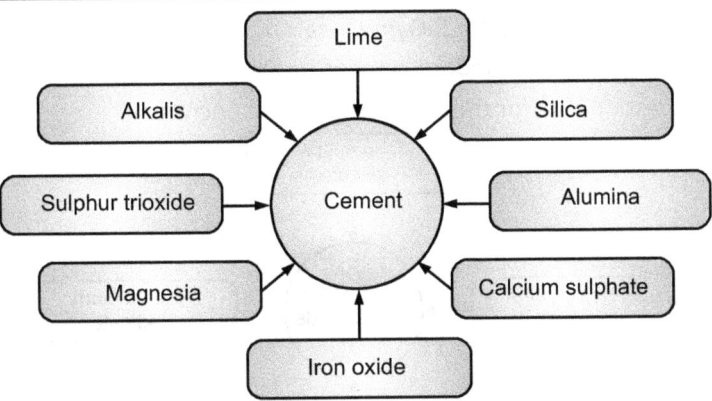

Fig. 1.6: Chemical Composition of Cement

5. **Iron oxide (Fe_2O_3):** Iron oxide imparts colour, hardness and strength to the cement. A good cement should have 3% to 4% of iron oxide.
6. **Magnesia (MgO):** Magnesia, if present in small amount, imparts hardness and colour to the cement. However, a high content of magnesia makes the cement unsound. Therefore, an ideal concentration of magnesia is between 0.5% to 4%.
7. **Sulphur trioxide (SO_3):** A very small amount of sulphur is present in the form of sulphur trioxide. It is useful in making the cement sound. However, if it is in excess, the cement becomes unsound. Therefore, sulphur trioxide should be present in the range of 1% to 2%.
8. **Alkalies:** Most of the alkalies present in raw materials are carried away by the flue gases during heating and the cement contains generally Na_2O and K_2O. It should be tried that the presence of these alkalies should be as low as possible (not more than 1%). If they are present in excess, they cause a lot of problems such as alkali-aggregate reaction, efflorescence etc.

1.5 Chief Constituents of Cement

As mentioned above the oxides present in the raw materials when subjected to high clinkering temperature combine with each other to form complex compounds. The identification of the major compounds is largely based on R.H. Bogue's work and hence it is called "Bogue's Compounds". The four compounds usually regarded as major compounds are:

1. **Tri-calcium silicate ($3CaO \cdot SiO_2$):** Tri-calcium silicate is designated as C_3S. The average C_3S content in a modern cement is 30% to 50% by mass. C_3S rapidly reacts with water and produces comparatively more heat of hydration. It is responsible for the early strength of concrete. A cement with more C_3S content is better for cold weather concreting.

2. **Di-calcium silicate (2CaO · SiO₂):** Di-calcium silicate is designated as C_2S. The average C_2S content in a modern cement is 20% to 45% by mass. C_2S hydrates rather slowly. It is responsible for the later strength of concrete.

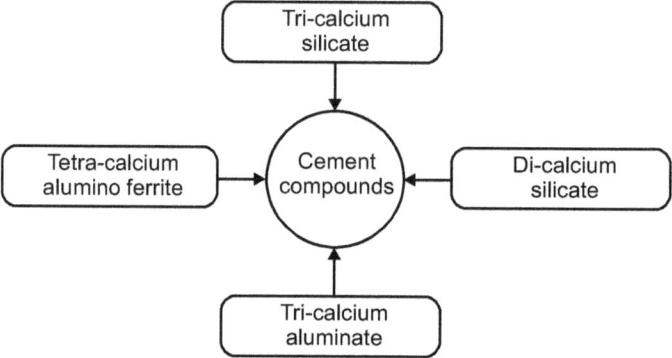

Fig. 1.7: Bouge's Cement Compound

3. **Tricalcium aluminate (3CaO · Al₂O₃):** Tri-calcium aluminate is designated by C_3A. The average content of C_3A in a modern cement is 8% to 12% by mass. The reaction with water is very fast and this may lead to flash set. To prevent this flash set, gypsum is added to the time of grinding the cement clinker. The hydrated aluminates do not contribute anything to the strength of the paste. It is responsible for initial setting of cement.

4. **Tetra-calcium alumina ferrite (4CaO · Al₂O₃ · Fe₂O₃):** It is designated as C_4AF. The average content of C_4AF in a modern cement is 6% to 10% by mass. The contribution of the hydrated product of C_4AF towards the strength is negligible, but it gives the higher resistance to the attack of sulphate.

In Fig. 1.8 and Fig. 1.9 the two graphs are showing the development of strength of pure compounds with respect to time and the rate of hydration of pure cement compounds.

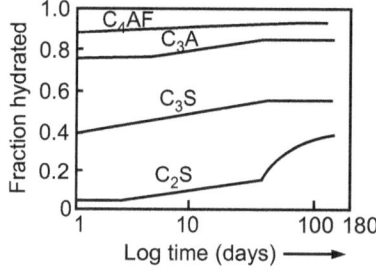

Fig. 1.8: Rate of Hydration of Pure Cement Compounds

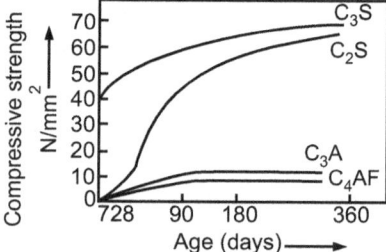

Fig. 1.9: Contribution of Cement Compounds to the Strength of Cement

1.6 Hydration of Cement

When the water is added to cement, a chemical reaction starts which is exothermic in nature and produces a significant amount of heat. This is known as *hydration* and the liberated heat is called the *heat of hydration*. The process of hydration is not an instantaneous. It is faster in the early periods and continues indefinitely at slower rate. In about a month's time, 85 to 90 per cent of the cement hydrates and the cement attains almost its full strength. The hydration still continues and cement grows stronger with time. The process of hydration may be explained as follows:

In a cement paste i.e. a thorough mixture of cement and water, chemical reaction soon starts and after a lapse of some time, the paste consists of hydrates of various compounds, collectively called gel, unhydrate cement, water and residue of the water-filled spaces in the fresh paste. These voids are called *capillary pores*. The cementing gel consists of thin fibrous crystals which is porous in nature. These pores are called gel-pores. About 23% of water by mass of cement is required for chemical reaction of cement with water and is known as bound water. About 15% of water by mass of cement is required to fill the gel-pores and is known as gel-water. Thus, a total of 38% of water by mass of cement is required for complete hydration. In this discussion, it is assumed that the reaction takes place in a sealed container. The remaining water mixed with cement causes undesirable capillary cavities. If only 38% of water is added, the capillary cavities can be eliminated. The products of hydration are colloidal and because of this, during hydration the surface area of solid phase increases enormously. This absorbs a large amount of free water. If water added is 38%, all the colloids are not sufficiently saturated which decreases the relative humidity of the paste.

This leads to a lower hydration as the gel can be formed only in water filled space. This requires a minimum of 50% of water by mass of cement or in other words, a water-cement ratio in excess of 0.5 is sufficient for hydration. In actual conditions, the reaction does not take place in a sealed container and with lower percentage of water, the concrete mix would not be workable. A mix is workable if it can be easily mixed, placed and compacted at the required place. Usually about 50 to 60% of water by mass of cement is added to manufacture the concrete. The rate of hydration is mainly influenced by:

1. **The temperature at which hydration takes place:** At high temperatures the reaction is rapid. Only 10 to 15 minutes of hydration at higher temperature is equivalent to 10 to 12 hours of hydration at lower temperatures. It is for this reason that in cold weather, sometimes the aggregates are heated before they are used for making concrete.
2. **The fineness of cement:** The finer the cement, the more rapid is the reaction. As the hydration starts at the surface of the cement particles, the larger the available surface

area, the more rapid is the hydration. Finer cements have larger surface areas and therefore the hydration is rapid. However, a very fine ground cement is susceptible to air-set and deteriorates earlier.

3. **The ingredients of cement:** The reaction can be made rapid or slow by changing the properties of the ingredients of the cement.

1.7 Classification of Cement

Portland cements are classified under the American Society for Testing Materials (A.S.T.M.) standards. As per ASTM, cement is designated as Type I, Type II, Type III, Type IV, Type V and other minor types like Type IS and Type IP etc.

Type I: Normal portland cement: This is the general purpose cement suitable for all use when the special properties of the other types are not required.

Type II: Modified portland cement: This cement has a lower heat of hydration than type I and generates heat at a slower rate. It also has improved resistance to sulphate attack.

Type III: High early strength portland cement: This cement is used where high strengths are desired at very early periods.

Type IV: Low heat portland cement: This is a special cement for use where the amount and rate of heat generated must be kept to a minimum. The development of strength is also at a slower rate. It is intended for use only in large masses of concrete such as large gravity dams where temperature rise resulting from the heat generated during hardening is a critical factor.

Type V: Sulphate resistant portland cement: This is a special cement intended for use only in structures exposed to severe sulphate action, such as in soils, and waters of high alkali content. It has a slower rate of hardening than normal portland cement.

1.8 Types of Cements

By changing slightly the chemical composition, it is possible to obtain cement exhibiting different properties. Hence, cement can be manufactured to suit the desired properties. The following are the types of cement.

(a) Ordinary portland cement (OPC).
(b) Rapid hardening portland cement (RHPC)
(c) Extra-rapid hardening portland cement.
(d) Portland blast-furnace cement.
(e) Low heat portland cement.

(f) Sulphate resisting portland cement.
(g) White portland cement.
(h) Coloured portland cement.
(i) Super-sulphate cement.
(j) Masonry cement.
(k) Expansive cement.
(l) Oil-wet cement.
(m) Hydrophobic cement.
(n) Pozzolana cement.
(o) High-Alumina cement.
(p) High-strength cement.
(q) Acid-resisting cement.
(r) Quick setting cement.
(s) Blended cement.

Some of them are described below:

Ordinary Portland Cement:

It is a widely used cement for most of the works. It is suitable for general construction works when there is no exposure to sulphates in the soil or in the ground water. The manufacturing of cement as discussed in Art. 1.3, pertains to the ordinary portland cement.

For using the portland cement to produce high strength concrete (M35 and above) for specialized works; high strength cement is required. The Bureau of Indian Standards has therefore introduced three different grades of ordinary portland cement. Consequently, ordinary portland cement is now available in three different grades as follows:

1. Grade 33 (IS : 269 – 1989)
2. Grade 43 (IS : 8112 – 1987)
3. Grade 53 (IS : 12269 – 1987)

The grade indicates the compressive strength of cement at 28 days. Testing according to IS : 4031 (Methods of physical tests for hydraulic cement). Higher strength of cement (grade 43 and grade 53) is achieved by:

1. Selecting good quality of limestone as a raw material.
2. Using low ash coal firing as the coal ash is detrimental to the quality of clinker.
3. Ratio of CaO with SiO_2, Al_2O_3 and Fe_2O_3 is always maintained during manufacturing.
4. At all stages of manufacturing, required quality controls are carefully exercised.

With a better quality of limestone, having higher percentage of $CaCO_3$, the cement of higher grade (even 63 grade) can be produced. In India, good quality limestone deposits are localised at Ranavav in Gujrat, Ariyalur deposits in Tamil Nadu, Gotan of Rajasthan etc.

The chemical properties of 33 grade, 43 grade and 53 grade cements are tabulated in Table 1.1.

Table 1.1

Chemical properties	33 grade IS : 269 - 1989	43 grade IS : 8112 - 1989	53 grade IS : 12269 - 1987
1. Loss on ignition, percent, maximum	5.0	5.0	4.0
2. Insoluble residue, percent, by mass, maximum	4.0	2.0	2.0
3. Magnesia, (MgO), percent, maximum	6.0	6.0	6.0
4. Sulphur, percent, maximum as SO_3	2.5	2.5	2.5
5. Tricalcium aluminate (C_3A), maximum	0.66	0.66	0.66
6. Lime saturation factor (LSF)	0.66 to 1.02	0.66 to 1.02	0.8 to 1.02

Rapid Hardening Cement (IS : 8041 – 1990):

As the name implies, it hardens and attains its strength earlier than ordinary portland cement. Three days hardening of this cement is equivalent to seven days hardening of ordinary portland cement. The rapid hardening property of this cement is achieved by a higher C_3S content and by finer grinding of the cement clinker. Due to this property, early stripping of concrete formwork becomes possible.

This is advantageous where repeated use of the same shuttering is made i.e. precast works or where speedy development of strength is important. For example, road repair works. Rapid hardening cement should not be confused with quick setting cement which sets quickly but does not harden quickly. In the early stages this cement gives out a large quantity of heat of hydration. This cement must not be used for mass concrete or for large structural sections because due to a large quantity of heat of hydration, the temperature inside the concrete increases, leading to formation of undesirable cracks on cooling.

Extra-rapid Hardening Portland Cement:

It is manufactured by intergrinding about 2% calcium chloride and rapid hardening portland cement. While using this cement, maximum time of 10 minutes is available for mixing, transporting and placing the concrete. Also this cement should be used within one month. This cement attains strength more rapidly than rapid hardening cement and is used for special purposes like repair works, especially in cold weather.

Low Heat Portland Cement (IS : 12600 – 1989):

It is manufactured by reducing the percentage of C_3S and C_3A of ordinary portland cement. As a result, this cement gets the strength at a slower rate and the heat of hydration is less. This will require long time curing and keeping forms for a long time. This cement is particularly useful for mass concrete works. According to IS : 12600, the heat of hydration for this cement is limited to 314 kJ/kg at 28 days. Ordinary portland cement generates about 502 kJ/kg heat of hydration at 28 days.

Sulphate Resisting Cement (IS : 12330 – 1988):

It is similar to ordinary portland cement except that it contains more silicates and less quantity of aluminates. The heat of hydration of this cement is low and it develops higher ultimate strength, although the early strength of this cement is low. It is used for underwater structures particularly exposed to alkali actions.

Quick Setting Cement:

As the name implies, it sets quickly. This does not mean that it achieves the strength quickly. It sets quickly but does not harden quickly. In the manufacture of this cement, gypsum content is reduced to get the quick setting property. It is particularly used for underwater constructions. It sets very quickly so that the time available for mixing, transporting and placing the concrete is very short and its use in general works must be avoided.

High Strength Cement:

It has very high strength as compared to ordinary portland cement and is used in special works such as prestressed concrete and precast concrete works. This cement must not be confused with rapid hardening cement.

High Alumina Cement (IS : 6452 – 1989):

It is a non-portland cement. It is manufactured by melting mixture of aluminous and calcareous materials in suitable proportion and grinding the resulting clinker to fine powder which is black in colour. It hardens and develops strength very rapidly, giving out a great amount of heat. Its one day's strength is equal to 28 day's strength of ordinary cement. It is strongly resistant to chemical attack and is suitable to sea and underwater works. It is not recommended in tropical region.

White Cement (IS : 8042 – 1989):

It is manufactured in the same way as portland cement. The grey colour of portland cement is due to the presence of iron oxide (about 4%). If the raw materials selected for manufacturing portland cement are such that they do not contain iron oxide, the resulting cement is white in colour. The raw materials are chosen to see that the maximum Iron oxide content is less than one per cent. White clay and China clay are used as raw materials in the manufacturing of this cement and coal firing is replaced by oil fuel firing. This results in white coloured cement. It is used for white concrete (as may be required architecturally) or for white finishing works.

Coloured Cement:

These are manufactured by adding 5 to 10% of ground pigments to ordinary or white portland cement. The pigments are chemically inert and have fast colours. The proportion and type of pigments added vary according to the colour desired. Thus, iron oxide is added to give red and yellow, cobalt to give blue and magnese dioxide to give black colour.

Hydrophobic Cement (IS : 8043 – 1978):

It is manufactured by grinding ordinary portland cement clinker with 0.1 to 0.4 % of oleic acid, stearic acid. This addition forms water repellent film around each particle of cement and therefore transportation and storage of this cement is not affected by the moisture content of atmosphere. When concrete is prepared using this cement, the water repellent film breaks out which improves the workability of concrete. The storage of ordinary portland cement in humid places causes deterioration in the quality of cement. For such places this cement is useful.

Masonry Cement (IS : 3466 – 1988):

It is specially manufactured for masonry works, plaster works etc. by intergrinding very finely ground portland cement, limestone and an air-entraining agent. It can also be manufactured by intergrinding portland cement and hydrated lime, granulated cement or crushed stone. Addition of these materials give good workability, reduces shrinkage and water retentivity. The cement mortar prepared from this cement is more plastic, cohesive and strong and yet workable, than that prepared from ordinary portland cement which produces a harsh mortar. When ordinary portland cement is used, due to its less water retentivity, the masonry absorbs water from the mortar resulting in a poor bond. This difficulty is overcome when masonry cement is used. However, the strength of mortar is reduced. This cement must not be used for concrete works.

Expansive Cement:

It is used to neutralize the shrinkage of concrete to eliminate cracks. An ordinary portland cement shrinks while setting due to the loss of free water, whereas the volume of expanding cement increase on hardening. This does not mean that expanding cement produces a 'shrinkless' concrete but the magnitude of expansion can be adjusted in such a way that strinkage and expansion of volume are numerically equal. A small percentage of this cement when added to the concrete, will eliminate cracks. This is specially used for hydraulic structures.

Super-sulphate Cement:

This cement is made from well-granulated slag (80 to 85%) and calcium sulphate (10 to 15%) together with 1 to 2% of portland cement. Its specific surface is between 3500 and 5000 cm²/g. It is free from false set having initial setting time between $2\frac{1}{2}$ to 4 hours and final setting between $4\frac{1}{2}$ and 7 hours.

Its total heat of hydration is very low, about 165 to 190 kJ/kg at 7 days and 190 to 210 kJ/kg at 28 days, which make it very suitable for mass concreting but requires great care while concreting in cold weather.

Concrete made from supersulphate cement may expand or contract slightly on setting according to conditions and hence should be properly cured.

Super-sulphate cement can be used for all purposes. Its setting action is different from other cements and admixtures should not be used with it. If used in R.C.C. work, a minimum cover 35 mm is necessary. It must not be mixed with high alumina cement since the action will be different. It is highly resistant to chemical attack. If cured in air, the surface gets softened by atmospheric CO_2. Hence, water curing is always preferable.

In a normal 1: 2: 4 mix, with W/c ratio 0.55, the strengths are 350 kg/cm² at 7 days; nearly 500 kg/cm² at 28 days and between 500 to 700 kg/cm² at 6 months.

This cement gives comparatively high resistance to chemical attack. Its rate of hardening increases with the temperature upto about 38°C but above that it decreases.

Blended Cement:

We are facing the problem of waste disposal due to industrialization. Many industries like iron, and metal manufacturing industry, thermal power station produces extensively large amount of waste produces such as blast furnace slag, flyash respectively. So using waste materials such as blast furnace slag, flyash as pozzolanic substitutes for portland cement can result in reduction of environmental pollution. The goal, then, is to specify blended cements.

Blended cement is the cement with a fixed percentage of pozzolana, replacing the portland cement clinker portion of the cement mix. The pozzolanic material should be mixed within the percentage given by ASTM. This percentage of substitution is generally 20 – 60% of total volume.

The pozzolanic materials which are mixed in the blended cement are: Fly ash, Ground granulated blast furnace slag, Rice husk, Silica fume etc.

Table 1.2 shows the allowable composition of blended cements:

Table 1.2

Cement type	Component %		
	Clinker	Flyash	Slag
Portland flyash	65 - 94	6 - 35	Nil
Portland slag	65 - 94	Nil	6 - 35
Blast furnace	20 - 64	Nil	35 - 80

On top of that, appropriate percentage of gypsum may be added.

Blended cement is more advantageous than other cements in the following respect:

1. Blended cement is more economical than other cements as it contains many industrial waste products.
2. Generation of green house gases can be minimised. As blended cement contains burnt material.
3. Less heat of hydration is produced in blended cement concrete.
4. Problem of waste disposal can be solved. As blended cement contains industrial waste.
5. Eco-friendly behaviour of concrete produced by blended cement.
6. The use of blended cement is advantageous particularly when dealing with sulphate resistance, alkali-silica resistance or chloride induced corrosion resistance. Hence it can be easily used in Marine construction.
7. Concrete with blended cements require less amount of water for same workability level.

Blended cements are used in the following constructions:
(a) Wall, floors and columns of building, bridges and industrial plants.
(b) All types of foundations.
(c) Concrete pipes, blocks; precast concrete elements.
(d) Prestressed piles, concrete roads; soil stabilization.
(e) Bridge in sea water environment; sewage systems etc.

Examples: Portland pozzolana cement, blast furnace slag portland cement etc.

Portland Pozzolana Cement:

This cement is manufactured by grinding portland cement clinker with pozzolana and required quantity of gypsum. The pozzolanas are materials which at ordinary temperatures, react with lime in presence of water, resulting in cementing materials. Fly ash, burnt clay and pumicite are used as pozzolana. Addition of pozzolana is 10 to 25% of the pozzolana cement by mass. The advantages of this cement are: reduced cost, increased impermeability, increased workability, less heat of hydration and if offers greater resistance to the attack of aggressive waters. However, the rate of hydration is low and gaining of strength is slower upto 14 days. If the concreting done by this cement is properly cured at 28 days, the strength of this cement is equal to that of ordinary portland cement.

Blast Furnace Slag Portland Cement:

It is manufactured by mixing portland cement clinker with granulated blast furnace slag (a waste product from blast furnace which contains oxide of lime, silica and alumina) and gypsum in suitable proportions and grinding the mixture to the required fineness. The slag proportion is limited to 65% of the mass of the mixture. According to IS : 455 - 1976, the slag content should not be less than 25% and not more than 65% of the total mass of the mixture. It has low heat of hydration, more durability and is better resistant to soil and water containing excessive amounts of sulphates; alkalies, metals as well as acidic waters. It is helpful for marine works.

1.9 Testing of Cement

To ensure the quality of cement, specifications are drawn in various Indian standards. The cement should conform to the requirements of these specifications. For this, a number of tests on cement are carried out to ensure that the cement is of required standards. Test are also necessary to check the quality of cement periodically. Testing of cement may be field testing and/or laboratory testing. Field testing is used only to get an idea of the quality. If a cement satisfies field testing, it can be said that the cement is not bad. However, to conclude finally that the cement is of a good quality, the laboratory testing is required.

The following are the field tests:

1. The cement should look greenish grey in colour. There should not be any presence of lumps.
2. The cement should give smooth feeling when rubbed between the fingers.
3. It should give a cool feeling when a hand is thrust into a cement bag.
4. If a handful of cement is thrown in water, the cement should float for a few minutes before it sinks.

The laboratory tests include the methods of sampling, methods of physical tests and methods of chemical tests. All these are discussed in details in respective Indian Standard specifications.

The methods of sampling are described in IS : 3535 - 1986 (Method of sampling hydraulic cement) and may be referred. The chemical tests are described in IS : 4032 - 1985

(Methods of chemical analysis) and may be referred. In the following articles, some physical tests for cement are described and are in accordance with IS : 4031 - 1988/91. The following tests are usually conducted in the laboratory as shown in Fig. 1.10.

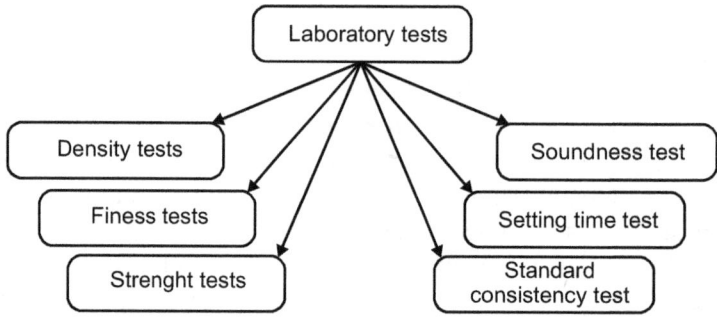

Fig. 1.10

1.9.1 Fineness Test

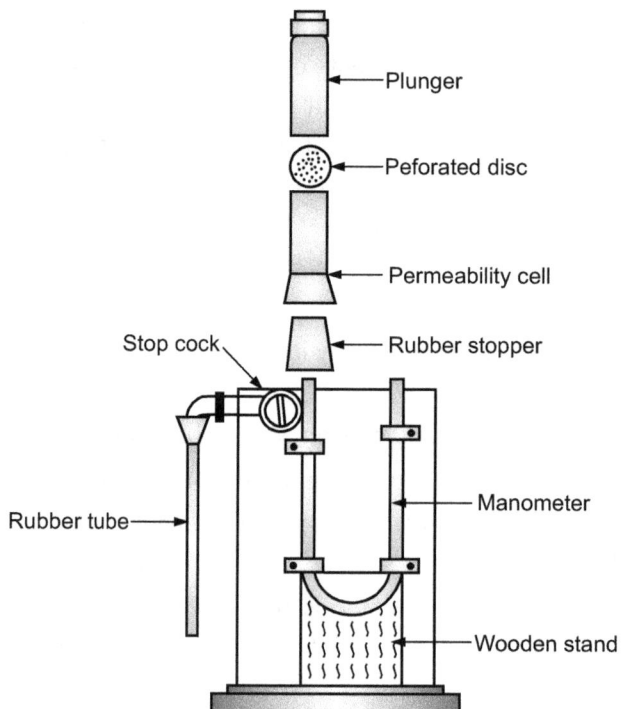

Fig. 1.11: Blaine Air Permeability Apparatus

Strength development of concrete is the result of the reaction of water with cement particles. The reaction start with the cement available at the surface of the particles. Thus, larger the surface area available for reaction, greater is the rate of hydration. Repaid development of strength requires greater degree of fineness. Rapid Hardening Cement, therefore, requires greater degree of fineness.

However, too much fineness is also undesirable, because the cost of grinding the cement to higher fineness is considerable. Finer cement deteriorates more quickly when exposed to air and likely to cause more shrinkage, but less prone to bleeding. Greater fineness also requires greater amount of gypsum for proper retardation. Also amount of water requirement for the paste of standard consistency is greater.

It is, therefore, necessary to ensure certain amount of coarseness in the cement, but maximum limit to this coarseness is prescribed by BIS to ensure minimum degree of grinding.

Procedure: Refer Appendix – Experiment 4.

1.9.2 Standard Consistency Test

Cement paste of normal consistency is defined as percentage of water by weight of cement which produces a consistency which permits a plunger of 10 mm diameter. To penetrate up to a depth of 5 mm to 7 mm above the bottom of Vicat's Mould.

Before performing the test for initial setting time, final setting time, compressive strength, tensile strength and soundness of cement etc., it is necessary to fix the quantity of water to be mixed to prepare a paste of cement of standard consistency in each case. The quantity of water to be added in each of the above mentioned experiment bears a definite relation with the percentage of water for standard consistency. This experiment is intended to find out for a given cement, the quantity of water to be mixed to give a paste of standard consistency.

Percentage of water in the cement paste 'P' for standard consistency will vary from cement to cement and from batch to batch of the same cement, and the quantities of water used in the other tests will vary accordingly. Following are the quantities of water required for various tests:

(i) Quantity of water for setting time test expressed as percentage of weight of cement = 0.85 P

(ii) Quantity of water for soundness test expressed as percentage of weight of cement
    (a) Le Chatelier method = 0.78 P
    (b) Autoclave method = P

(iii) Quantity of water for compressive strength on 1 : 3 cement and standard sand mortar expressed as percentage of weight of dry cement and aggregate = P/4 + 3.0 Where, P is the percentage of water for standard consistency.

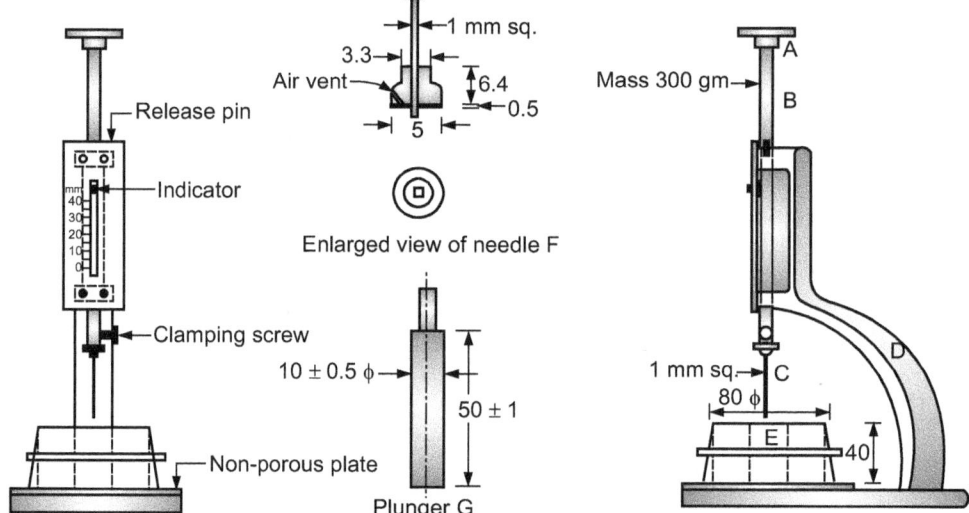

Fig. 1.12: Vicat Apparatus

Procedure: Refer Appendix – Experiment 1.

1.9.3 Setting Time Test

When water is mixed with cement to form a paste, reaction starts. In its pure form, the finely ground cement is extremely sensitive to water. Out of the three main compounds viz. C_3A, C_3S and C_2S, the C_3A reacts quickly with water to produce jelly-like compound which start solidifying. This action of changing from a fluid state to a solid state is called 'Setting' and should not be confused with 'Hardening'.

During the next stage of hydration, cement paste starts hardening owing to the reaction of C_3S and C_2S and the paste gains strength. In the first few minutes, the seting action is more predominant and after some time hardening action becomes rapid.

In practice, such solidifying action or loss of plasticity is required to be delayed, because some time is needed for mixing transporting and placing of concrete into final position before the mix looses its plasticity due to setting action.

It is usually specified that the plastic concrete should be placed and consolidated before initial set has occurred, it should not then be disturbed until concrete has hardened. This initial setting time should not be too small and therefore, the standards specify minimum initial setting time.

Once initial stiffening of concrete has taken place it is desirable that it should harden or gain strength as rapidly as possible, so that there is minimum of delay before shuttering can be removed and risk of frost-damage minimized. Standards, therefore, specify maximum value of final setting time.

It is not possible, however, in practice to exactly locate the initial setting time and final setting time. The Indian standards have selected two arbitrary points which relate strength of cement to time from adding water.

'Initial setting time' is defined as 'the period elapsing between the time when the water is first added to the cement and the time at which the needle of 1 mm square section (Fig. 1.12), fails to pierce the test block, to a depth of about 5 mm from the bottom of mould'. 30 minutes is minimum initial setting time specified by ISI for ordinary, rapid hardening and other cement and 60 min. for low heat cement.

The 'Final setting time' is defined as 'the period elapsing between the time when the water is added to the cement and the time at which the needle of 1 mm square with 5 mm diameter attachment (shown in the Fig. 1.12) makes an impression on the test block, while the attachment fails to make an impression on the test block. 600 minutes is the maximum time specified for final set for all the above mentioned Portland cements.

Procedure: Refer Appendix – Experiment 2.

1.9.4 Soundness Test

It is essential that cement concrete does not undergo large change in volume after it has hardened. This is ensured by limiting the quantities of free-lime (CaO) and magnesia (MgO) in cement. During manufacture of cement, free-lime is produced. Free-lime reacts with water and increases in volume considerably. Magnesia also has the same effect but its rate of reaction is slow. Larger percentage of free-lime and magnesia, if present, therefore, tends to increase the volume of the hardened concrete, thus causing disintegration. The cement is, therefore, said to be unsound when the percentage of free-lime and magnesia is more than that specified by Bureau of Indian standard.

Unsoundness is measured with the help of the Le-Chateliar mould as explained in the procedure.

It must be specially mentioned here that in the event of the cements failing to comply with the above requirement, a further test should be made by the "Le-Chatelier Method" from another portion of the sample after aeration by spreading it out to a depth of 75 mm at a relative humidity of 50 to 80 per cent for a total period of 7 days. The expansion of the aerated sample is determined with the "Le-Chatelier Method" which shall not be more than 5 mm as given in BIS.

Procedure: Refer Appendix – Experiment 3.

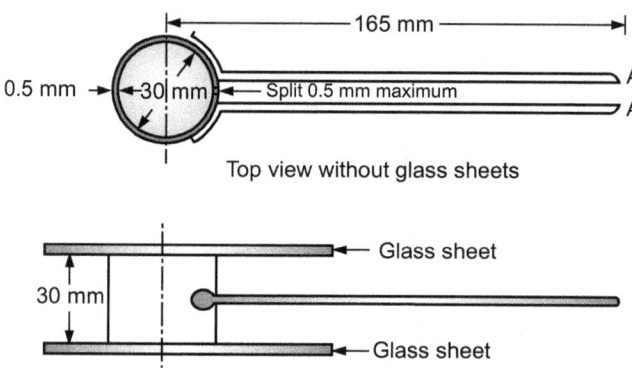

Fig. 1.13: Le Chatelier's Apparatus

1.9.5 Compressive Strength Test

The compressive strength test is the final check on the quality of cement. The compressive strength is measured by determining the compressive strength of cement mortar cubes of 1 : 3 proportions. The fine aggregate used is the standard sand specified by IS 650. The compression test enables also to distinguish rapid hardening cement from low heat and ordinary cement. The O.P.C. is now being classified as 33 Gr. O.P.C., 43 Gr. O.P.C. and 53 Gr. O.P.C. depending on the strength of cement. C.R.R.I. has developed curves for concrete compressive strength v/s water cement ratio corresponding to the 7 and 28 days compressive strengths of cement. The compressive strength of cement enables us to distinguish cements of different strength and maximum use can be made of high strength cement.

Procedure: Refer Appendix – Experiment 5.

1.9.6 Density Test

The object of this test is to determine the density of cement. Refer IS : 4031 - part XI.

Apparatus : Standard Le Chatelier flask

Materials : Kerosene (light oil) free from water

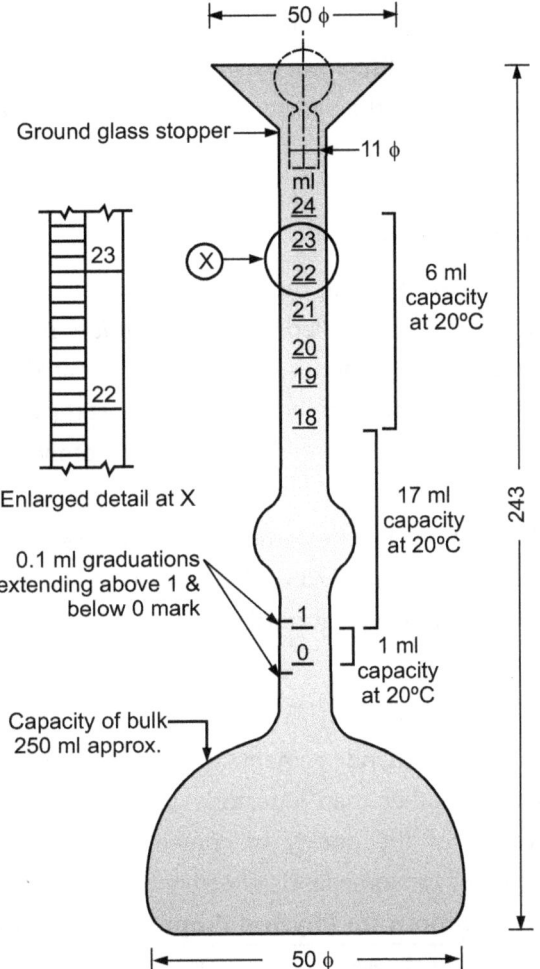

Fig. 1.14: Le Chatelier Flask for Density Test

Procedure: Fill the flask with kerosene to a point on the stem between zero and 1 ml mark. The inside of the flask above the level of the liquid, shall be dried if necessary, after pouring. Immerse the flask in a constant temperature water bath and record the first reading. About 64 gm of cement is then introduced in small amounts at the same temperature of the liquid. Care shall be taken that cement does not stick to the portion of the flask above the surface of the oil. After all the cement has been introduced, the flask is fitted with stopper and rolled in an inclined position so that the cement is free from air, until no further bubbles rise to the surface of the liquid. The final reading of the oil in the flask is then taken after the flask has been immersed in water bath to maintain the temperature.

Calculation: The difference between the first reading (R_1) and the final reading (R_2) represents the volume of liquid displaced by the cement and is equal to the volume of cement. If mass of the cement is m, the density (ρ) of the cement is calculated as

$$\rho = \frac{m}{R_1 - R_2} \text{ gm/cm}^3$$

1.9.7 Heat of Hydration Test

When water is added to the cement, the hydration of cement starts. This is exothermic and releases a large amount of heat called *heat of hydration*. It is estimated that 1 gm of ordinary portland cement generates about 500 Joules of heat during hydration. This is a particularly serious matter in the case of large mass concreting works such as dams where the high temperature developed in the interior of the concrete will cause serious crackings. Therefore, in such works, low heat cement is used.

The test for heat of hydration shall be carried out for low heat cement only. When tested by the standard method as specified by IS : 4031 (Method of physical test for hydraulic cement), the heat of hydration of low heat portland cement shall not be more than 272 kJ/kg at 7 days and 314 kJ/kg at 28 days.

1.9.8 Specific Gravity

The specific gravity of portland cement is generally 3.15, but that of cement manufactured from materials other than limestone and clay, the value may vary. Specific gravity is not an indication of the quality of cement. It is used in calculation of mix proportions. The specifications for some kinds of cements are tabulated in Table 1.3.

Table 1.3: Specifications for Physical Properties of Portland Cements

Sr. No.	Properties	IS : 269 ordinary 33 grade	IS : 8112 ordinary 43 grade	IS : 12269 ordinary 53 grade	IS : 12600 low heat	IS : 8041 rapid hardening	IS : 1484 portland pozzolana	IS : 6452 High alumina
1.	**Fineness**							
	Residue by mass on IS sieve 90 not to exceed percent*	10	10	10	5	–	5	–
	Specific surface (m²/kg) by air permeability method, not less than	225	225	225	320	325	300	225

contd. ...

2.	Setting time							
	Initial setting time in minutes, not less than	30	30	30	60	30	30	30
	Final setting time in minutes, not more than	600	600	600	600	600	600	600
3.	**Soundness**							
	By Le Chatelier method specimen shall not have expansion of more than (mm)	10	10	10	10	5	10	5
4.	**Compressive strength (N/mm^2)**							
	At 24 hours ± 30 min, not less than	–	–	–	–	16	–	30
	At 72 ± 1 hours, not less than	16	23	27	10	27.5	16	35
	At 168 ± 2 hours, not less than	22	33	37	16	–	22	–
	At 672 ± 4 hours, not less than	33	43	53	35	–	33	–

*This specification is not included in the new editions of respective IS standards.

[B] AGGREGATES

1.10 Introduction

Water, cement and crushed rock or gravel and sand – are the chief ingredients of concrete. About 75% of volume of concrete is composed of aggregates and hence properties of aggregate greatly affect the properties of concrete such as workability, strength, durability and economy. Originally, aggregate was looked upon an inert material dispersed throughout the cement paste mainly for economic reasons. But, in fact, its physical, thermal and sometimes also chemical properties influence the performance of concrete. Aggregate being cheaper than cement, it is economical to put into the concrete as much of the aggregate as possible. But the aggregate is not used only from the economical viewpoint but the higher volume stability and better durability (than the cement paste alone), which is due to the aggregate, is more valuable.

1.11 Classification of Aggregates

The classification of the aggregates is generally based on their geological origin, size, shape, unit weight etc.

1.11.1 Classification According to Geological Origin

The aggregates are usually derived from natural sources and may have been naturally reduced to size (e.g. gravel or shingle) or may have to be reduced by crushing. The suitability of the locally available aggregate depends upon the geological history of the region. The aggregate may be divided into two categories; namely the natural aggregates and artificial aggregates.

Natural Aggregate: These are generally obtained from natural deposits of sand and gravel, or from quarries by cutting rocks. Cheapest among them are the natural sand and gravel which have been reduced to their present size by natural agents, such as water, wind and snow etc. The river deposits are the most common and have good quality. The second most commonly used source of aggregates is the quarried rock which is reduced to size by crushing. Crushed aggregates are made by breaking rocks into requisite graded particles by blasting, crushing and screening etc. from the petrological stand point. The natural aggregates, whether crushed or naturally reduced in size, can be divided into several groups of rocks having common characteristics. Natural rocks can be classified according to their geological mode of formation. i.e. igneous; sedimentary or metamorphic origin, and each group may be further divided into categories having certain petrological characteristics in common. Such a classification has been adopted in IS : 383: 1970.

Artificial Aggregate: The most widely used artificial aggregates are clean broken bricks and air-cooled fresh blast-furnace slag. The broken bricks of good quality provide a satisfactory aggregate for the mass concrete and are not suitable for reinforced concrete work if the crushing strength of brick is less than 30 to 35 N/mm^2. The bricks should be free from lime mortar and lime sulphate plaster. The brick aggregate is not suitable for waterproof construction. It has poor resistance to wear and hence it is not used in concrete for the road work.

The blast-furnace slag is the byproduct obtained simultaneously with pig iron in the blast furnace, which is cooled slowly in air. Carefully selected slag produces concrete having properties comparable to that produced by using gravel aggregate. However, the corrosion of steel is more due to sulphur content of slag, however, the concrete made with blast-furnace-slag aggregate has good fire resisting qualities. The other examples of the artificial slag are the expanded shale, expanded slag; cinder etc. Such aggregates should not contain more than one per cent of sulphates and should not absorb water more than 10% of their own mass.

1.11.2 Classification According to Size

The aggregates used in concrete range from few centimetres or more, down to a few microns. The maximum size of the aggregate may vary, but in each case it is to be so graded that the particles of different size fractions are incorporated in the mix in appropriate proportions. The particle size distribution is called the *grading of aggregate*. According to size, the aggregate is classified as: fine aggregate, coarse aggregate and all-in-aggregate.

Fine aggregate: It is the aggregate most of which passes through a 4.75 mm IS sieve and contains only so much coarser material as is permitted by the specifications. Sand is generally considered to have a lower size limit of about 0.07 mm. Material between 0.06 mm and 0.002 mm is classified as silts, and still smaller particles are called *clay*. The soft deposit consisting of sand, silt and clay in about equal proportions is termed *loam*. The fine aggregate may be one of the following types:

(a) Natural sand, i.e. the fine aggregate resulting from natural disintegration of rock and/or that which has been deposited by stream and glacial agencies.

(b) Crushed stone sand, i.e. the fine aggregate produced by crushing hard stone, or

(c) Crushed gravel sand, i.e. the fine aggregate produced by crushing natural gravel.

According to size, the fine aggregate may be described as coarse, medium and fine sands. Depending upon the particle size distribution, IS : 383 - 1970, has divided the fine aggregate into four grading zones. The grading zones become progressively finer from grading zone I to grading zone IV.

Coarse aggregate: The aggregate most of which are retained on the 4.75 mm IS sieve and contain only so much of fine material as is permitted by the specifications are termed as coarse aggregates. The coarse aggregate may be one of the following types:

(a) Crushed gravel or stone obtained by the crushing of gravel or hard stone,

(b) Uncrushed gravel or stone resulting from the natural disintegration of rock, or

(c) Partially crushed gravel or stone obtained as a product of the blending of the above two types.

All-in-aggregate: Sometimes combined aggregates are available in natural comprising different fractions of fine and coarse aggregates, which are known as all-in-aggregate. The all-in-aggregates are not generally used for making high quality concrete.

Singe size aggregate is the bulk of aggregate which passes one size on the normal concrete series and is retained on the next smaller size.

Graded aggregate is the aggregate comprising of a proportion of all sizes from a given normal maximum to 4.25 mm. When these sizes are so proportioned as to give a definite grading, it is a well graded aggregate.

1.11.3 Classification According to Shape

The aggregate shape is important as it affects the workability of concrete. The shape of aggregate is defined using certain geometrical characteristics of particles. Classification of aggregates based on the shape of aggregate as given by IS : 383 - 1963 is tabulated in Table 1.4.

Table 1.4: Particle Shape

Classification	Description	Example
Rounded	Fully water-worn or completely shaped by attrition.	River or sea shore gravels, desert, and wind blown sand.
Irregular or partly rounded	Naturally irregular or partly shaped by attrition and having rounded edges.	Pit sands and gravels, dug flints or rocks.
Angular	Processing well defined edges formed at the intersection of roughly plane faces.	Crushed rock of all types, talus, screes.
Flaky	Material usually regular of which the thickness is small relative to the width and/or length.	Laminated rocks.

To achieve the best possible strength, concrete should be as dense as possible i.e. it should contain minimum voids. The voids are greatly influenced by the shape of aggregates. The rounded particles can be packed to produce a concrete with 33% voids i.e. 67% of the volume of concrete is occupied by the aggregates. The rounded particles produce smoother mix for a given Water/Cement (W/C) ratio. On the other hand, the angular and flaky particles reduce the workability and demand more cement and water to give the specified strength of concrete mix. Not more than 10 to 15% of flaky particles should be used in concrete.

1.11.4 Classification According to Surface Texture

According to surface texture the aggregates are classified as glassy, smooth, granular, rough, crystalline and honeycombed. This classification is based on degree to which the particle surfaces are polished or dull and smooth or rough. The surface texture of aggregate depends on the properties of parent materials. Such as hardness, grain size and pore characteristics. Examples of surface texture are as follows:

(a) Glassy : Black flint
(b) Smooth : Chert, slate, marble
(c) Granular : Sandstone, oolite
(d) Rough : Basalt, limestone
(e) Crystalline : Granite, gabbro, gnesis
(f) Honeycombed : Brick, pumice, trass, clinker.

1.11.5 Classification Based on Unit Weight

The aggregates can also be classified according to their unit weights as normal-weight, heavy-weight and light-weight aggregates.

Normal-weight aggregates: The commonly used aggregates i.e. Sands and gravels; crushed rocks such as granite, basalt, quartz, sandstone and limestone; and brick ballast etc., which have specific gravities between 2.5 and 2.7 produce concrete with densities ranging from 2300 kg/m^3 to 2600 kg/m^3 and crushing strength at 28 days between 15 to 40 N/mm^2 are termed as normal-weight aggregates.

Heavy-weight aggregates: Some heavy-weight aggregates having specific gravities ranging from 2.8 to 2.9 but unit weights from 2800 kg/m^3 to 2900 kg/m^3 such as magnetite (Fe_3O_4), barytes ($BaSO_4$) and scrap iron are used in the manufacture of heavy weight concrete. Concrete having densities of about 3000 kg/m^3, 3600 kg/m^3 and 5700 kg/m^3 can be produced by using magnetite, baryte and scrap iron, respectively.

Light-weight aggregates: The light-weight aggregates having bulk density upto 1200 kg/m^3 are used to manufacture the structural concrete and masonry blocks for reduction of the self weight of the structure. These aggregates can be either natural, such as diotomite, pumice, volcanic cinder etc. or manufactured, such as bloated clay, sintered flyash or foamed blast-furnace-slag. In addition to reduction in the weight, the concrete produced by using light-weight aggregate provides better thermal insulation and improved fire resistance.

1.12 Properties of Aggregates

1.12.1 Mechanical Properties

The following important mechanical properties of aggregate when the aggregate is subjected to wearing surfaces, are:

1. Toughness
2. Hardness
3. Crushing value of aggregate (compressive strength).

The toughness of aggregate which is measured as the resistance of the aggregate to failure by impact is determined in accordance with IS : 2386 (part - IV) - 1963. The aggregate impact value shall not exceed 45% by weight for aggregate used for concrete other than those used for wearing surfaces and 30% for concrete for wearing surfaces.

The hardness of aggregate defined as 'its resistance to wear' and obtained in terms of aggregate abrasion value is determined by using Los Angeles machine as described in IS : 2386 (part-IV)-1963. The method combines the test for attrition and abrasion. A satisfactory aggregate should have an abrasion value of not more than 30% of aggregates used for wearing surfaces and 50% for aggregates used for non-wearing surface.

The aggregate crushing value is a relative measure of the resistance of an aggregate sample to crushing under gradually applied compressive load. The crushing value of aggregate is restricted to 30% for concrete used for road pavements and 45% for other structures.

1.12.2 Physical Properties

The physical properties of aggregates depend on:
(i)   Size of aggregate
(ii) Shape of aggregate
(iii) Surface texture of aggregate
(iv) Bulk density
(v)   Specific gravity
(vi) Moisture content of aggregate
(vii) Porosity and water absorption.

The shape of the aggregates, influence the workability of fresh concrete and bond between the aggregate and the mortar phase. The shape of aggregates are of four categories like rounded, irregular, angular and flaky. The angular aggregates having thickness smaller than the width and/or length are termed as flaky. The rounded aggregate requires lesser amount of water and cement paste for a given workability. On the other hand, the use of crushed aggregate may result in 10 to 20% higher compressive strength due to development of stronger aggregate-mortar bond. The flakiness index of a coarse aggregate is generally limited to 25%.

The surface texture is a measure of the smoothness or roughness of the aggregate. The surface texture may be classified as glassy, smooth, granular, rough, crystalline, porous and honeycombed.

Shape and surface texture of aggregate influence considerably the strength of concrete. The flexural strength is more affected than the compressive strength and the effects of shape and texture are more significant in the case of high strength concrete.

The bulk density of an aggregate can be used for judging the quality of aggregate by comparison with normal density for that type of aggregate. It is also required for converting proportions by weight into the proportions by volume.

The specific gravity is required for the calculations of the yield of concrete or of the quantity of aggregate required for a given volume of concrete. The specific gravity of an aggregate gives valuable information on its quality and properties. Higher the specific gravity of an aggregate, indicates the stronger and harder aggregate.

There is no theoretical relation between the strength of concrete and the water-absorption of the aggregate used. The pores of surface of the particle affect the bond between the aggregate and cement paste. Thus, affecting the strength. Also the porosity affect the bond between the aggregate and the cement paste, the resistance of concrete to freezing and throwing, resistance to abrasion and the specific gravity of aggregate.

1.13 Impurities in Aggregates

The materials whose presence may adversely affect the strength, workability and long-term performance of concrete are termed *deleterious materials*. These are considered undesirable as constituent because of their intrinsic weakness, softness, fineness or other physical or chemical characteristics harmful to the concrete behaviour.

The aggregate may contain deleterious substances such as:

1. Product of decay and vegetable matter.
2. Organic impurities which interfere the hydration of cement.
3. Surface coatings which prevent the development of good bond between aggregate and cement paste.
4. Salt when aggregate is obtained from sea-shore etc.
5. Weak or unsound particles.

These are described below in brief:

1.13.1 Organic Impurities

The organic impurities in aggregate usually consists of products of decay or vegetable matter (mainly tunic acid and its derivatives). They may interfere with the chemical reactions of hydration. These impurities can be easily washed away. The impurities sometimes may be temporary i.e. they initially interfere with the hydration but they are not effective later on. Concrete made out of these aggregates shows lower strength in earlier periods but at 28 days give satisfactory results. All the organic matter is not harmful. However, if aggregate contains organic impurities, it shall be tested according to IS : 2386 (part-II).

1.13.2 Surface Coatings

Clay, silt and crusher dust may be present in the aggregates. Because of the extreme fineness of these materials, they completely coat the aggregate, increase the amount of water needed for mixing and interfere with the bond between aggregate and cement paste. These impurities can be harmful if the coatings are chemically reactive. Before using such aggregates, they should be washed. The quantities of these materials can be determined by laboratory test as per IS : 2386 (part-II).

1.13.3 Salt Contamination

Sand obtained from sea-shore or from a river estuary contains salt. This salt is harmful as it absorbs water from air, causes efflorescence and corrosion of reinforcement. The simplest method is to wash the aggregate in fresh water.

1.13.4 Unsound Particles

The aggregate may contain unsound particles such as shale, clay lumps, coal, wood etc. These particles may adversely affect the strength and durability of concrete. IS :383-1963 gives limiting values of such impurities and should be observed. The total amount of deleterious materials should not exceed 5% as per IS :383-1970. The limits of deleterious materials are given in Table 1.5.

Table 1.5: Limits of Deleterious Materials (Maximum Percentage of Mass)

Deleterious substances	Fine aggregate		Coarse aggregate	
	Uncrushed	Crushed	Uncrushed	Crushed
Coal and lignite	1.0	1.0	1.0	1.0
Clay lumps	1.0	1.0	1.0	1.0
Soft fragments	–	–	3.0	–
Material passing 75 µm IS sieve	3.0	3.0	3.0	3.0
Shale	1.0	–	–	–

1.14 Grading Requirements

The strength of full compacted concrete depends only upon the water-cement ratio and not on the grading of aggregate. But the grading of aggregate affects the workability which is in turn affects the water and cement requirements, controls segregation, has some effect on bleeding, and influence the placing and finishing of the concrete. These factors represent the important characteristics of fresh concrete and affect also its properties in the harden state. viz. strength, shrinkage and durability.

The main factors, which govern the desired aggregate grading are: the surface area of the aggregate, the relative volume occupied by the aggregate, the workability of the mix, and the tendency to segregation. Of course, economy is also an important factor.

1.15 Standard Grading

IS : 383 (specifications for coarse and fine aggregates from natural sources for concrete), the aggregates are graded as follows:

(a) Coarse aggregates: Single sized coarse aggregates should be supplied in the nominal sizes as shown in Table 1.6. Graded coarse aggregates should be supplied in the nominal sizes given in table 1.6. Fig. 1.15 and 1.16 indicates the practical grading curves produced by road research laboratory (U.K.) for all in aggregates graded down from 20 mm and 40 mm respectively. This is published as Road Research Note No. 4 on the design of concrete mixes. Similar curves for aggregates with maximum size of 10 mm and below have been prepared by MCIntosh and Erntroy's (Fig. 1.17).

Curve No. 1 at the bottom indicates the coarse set grading and curve No. 4 at the top represents the fine grading. Zones A, B, C are the grading zones between these curves. The coarse grading produces more workable even with the low W/C ratio, but it may segregate readily. The finer grading is more cohesive but less workable concrete i.e. for the same workability and aggregate/cement ratio, the fine grading requires higher water content and it reduces the strength of concrete. In case of grading of aggregate lying partly in one zone and partly in another zone with absence of too many intermediate sizes, it represents the gap grading. The gap graded aggregate is liable to segregate.

In practice, the grading of aggregate may not confirm to any one of standard grading curves exactly. The coarse and fine aggregates are supplied separately. Knowing their gradings, it is possible to control the proportion of each fraction in the mix such that the grading of all in aggregate conforms the standard grading limits.

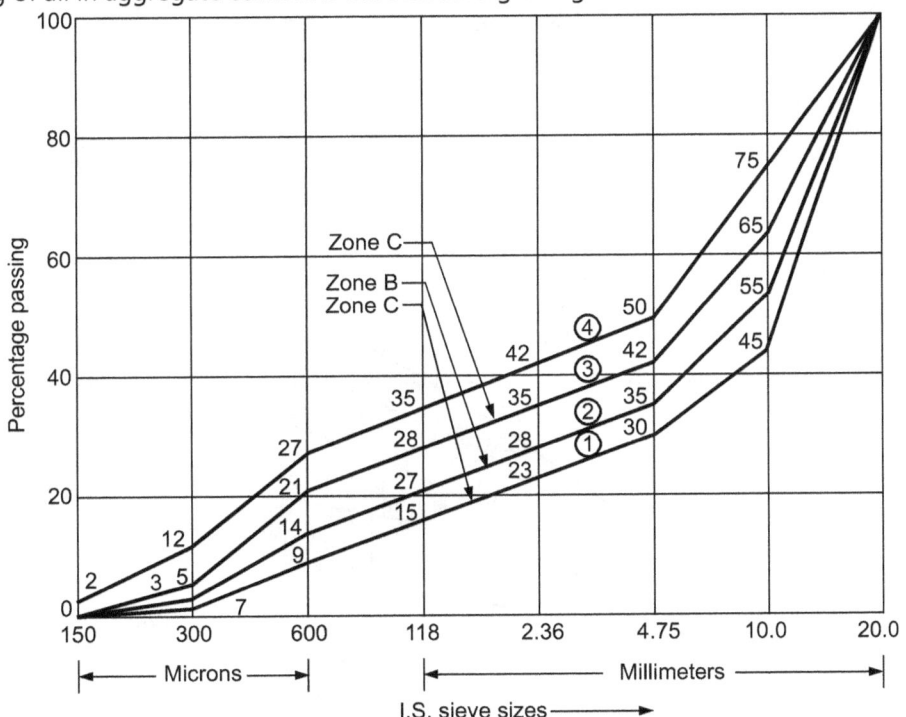

Fig. 1.15: Grading Curves for 20 mm Aggregate

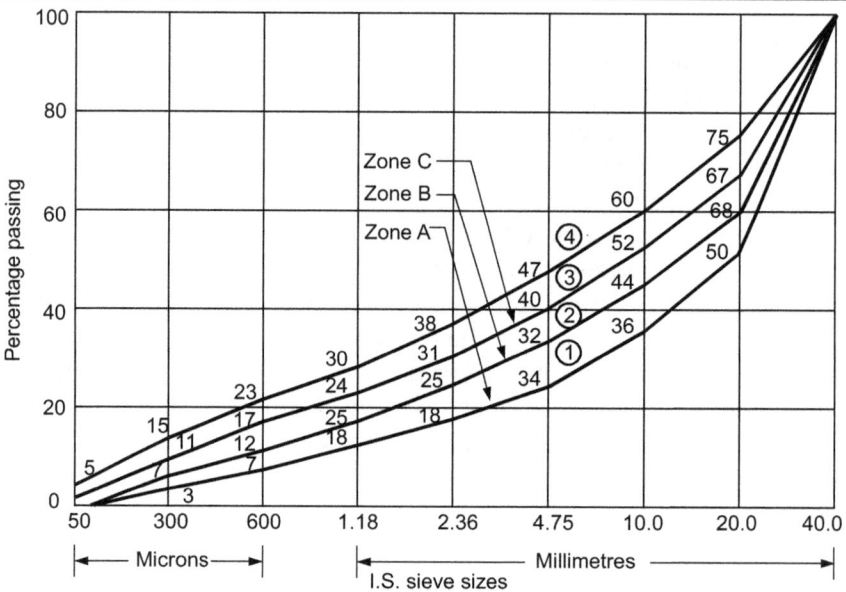

Fig. 1.16: Grading Curves for 40 mm Aggregate

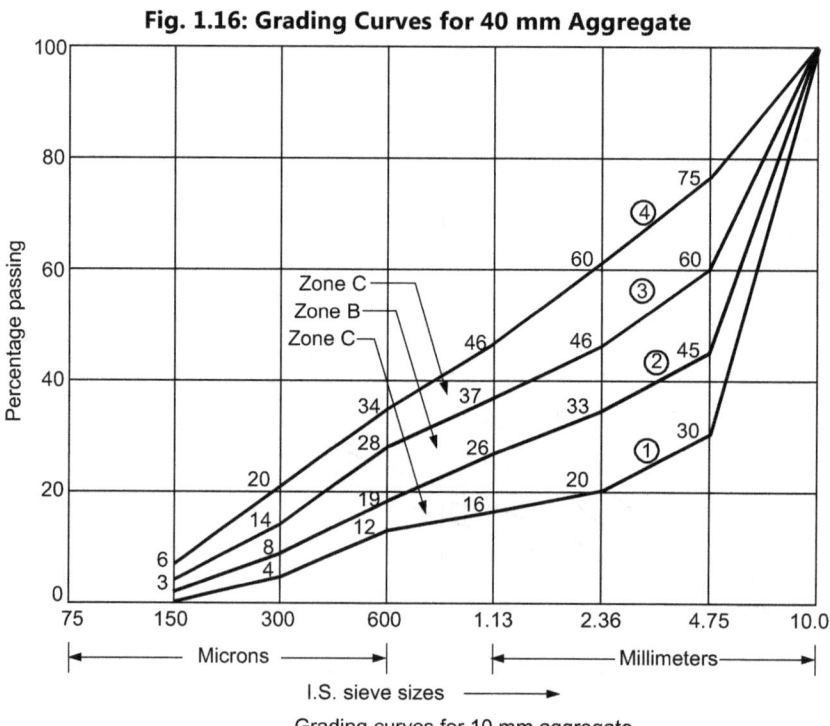

Grading curves for 10 mm aggregate

Fig. 1.17: Grading Curves for 10 mm Aggregate (MCIntosh and Erntroy's type)

Table 1.6: Coarse Aggregate

IS sieve designation	Percentage passing for single-sized aggregate of nominal size						Percentage passing for graded aggregate of nominal size			
	63 mm	40 mm	20 mm	16 mm	12.5 mm	10 mm	40 mm	20 mm	16 mm	12.5 mm
(1)	(2)	(3)	(4)	(5)	(6)	(7)	(8)	(9)	(10)	(11)
80 mm	100	–	–	–	–	–	100	–	–	–
63 mm	85 to 100	100	–	–	–	–	–	–	–	–
40 mm	0 to 30	85 to 100	100	–	–	–	95 to 100	–	–	–
20 mm	0 to 5	0 to 20	85 to 100	100	–	–	30 to 70	95 to 100	100	100
16 mm	–	–	–	85 to 100	100	–	–	–	90 to 100	–
12.5 mm	–	–	–	–	85 to 100	100	–	–	–	90 to 100
10 mm	0 to 5	0 to 5	0 to 20	0 to 30	0 to 45	85 to 100	10 to 35	25 to 55	30 to 70	40 to 85
4.75 mm	–	–	0 to 5	0 to 5	0 to 10	0 to 20	10 to 5	0 to 10	0 to 10	0 to 10
2.36 mm	–	–	–	–	–	0 to 5	–	–	–	–

Table 1.7: Grading of Fine Aggregates

IS sieve designation	Percentage passing for			
	Grading Zone I	Grading Zone II	Grading Zone III	Grading Zone IV
10 mm	100	100	100	100
4.75 mm	90 – 100	90 – 100	90 – 100	95 – 100
2.36 mm	60 – 95	75 – 100	85 – 100	95 – 100
1.18 mm	30 – 70	55 – 90	75 – 100	90 – 100
600 microns	15 – 34	35 – 59	60 – 79	80 – 100
300 microns	5 – 20	8 – 30	12 – 40	15 – 50
150 microns	0 – 10	0 – 10	0 – 10	0 – 15

Note 1: For crushed stone sands, the permissible limit on 150 micron IS sieve is increased to 20 per cent. This does not affect the 5 per cent allowance permitted in applying to other sieve sizes.

Note 2: Fine aggregate complying with the requirements of any grading zone in the above table is suitable for concrete but the quality of concrete produced will depend upon a number of factors including proportions.

Note 3: Where concrete of high strength and good durability is required, fine aggregate conforming to any one of the four grading zones may be used, but the concrete mix should not be properly designed. As the fine aggregate grading becomes progressively finer, that is, from grading zones I to IV, the ratio of fine aggregate to coarse aggregate should be progressively reduced. The most suitable fine to coarse ratio to be used for any particular mix will, however, depend upon the actual grading, particle shape and surface texture of both fine and coarse aggregates.

Note 4: It is recommended that fine aggregate conforming to grading zone IV should not be used in reinforced concrete unless tests have been made to ascertain the suitability of proposed mix proportions.

(b) Fine aggregates: Fine aggregates are graded in four different zones as given in table 1.8 known as grading zones I, II, III and IV where the grading falls outside the limits of any particular grading zone of sieves other than 600 micron IS sieve by a total amount not exceeding 5%, it should be regarded as falling within that grading zone. This tolerance shall not be applied to percentage passing the 600 micron IS sieve or to percentage passing any other sieve size on the coarse limit of grading zone I or the finer limit of grading zone IV. The sand falling in grading zone II is a normal sand. The sands falling in zone I and II are respectively coarser and finer sands. The sand of zone IV is too fine and is generally not used for concrete work.

(c) All-in-aggregate: In the case of all-in-aggregate the necessary adjustment may be made in the grading by the addition of single-sized aggregate without separating into fine and coarse aggregate. The grading of the all-in-aggregate should be confirmed to table 1.8.

Table 1.8: All-in-aggregate Grading

IS sieve designation	Percentage passing for all-in-aggregate of	
	40 mm nominal size	20 mm nominal size
80 mm	100	–
40 mm	95 to 100	100
20 mm	45 to 75	95 to 100
4.75 mm	25 to 45	30 to 50
600 micron	8 to 30	10 to 35
150 micron	0 to 6	0 to 6

1.16 Tests on Aggregates

The following are the important test of aggregates which influences the properties of concrete.

1.16.1 Test for the Determination of Aggregate Crushing Value

The *'Aggregate crushing value'* gives a relative measure of the resistance of an aggregate to crushing under a gradually applied compressive load. It is the percentage by weight of the crushed (or timer) material obtained when the test aggregates are subjected to a specified load under standardized conditions, and is a numerical index of the strength of the aggregate used in road construction. Aggregates with lower crushing value indicate a lower crushed fraction under load and would give a longer service life to the road and hence a more economical performance. Weaker aggregates if used would get crushed under traffic loads and produce smaller pieces not coated with binder and these would be easily displaced or loosened out resulting in loss o1 the surface/layer. In short, the aggregates used in road construction must be strong enough to withstand crushing under roller and traffic.

Procedure: Refer Appendix – Experiment 14.

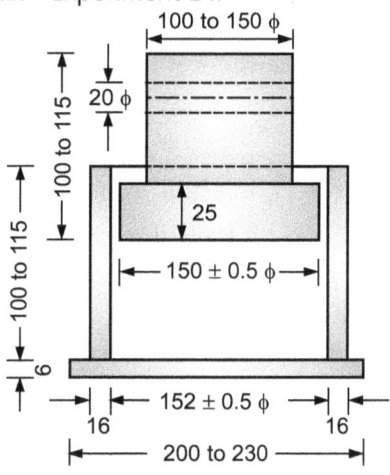

Fig. 1.18

1.16.2 Test for the Determination of Aggregate Impact Value

The property of a material to resist impact is known as *toughness*. Due to movement of vehicles on the road, the aggregates are subjected to impact resulting in their breaking down into smaller pieces. The aggregates should therefore have sufficient toughness to resist their disintegration due to impact. This characteristic is measured by impact value test. The *aggregate impact value* is a measure of resistance to sudden impact or shock, which may differ from its resistance to gradually applied compressive load.

Procedure: Refer Appendix – Experiment 15.

1.16.3 Test for Determination of Aggregate Abrasion Value

The aggregate abrasion value is a measure of hardness which is defined as 'the resistance to wear subjected to heavy traffic'. The test sample consisting of clean aggregate dried in an oven at 105° to 110°C to substantially constant weight and in sufficient quantity as specified in the specifications and the abrasive charge (cast iron or steel spheres approximately 48 mm in diameter each weighing between 390 to 445 gm) is placed in the Los Angles machine. This machine is rotated at a uniform speed of 20 to 33 rev./min. The number of revolutions should be specified in the specifications for the particular grade of aggregate. After the revolutions are over, the material is taken out from the machine and a preliminary separation of the sample is made on a sieve coarser than 1.70 mm IS sieve. The finer portion is then sieved on a 170 mm IS sieve and accurately weighted to the nearest gram.

Let, Mass of test sample = W_1 kg

Mass of the material passing through 1.70 mm IS sieve = W_2 kg

Then, Aggregate abrasion value = $\dfrac{W_2}{W_1} \times 100$ per cent

The aggregate abrasion value for a good stone should not exceed 16%.

1.16.4 Test for Determination of Bulk Density

Bulk density is the weight of aggregate required to fill a container of unit volume. This unit volume, therefore, consists of volume of solid material plus the volume of voids and is measured in kg/litre. These values are required to convert the quantity of aggregate by weight to quantities by volume when volume batching is done and vice versa.

Value of the bulk density of the aggregate depends upon the amount of effort used to fill the container as densely as possible, size distribution, shape and specific gravity. More graded the aggregate, greater is the bulk density. Angular and flaky shape of the material reduce the bulk density.

If this bulk density test is carried on frequently on the site, the appreciable change in the value of the bulk density at any one time helps to detect the change in grading or the shape of the material and enables the engineer on site to conduct further elaborate test, if necessary.

For batching purposes where the materials are measured, the bulk density of the 'loose' material should be calculated.

When the bulk density test is carried out to detect the change in grading and shape, the rodded bulk density test will have to be done to compare the results. Also for comparison of results size of two aggregates to be compared should be the same.

Procedure: Refer Appendix, Experiment 10.

1.16.5 Test for Determination of Specific Gravity and Water Absorption

As the aggregate generally contains pores, both permeable and impermeable. Therefore there are two types of the specific gravities of the aggregate are defined in concrete technology. These are:

(a) Apparent specific gravity.

(b) Specific gravity based on saturated surface dry basis.

These are discussed below.

The specific gravity is defined as 'the ratio of the weight of solid, referred to vacuum, to the weight of an equal volume of gas-free distilled water, both taken at a stated temperature'.

(Different test procedures are described for aggregates of sizes such as larger than 40 mm, between 10 to 40 mm, and smaller than 10 mm etc. These tests cover the tests for determining specific gravity, apparent specific gravity and water absorption of aggregates. The procedure given below is for an aggregate larger than 40 mm).

A sample of weight more than 2 kg is taken. It is thoroughly washed to remove finer particles and dust, drained and then placed in the wire basket and immersed in distilled water at a temperature of between 22°C and 32°C. A minimum cover of atleast 50 mm of water is provided above the top of the basket. Immediately after immersion, the entrapped air is removed from the sample by lifting and lowering the basket for 25 times. During this operation care is taken so that the basket and the aggregate will be in water. They are kept in water for a period of $24 \pm \frac{1}{2}$ hrs. The basket and aggregate are then jolted and weighted (W_1) in water at a temperature of 22°C to 32°C. The basket and the aggregate is then removed from water, allowed to drain for few minutes, and then the aggregate is gently taken out from the basket on to one of the dry clothes. The empty basket is again immersed in water, jolted 25 times and is weighed in water (W_2). The aggregate is surface dried with the clothes and then exposed to atmosphere until it appears to be completely surface dry. The weight of this aggregate is taken (W_3). Then the aggregate is kept in oven at a temperature of 100°C to 110°C for about 24 hours. Then it is cooled in the air-tight container and weighed (W_4). Then required results are calculated as:

$$\text{Specific gravity} = \frac{W_4}{W_3 - (W_1 - W_2)}$$

$$\text{Apparent specific gravity} = \frac{W_4}{W_4 - (W_1 - W_2)}$$

$$\text{Water absorption (\% of dry weight)} = \frac{(W_3 - W_4)}{W_4} \times 100$$

The majority of natural aggregates have a specific gravity of between 2.6 to 2.7.

The absorption capacity of coarse aggregate is about 0.5 to 1% by weight of aggregate.

Procedure: Refer Appendix – Experiment 8.

1.16.6 Test for Determination of Moisture Content of Aggregate

The surface moisture is expressed as a percentage of the weight of saturated and surface-dry aggregate, and is termed as *moisture content*. Since absorption represents the water contained in aggregate in a saturated and surface dry condition, and the moisture content is the water in excess of that state, the total water content of a moist aggregate is equal to the sum of absorption and moisture content.

If aggregates are exposed to rain, then they will absorb some water. This is especially true for fine aggregates. The moisture content of the aggregate-changes with weather and also from one stock pile to another, the value of the moisture content has to be determined frequently.

IS : 2386 (part-III) - 1963 describes the test to determine the moisture content of aggregate. When all the pores of aggregate are full of water, it is said to be **saturated and surface dry**. If it is allowed to dry in air, some of the water pores will evaporate. This is called **air dry**. If the aggregate is oven-dried, all water will evaporate and is called **bone dry**. Fig. 1.19 shows the diagrammatic representation of moisture in aggregate.

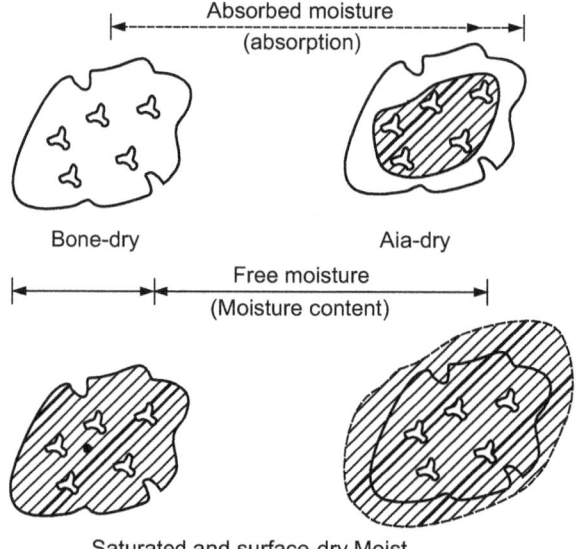

Fig. 1.19: Diagrammatic Representation of Moisture in Aggregate

IS : 2386 (part-III) - 1963 gives two methods for the determination of moisture content. The first method, namely, the displacement method, gives the moisture content as a percentage by mass of the saturated surface dry sample whereas the second method namely the drying method, gives the moisture content as a percentage by mass of the dried sample. The moisture content obtained by these two methods are quite different. The moisture content given by the drying method will normally be the total moisture content due to free plus absorbed water.

1.16.7 Test for Determination of Flakiness Index and Elongation Index (Shape Tests)

The aggregates which are flaky or elongated are not desirable because the large number of flaky aggregates create larger percentage of voids, which inturn will require larger amount of fine materials and also more water for the same workability, since such shapes offer more surface area for lubrication. It also tends to harm durability, because the particles tend to be oriented in one plane thus causing laminations.

The aggregate is said to be flaky when its least dimension is less than $3/5^{th}$ of its mean dimension. Mean dimension is the average of sieve size through which the particles pass and the sieve size on which it is retained. For example, a mean sieve size of the particle passing through 25 mm and retained on 20 mm is 20 + 25/2 = 22.5 mm. If the least dimension is less than $3/5 \times 22.5$ = 13.5 mm, then material is classified as flaky.

The material is said to be elongated when its length is greater than 9/5 times the mean sieve size.

Flakiness index or elongation index is the weight of flaky or elongated particles measured as percentage of the total weight of the sample. Flakiness index in excess of 35 to 40 per cent is considered undesirable. No limits for elongation index are known to have been prescribed as yet. The presence of elongated particles in excess of 10 to 15% is generally considered underside.

Procedure: Refer Appendix – Experiment 7.

1.16.8 Bulking of Sand

Due to presence of moisture content, aggregates bulk in volume. The moisture particles form a thin film around the aggregates and exert surface tension. This keeps the particles away from each other and thus aggregates bulk in volume. This phenomenon, practically negligible in case of coarse aggregate is however, of great importance in case of fine aggregate or sand. For sand, the volume goes on increasing until the moisture content is about 4% (for fine sand) by mass of sand. The bulking increases with the fineness of aggregates. With further addition of moisture content, the thin film of water coated round the sand, starts disappearing and the volume of sand begins to decrease and the volume of sand returns to its original volume, when it is dry.

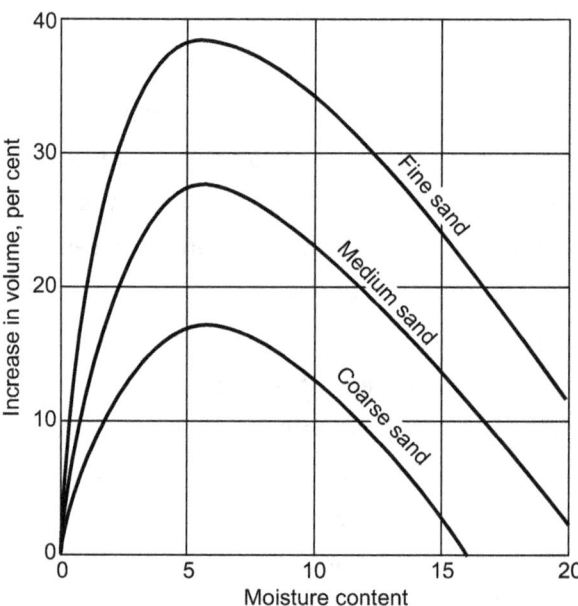

Fig. 1.20: Effect of Moisture Content on the Bulking of Sand

When the materials are proportional by volume batching, bulking of sand, the actual amount of sand mixed is less than required. This results in a strong mix and also the concrete will be honeycombed. Thus, the amount of sand to be added shall be suitably modified when moisture is present. The bulking of sand directly affects the quantity of sand required.

Bulking Factor: In connection with the bulking of sand, the bulking factor is defined as 'the ratio of the volume of moist sand to volume of the sand when dry'.

To find the bulking factor, take 500 gm (V_1) of dry sand by mass. Put it in a mixing pan and add 1% water (5 c.c.). Mix it thoroughly to get uniform colour. Fill the cylinder gently and note the volume V_2. The increase in volume is ($V_2 - V_1$) and the percentage bulking = $\frac{(V_2 - V_1)}{V_1}$. The bulking factor from the definition is $\frac{V_2}{V_1}$. Repeat the experiment using different percentage of water. Plot the graph of bulking factor V/s moisture content, by per cent of dry mass of sand. This is known as *bulking curve*. Typical bulking curves are shown in Fig. 1.20. Note that the finer sand has higher maximum bulking factor than that of a coarser sand, as large surface area is available with finer sand.

1.16.9 Test for the Determination of the Percentage of Bulking of Fine Aggregate (Field Method)

The damp sand, consolidated by shaking is poured in a 250 ml measuring cylinder until it reaches the 200 ml mark. Then it is filled with water and the sand is stirred well. In this operation, the sand should be in submerged condition. The level of the surface of sand is noted, say mark x ml. Then the % of the bulking of the sand due to moisture is calculated as:

$$\% \text{ bulking} = \left(\frac{200}{x} - 1\right) \times 100$$

1.17 Effects of Aggregate on Strength of Concrete

When we talk of strength we do not imply the strength of the parent rock from which the aggregates are produced, because the strength of the rock does not exactly represent the strength of the aggregate in concrete. Since concrete is an assemblage of individual pieces of aggregate bound together by cementing material, its properties are based primarily on the quality of the cement paste. This strength is dependant also on the bond between the cement paste and aggregate is low, a concrete of a poor quality will be obtained irrespective of the strength of the rock or aggregate. But when cement paste of good quality is provided and its bound with the aggregate is satisfactory, then the mechanical properties of the rock or aggregate will influence the strength of concrete. From the above it can be concluded that while strong aggregates cannot make strong concrete, for making strong concrete, strong aggregates are an essential requirement. In other words, from a weak rock or aggregate strong concrete cannot be made. By and large naturally available mineral aggregates are strong enough for making normal strength concrete. The test for strength of aggregate is required to be made in the following situations:

(i) For production of high strength and ultra high strength concrete.
(ii) When contemplating to use aggregates manufactured from weathered rocks.
(iii) Aggregate manufactured by industrial process.

1.18 Quantity of Water for Concrete

'The ratio of weight of water to the weight of cement in a concrete mix' is called *water cement ratio*. It is usually expressed in litres of water required per bag of cement.

The strength of concrete is controlled by the quantity and quality of its ingredients. Excess quantity of water creates segregation and bleeding, whereas insufficient quantity of water makes the concrete harsh and unworkable. Therefore, it is necessary to add optimum quantity of water to allow hydration of cement completely and to make the mix workable enough such that it can be easily placed inside the form-works and around the reinforcement. Water is used for making concrete for three different purposes.

(i) For mixing,
(ii) For curing, and
(iii) For washing.

Out of these, the quality and quantity of water in mixing is of paramount importance because it ultimately affects the strength of concrete.

1.18.1 Quality of Water

It is a popular belief and a yardstick that 'if water is fit for drinking, it is fit for making concrete'. Suitability of water for concrete making is checked by comparing its seventh days and 28th days strength with companion cubes made with distilled water. If the compressive strength is upto 90%, the source of water may be accepted. This criterion can be adopted safely in places like coastal area or marshy area or in other places, where the available water is brackish. Carbonates and bi-carbonates of sodium and potassium also affect the setting time of cement. Salts of manganese, tin, zinc, copper and lead cause a significant reduction in strength of concrete. Silt and suspended particles have been found to be undesirable as these interfere with setting, hardening and bonding. Algae in mixing water causes a reduction in strength of concrete by combining with cement to reduce the bonding or by causing air entrainment in concrete. It has been found that sea water does not appreciably reduce the strength of concrete although it may lead to corrosion of reinforcement embedded in concrete. Sea water slightly accelerates the setting process of cement, but it reduces the 28 days strength of concrete by 10-15%. Water containing large quantities of chlorides may cause efflorescence and dampness.

Table 1.9: Tolerable Concentrations of Some Impurities in Mixing Water

Impurity	Tolerable Concentration
Sodium and potassium carbonates and bi-carbonates	1,000 ppm (total). If this is exceeded, it is advisable to make test both for setting time and 28th days' strength.
Chlorides	10,000 ppm
Sulphuric anhydride	3,000 ppm
Calcium chloride	2 per cent by weight of cement in non-prestressed concrete.

contd. ...

Sodium iodate, sodium sulphate, sodium arsenate, sodium borate	Very low
Sodium sulphide	Even 100 ppm warrants testing.
Sodium hydroxide	0.5 per cent by weight of cement, provided quick set is not induced.
Silt and suspended particles	2,000 ppm. Mixing water with a high content of suspended solids should be allowed to stand in a settling basin before use.
Total dissolved salts	15,000 ppm.
Organic material	3,000 ppm. Water containing humic acid or such organic acids may adversely affect the hardening of concrete; 780 ppm of humic acid are reported to have seriously impaired the strength of concrete. In the case of such waters, therefore, further testing is necessary.
pH	4.5 to 8.5.

1.18.2 Hydration of Cement

Cement when mixed with water forms hydrated compounds of very low solubility. The reaction of cement with water is exothermic in nature. The reaction releases a lot of heat which is called "heat of hydration". Different compounds hydrate at different rates and liberate different quantities of heat.

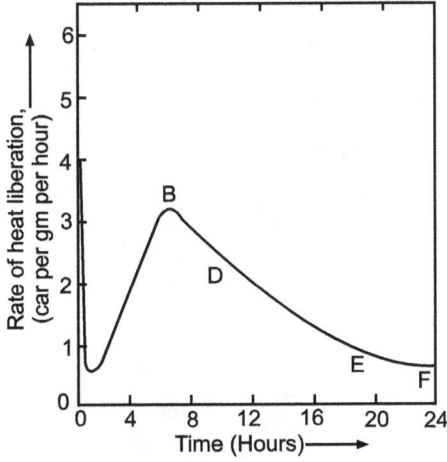

Fig. 1.21: Heat Liberation from a Setting Cement

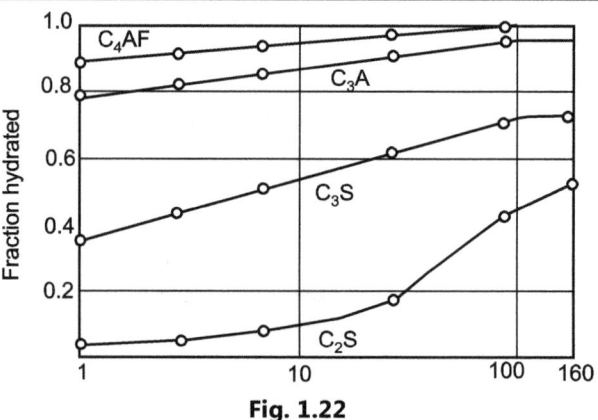

Fig. 1.22

Fig. 1.22 shows the rate of hydration of pure compounds of cement. As retarders are added to control the flash setting of C_3A, the early heat of hydration comes mainly from hydration of C_3S. Fineness of cement also affects the rate of development of heat but it does not affect the evolution of the total heat. Total heat depends upon the relative quantities of the major compounds present in cement. C_3S readily reacts with water and produces more heat of hydration. It is the responsible compound of cement for early strength of concrete. A cement with more C_3S is suitable for cold weather concreting. The quality and density of hydrated C_3S is slightly inferior to that formed by C_2S. C_2S hydrates rather slowly. It is the responsible compound of the cement for latter strength of concrete. It releases less heat of hydration. C_2S hydrated is rather dense and compact. Normally, the quality of the product of hydration of C_2S is better than that produced in the hydration of C_3S. Fig. 1.4 shows the development of strength of pure compounds.

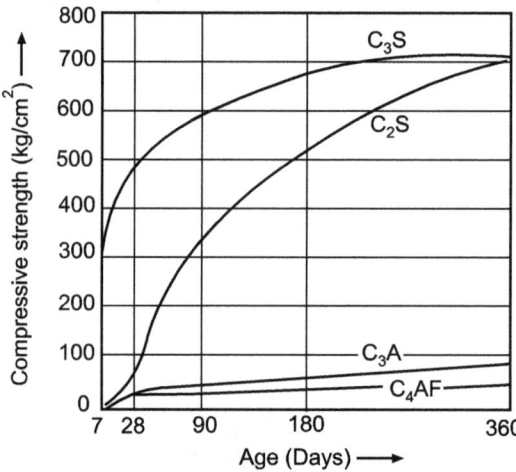

Fig. 1.23: Development of Strength of Pure Compounds

The hydrated aluminates do not contribute anything to the strength of paste. Rather their presence is harmful to the durability of concrete, particularly, where the concrete is likely to be attacked by sulphates. The hydrated C_4AF also does not contribute anything to the strength. The hydrates of C_4AF show a comparatively high resistance to the attack of sulphates than the hydrates of C_3A.

Exercise

1. Describe the manufacture of Portland Cement. In what way does it differ from rapid hardening cement.
2. What is the influence of the tri and di calcium silicates and tri calcium aluminate on the properties of cement?
3. What is hydration? On which factors the rate of hydration depends?
4. What is the importance of testing fineness of cement? How is the surface area method more reliable than sieve test for testing fineness of cement?
5. (a) Define consistency of standard cement paste.
   (b) How is the initial setting time of cement determined? What is its significance?
6. (a) Differentiate between setting and hardening of cement. Is setting time of cement related with setting time of concrete?
   (b) How is the setting time of cement controlled?
   (c) Why are the excess quantities of magnesium oxide, free lime in cements considered undesirable?
7. (a) Explain the roles of C_2S, C_3S, C_3A and C_4AF in hydration of cement. State the role of gypsum in setting of cement.
   (b) State the important field test and their significance for OPC. State various grades of cements and their significance to construction engineer. State the limitations of initial and final setting time as per IS code.
8. (a) List the various types of cement. Explain them briefly.
   (b) List out various laboratory tests to be carried out on cement. Which test is very important? Justify your stand.
   (c) Write a brief note on:
      (i) Hydration of cement.
      (ii) Initial and final setting time of cement.

9. (a) State and explain the term "Heat of Hydration".
   (b) Explain briefly how 'Portland Cement' is manufactured.
   (c) Explain in short the 'Rapid Hardening Cement". Where is it recommended?
   (d) Write brief notes on:
      (i) Compressive strength of cement.
      (ii) Sulphate resisting cement.

10. (a) Which are the field tests to be carried out on cement?
    (b) With neat sketch explain "Vicat Apparatus". Where is it employed?
    (c) State and explain the different grades of cement.

11. (a) Draw and explain the flow chart of dry process of manufacturing of cement.
    (b) State approximate values of oxides in composition of ordinary portland cement in percentage.
    (c) List out the various laboratory tests to be conducted on cement. Determine the quantity of water in ml required to conduct all above tests on 400 gm of cement if standard consistency (P_n) is 30%.

12. (a) Explain how aggregates can be classified based on weight, size, shape and texture.
    (b) Write a short note on "Deleterious material in aggregates".
    (c) What is "grading of aggregate". How do you determine the "fineness modulus" of aggregate?

13. (a) What is the importance of sieve analysis in aggregates?
    (b) Discuss qualities of aggregates required to produce good concrete.
    (c) What are the laboratory tests on aggregates?
    (d) Comment on 'flakiness' of aggregates.

14. (a) Explain the term "Grading of Aggregate". Explain its effect on properties of concrete.
    (b) Write a short note on 'flakiness index".
    (c) Describe the test for finding "Aggregate impact value' with corresponding I.S. limit.

15. (a) Explain the alkali-aggregate reaction and state anyone method to control it.
    (b) Explain bulking of sand. Draw the graph indicating this phenomenon for fine and coarse sand. Explain the difference in bulking of fine and coarse sand.
16. (a) Write a note on classification of aggregates based on weight and size.
    (b) Comment on inter-relationship between strength of parent rock, strength of aggregate on concrete and strength of concrete.
    (c) Explain how well graded aggregates and poorly graded aggregates affect the strength of concrete.
17. (a) With reference to aggregates used in making concrete distinguish the following and state briefly significance of each in mix design process.
    (i) Absolute specific gravity,
    (ii) Apparent specific gravity,
    (iii) Bulk density.
    (b) Write a note on effect of grading of aggregates on concrete mix.
    (c) Write short notes on:
    (i) Gap graded aggregates.
    (ii) Bouge's compound.
18. (a) The IS sieve sizes are 40 mm, 20 mm, 10 mm, 4.75 mm, 2.36 mm, 1.18 mm, 600 micron, 300 micron and 150 micron. A sample of sand measuring 2 kg is seived, and it is found that 0.20 kg, 0.36 kg, 0.52 kg, 0.48 kg and 0.42 kg are retained on 2.36 mm, 1.18 mm, 600 micron, 300 micron, and 150 micron respectively. What is the fineness modulus of the sand and the range in size.
    (**Ans.:** 2.69; 600 micron)
    (b) Draw a grading curve for the sand of example (a). Specify the zone of sand.
19. (a) Enlist the basic ingredients of portland cement and also state the ill-effects of it, if used in excess.
    (b) Write short notes on:
    (i) Hydrophobic cement,
    (ii) Oil-wet cement.
    (c) What is fineness modulus of aggregate? How will you find fineness modulus of coarse aggregate in laboratory.

20. (a) State the Bogue's compounds along with their percentage by mass of cement and function of each.
    (b) Explain the classification of aggregates in the basis of:
        (i) Origin,
        (ii) Size,
        (iii) Shape and
        (iv) Unit weight.
    (c) Comment on "minimum water-cement ratio required is 38% of weight of cement".

■■■

Unit 2
FRESH AND HARDENED CONCRETE

[A] FRESH CONCRETE
2.1 Definition and Its Ingredients

Concrete and steel are the two most widely used materials in Construction Industry and these are complement to each other and sometimes, compete with each other, as the structures of a similar type and function can be built in either of these materials. But the engineers, quite often, have got the less knowledge of concrete than steel and that has been the main reason of failures of different structures in the past. Hence, one must have the complete knowledge of concrete making, as there is not much difference in good concrete and bad concrete as far as the ingredients of concrete are concerned. Bad concrete, which is honey-combed, having unsuitable consistency, non-homogeneous, poor in strength, is made of cement, aggregates and water. Surprisingly, the good concrete is also made of these ingredients only. It is only the proper quality control and technical know-how, which is responsible for the difference. It is also interesting to know that: and bad concrete do not differ much in cost.

Cement concrete looks simple but actually it is a very complex material. It is prepared at the site while other construction materials such as steel are readymade. Hence, it varies in great extent depending upon the quality of the ingredients, i.e. cement, aggregate and water, quality of workmanship, control over process etc. For making a good concrete, one must have the good knowledge of the interaction of various ingredients in plastic and hardened conditions. This kind of knowledge is essential for site engineers and concrete technologists. The subject "Concrete Technology" is devised to meet this demand.

2.1.1 Definition of Concrete

"Cement concrete is a mixture of coarse aggregates, fine aggregates, cement and water in a certain proportion so as to make a concrete of desired quality".

Sometimes, special ingredients known as 'Admixture' are also added to these so as to include or improve some property in concrete.

Fresh Concrete: The fresh mixtures of coarse aggregates, fine aggregates, cement and water in suitable proportions is termed as "Fresh Concrete".

Hardened Concrete: As the time passes, above mentioned mixture gets hardened. This hardened mixture is termed as "Hardened Concrete".

Grade of Concrete: As the concrete properties vary much with composition and method of mixing, many different types of concrete can be obtained, each suitable for a specific purpose.

Concrete mixes have been classified into various grades by BIS like M 5, M 7.5, M 15, M 20, M 25 etc. In the designation of a concrete mix, M refers to the mix and the number to the characteristic compressive strength of cube at 28 days, expressed in N/mm^2.

The "characteristic strength" is defined as the strength of material below which not more than 5% of the test results are expected to fall.

2.1.2 Importance of Concrete

Concrete is the most important construction material because it is difficult to find out another material of such versatility and mouldability at such a cheap price.

(i) It has got good compressive strength, durability, impermeability, fire resistance and abrasion resistance.
(ii) Its weakness in tensile strength can be made-up by the use of reinforcing and prestressing techniques and this has made the use of concrete widespread and now it is almost used everywhere.
(iii) In India, about 60% of plan outlay accounts for construction only. Out of this, cement and cement product would account for more than 50%. It means that 30% of the total outlay goes into cement concrete. Therefore, concrete has got a tremendous impact upon our economy and we should use this economically and judiciously.

2.1.3 Necessity of Supervision for Concreting Operation

In the process of concreting supervision is very necessary for following reasons:

(i) To cure the concrete properly.
(ii) To maintain w/c ratio for correct strength.
(iii) To mix ingredients in proper proportion.
(iv) To see that concrete does not set before placing it in the formwork.
(v) To avoid segregation and bleeding.
(vi) To make a concrete as a good finished product.

2.1.4 Process Diagram of Concrete

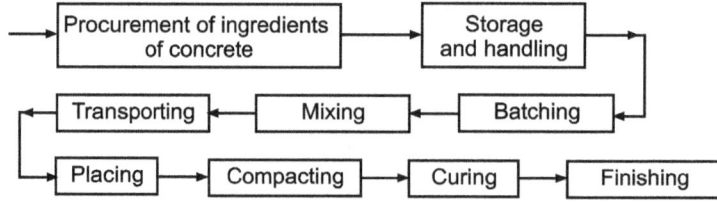

Fig. 2.1: Process Diagram of Concrete

Concrete Chain: This chain consists of the following operations in series.

(i) Procurement of ingredients of concrete.
(ii) Storage and handling of ingredients so that wastage does not take place.
(iii) Batching i.e. the measurement of materials for making concrete.
(iv) Mixing the ingredients in proper proportion.
(v) Transporting the mixed ingredients i.e. fresh concrete to the site.
(vi) Placing the fresh concrete in moulds.
(vii) Compacting the concrete.
(viii) Curing of concrete.
(ix) Testing of concrete in plastic and hardened stage.

Above mentioned steps in series known as concrete chain. A site engineer must be having the full knowledge of these operations and he must supervise the full procedure properly. So that a good concrete can be produced at the minimum cost.

2.1.5 Grades of Concrete

The concrete is generally graded according to its compressive strength. The various grades of concrete are stipulated in IS 456-2000. The concrete grades lower than M 20 are not suitable for reinforced concrete works and grades of concrete lower than M 35 are not to be used in the prestressed concrete works.

(a) Ordinary concrete:

Ordinary concrete mixes or nominal concrete mixes are classified as per IS: 456-2000 as M 10, M 15, M 20 having minimum compressive strength after 28 days as 10 N/mm^2, 15 N/mm^2, and 20 N/mm^2 respectively.

(b) Standard concrete:

Standard concrete mixes are classified as per IS: 456-2000 as M 25, M 30, M 35, M 40, M 45, M 50, M 55 having minimum compressive strength after 28 days as 25 N/mm^2, 30 N/mm^2, 35 N/mm^2, 40 N/mm^2, 45 N/mm^2, 50 N/mm^2 and 55 N/mm^2 respectively.

(c) High strength concrete:

These grades are classified as M 60, M 65, M 70, M 75, M 80 specially used for prestressed concrete giving minimum strengths of 60 N/mm^2, 65 N/mm^2, 70 N/mm^2, 75 N/mm^2 and 80 N/mm^2 respectively.

Table 2.1: Grades of concrete as per IS 456-2000

Group	Grade Designation	Specified characteristic compressive strength of 150 mm cube at 28 days in N/mm^2
Ordinate concrete	M 10	10
	M 15	15
	M 20	20
Standard concrete	M 25	25
	M 30	30
	M 35	35
	M 40	40
	M 45	45
	M 50	50
	M 55	55
High strength concrete	M 60	60
	M 65	65
	M 70	70
	M 75	75
	M 80	80

Minimum grades of concrete for different exposure conditions:

According to the purpose for which concrete is used minimum grade of concrete is used.

Minimum M_{10} grade is required for RCC. Minimum M30 grade is required for water retaining structure and in sea-water construction. Minimum grade M-40 and above it are required for prestressed concrete.

High strength and ultra-high strength concrete is used for runways of airport, for automic reactors, sky scrapers, very high buildings etc.

Notes:

In the designation of concrete mix, M refers to the mix and the number refers to the specified compressive strength of 150 mm size cube at 28 days, expressed in N/mm^2.

Minimum cement content, maximum water/cement ratio and minimum grade of concrete for different exposures with normal weight aggregate of 20 mm nominal maximum size as per IS: 456-2000.

Table 2.2

Sr. No.	Exposure	Plain concrete			Reinforced concrete		
		Minimum cement content kg/m³	Maximum free w/c ratio	Minimum grade of concrete	Minimum cement content kg/m³	Maximum free w/c ratio	Minimum grade of concrete
1.	Mild	220	0.60	–	300	0.55	M 20
2.	Moderate	240	0.60	M 15	300	0.50	M 25
3.	Severe	250	0.50	M 20	320	0.45	M 30
4.	Very severe	260	0.45	M 20	340	0.45	M 35
5.	Extreme	280	0.40	M 25	360	0.40	M 40

Notes:

Cement content prescribed in this table is irrespective of the grade of cement and it is inclusive of all supplementary cementitious materials. The addition of all supplementary cementitious materials may be taken into account in the concrete composition with respect to the cement content and W/C ratio, if the suitability is established and as long as the maximum amounts taken into account do not exceed the limit prescribed in the relevant codes.

(2) Minimum grade for plain concrete under mild exposure condition is not specified.

(a) **Minimum grade of concrete for water retaining structure:** For water retaining structure minimum grade used for concreting is M 30.

(b) **Minimum grade of concrete for sea water construction:** For sea water construction minimum grade used for concreting is M 30.

2.1.6 Concrete Grade in Sea Water Construction and Water Retaining Structure

Concrete in sea water or exposed directly along the sea-coast shall be at least M 20 grade in the case of plain concrete and M 30 in case of reinforced concrete. The use of slag or pozzolana cement is advantageous under such conditions.

Special attention shall be given to the design of the mix to obtain the densest possible concrete; slag, broken brick; soft sand stone, or other porous or weak aggregate shall not be used. As far as possible, preference shall be given to precast members unreinforced, well-cured and hardened, without sharp corners, and having trowel-smooth finished surface free from crazing, cracks or other defects; plastering should be avoided. No construction joint shall be allowed with 600 mm below lower water level or within 600 min of the high and low planes of wave action.

Where unusually severe conditions or abrasions are anticipated, such parts of the work shall be protected by bituminous or silico fluoride coating or stone facing beded within bitumen.

In reinforced concrete structure, care shall be taken to protect the reinforcement from exposure to saline atmosphere during storage, fabrication and use. It may be achieved by tearing the surface of reinforcement with cement wash or by suitable methods.

2.1.7 Durability of Concrete

The durability of concrete is its ability to withstand the environmental conditions to which it is exposed'. It is necessary to emphasize durability in the design and construction of concrete structure. Main requirements of durability are

1. An upper limit of W/C ratio.
2. A lower limit of the cement concrete.
3. A lower limit of the concrete cover to reinforcement.
4. Good compaction.
5. Adequate curing.

In addition, concrete should be free from effect of harmful ingredients like alkali aggregate reactions, volume changes due to non-compatibility of thermal and mechanical properties of aggregate and cement paste, presence of sulphate and chlorides. In case of reinforced concrete, the ingress of moisture or air will facilitate the corrosion of steel, leading to an increase in the volume of steel and cracking and spalling of concrete cover.

It is known that the permeability of cement-paste increases exponentially with increase in water/cement ratio above 0.45. High water/cement ratio will have evaporable water and the babbles of trapped air occupy space called voids. Permeability of concrete increases rapidly with the amount of voids. Factors which increase the strength of concrete are likely to reduce permeability and thus improve durability. It has been observed that when absorption of water in a sample exceeds 7%, there is likely to be corrosion of steel.

Corrosion of reinforcement can seriously affect the service life of concrete structures. A low permeability also makes the concrete better able to withstand the effect of weathering including effects of rain and disrupting effect of freezing and thawing.

The type of cement is also important in order to resist the sulphate solutions in solid and ground water. The ordinary Portland cement having C3A less than 5% has got the maximum resistance against-sulphate environment. The Portland slag-cement and the pozzolana cement are preferable in marine or sulpharic conditions.

Too high cement content may not always be good from durability point of view as it increases the risk of cracking due to drying, shrinkage in thin section or thermal stresses in thick section. Experience has also shown that too low a cement content makes it more difficult to obtain a durable concrete. It is therefore, often desirable in practice to specify a minimum cement content.

Thus, cement, in case of concrete, is to be decided on three conditions.

(i) Workability which again depends on placing conditions, cover thickness and the concentration of reinforcement.

(ii) To ensure sufficient alkalinity to provide a passive environment against corrosion of steel. Thus, in case of concrete in marine environment or in sea water, the maximum cement specified is more than in normal conditions.

(iii) The cement content and water cement ratio should be such as to result in sufficient volume of cement paste to fill voids in the compacted aggregates. This will depend on the type and nominal maximum size of aggregate.

Hence, the durability of cement concrete is its ability to resist weathering action, chemical attack, abrasion or any other process of deterioration. Durable concrete will retain its original form, quality and serviceability when exposed to its environment.

2.2 Significance of Water/Cement Ratio

It has been found that, on an average, 23% of water by weight of cement is required for chemical combination with Portland cement i.e. for complete hydration. This water used for the chemical reaction is called 'bound water'. In addition to bound water, a certain quantity of water is taken in, within the gel pores, known as 'gel water'. This gel water constitutes 15% by weight of cement. So, a total of 38% of water by weight of the cement is required for complete chemical reaction and to fill up the gel pores.

In the case when water/cement ratio is considerably less (less than 38% by weight of cement), water added is insufficient for complete hydration of each particle of cement. It will produce a weak physical structure of the hydrated cement, and thus, the strength of concrete is reduced. On the other hand, when the water/cement ratio is considerably more than that required for the complete hydration of cement, the excess water occupies more space than that needed by the gel pores formed during the hydration of cement. When the excess water evaporates, the additional space, which was occupied by the excess water, is converted into capillary pores. Thus, the more the water/cement ratio, the more the capillary pores. Thus, the more the water cement ratio, the more is the uncombined water which will produce more capillary voids in the physical structure of hydrated cement, and thus weakens the strength, durability and water tightness of concrete.

It has been observed that, with water/cement ratio of 0.4, the water available in the concrete mix is just sufficient to hydrate each cement particle completely and the cement gel formed during hydration of cement occupies all the space previously occupied by water. On the other hand, with a water/cement ratio less than 0.4, the cement will not hydrate completely.

With lower w/c ratio, the cement particles are closer together. With the progress of hydration, when the volume of anhydrous cement increases, the product of hydration also increases. The increase in the volume of gel, to complete hydration, could fill up the space earlier occupied by water upto w/c ratio of 0.6 or so. If the w/c ratio is more than 0.7, the increase in the volume of the hydrated product would never be sufficient to fill-up the voids created by water. Such concrete would become a porous mass.

The diagrammatic representation of the progress of hydration is shown in Fig. 2.2. Fig. 2.2 (a) represents the state of the cement.

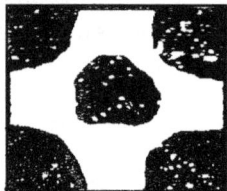

(a) Unhydrated cement particles

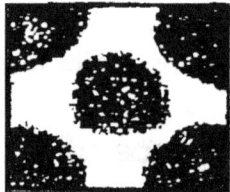

(b) Partially hydrated particles

(c) Fully hydrated with empty gel pores

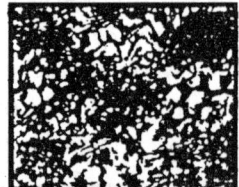

(d) Continuous hydration process with filled gel spaces

Fig. 2.2: Diagrammatic Representation off the Hydration Process and Formation of Cement Gel Particles Immediately After being Dispersed in the Aqueous Solution

During the first few minutes, the reaction rate is rapid, and calcium silicate hydrate forms a coating around the cement grains [Fig. 2.2 (b)]. As hydration proceeds, the hydration products, including calcium hydroxide, are precipitated from the saturated solution and bridge the gap between the cement grains and the paste stiffens into its final shape, [Fig. 2.7 (c)]. As the process continues, hydration involving some complex form of the diffusion process results in an even further deposition of the cement gel, at the expense of the unhydrated cement and the capillary pore water [Fig. 2.7 (d)].

Example 2.1: For casting cubes in the laboratory 12.5 kg cement is required. If w/c ratio is 0.41, calculate quantity of water to be added.

Solution: Given: Quantity of cement = 12.5 kg

$\dfrac{W}{C}$ = 0.41 C

∴   Quantity of water required, W = 0.41 × 12.5 = 5.125 lit.

2.3 Properties of Fresh Concrete

Fresh concrete is a freshly mixed material, which can be moulded into any shape. The relative quantities of constituent materials, i.e. cement, aggregates, water etc.; control the properties in the wet state as well as in the hardened state. Workability of fresh concrete depends upon the materials and environmental conditions. Workability is a complex phenomenon and the composite requirements of mixability, stability, transportability, placebility, mobility, compactibility, curability and finishability are the factors which define workability. Water plays an important role in the workability, as it lubricates the concrete so that the concrete can be compacted with specified effort forthcoming at the site of work. The lubrication required for handling concrete without segregation, for placing, for compacting with the amount of efforts forthcoming and for finishing it easily, the presence of a certain quantity of water is required.

2.3.1 Definition of Workability and Factors Affecting Workability

1. Definitions: Road Research Laboratory, U.K. defined workability as "the property of concrete which determines the amount of useful internal work necessary to produce full compaction". It can be also defined as the "ease with which concrete can be compacted 100% having regard to mode of compaction and place of deposition".

IS 6461-1973 defines workability as "the property of fresh mixed concrete or mortar which determines the ease and homogeneity with which it can be mixed, placed, compacted and finished".

Workable concrete is one which exhibits a little internal friction between particles or which overcomes the frictional resistance offered by the form work surface or reinforcement contained in the concrete with the just amount of compacting efforts.

2. Factors Affecting Workability: Following are the factors which affect the workability of concrete by creating lubricating effect to reduce internal friction for helping easy compaction.

(a) Water Content: Higher the water content per cubic metre of concrete, the higher will be the fluidity of concrete, thus affecting the workability. More water content, more workability. Therefore, higher water content can be used to increase the workability. It should be noted that from the durability point of view, increase of water content should be the last resort for improving the workability because increased water content may decrease the strength of concrete significantly.

(b) Mixed Proportions: The higher the aggregate/cement ratio, the leaner is the concrete. In lean concrete, less quantity of paste is available for providing lubrication and hence mobility of aggregate is restrained. On the other hand, in case of rich concrete with lower aggregate cement ratio, more paste is available to give better workability.

(c) Size of Aggregates: If bigger is the size of aggregate, lesser is the surface area per cubic metre of aggregate. Therefore, less amount of water will be required for wetting the surface and less paste is required for lubricating the surface. For a given quantity of water and paste, a bigger size of aggregate will always give higher workability.

(d) Shape of Aggregate: Angular, elongated or flaky aggregates make the concrete very harsh when compared to rounded aggregates. This is because the angular aggregates bear more surface area as compared to the rounded aggregates for the same volume. This explains the reason why river sand and gravel provide greater workability than crushed sand and aggregate.

(e) Surface Texture: Surface area of rough textured aggregate is more than the surface area of smooth aggregate of same volume. Reduction of inter particle frictional resistance offered by smooth aggregates also contributes to higher workability.

(f) Grading of Aggregate: A well-graded aggregate is the one which has least amount of voids in a given volume because if voids are less, excess paste is available to give better lubrication. The better the grading, the less is the void content and therefore, higher the workability.

(g) Use of Admixtures: Air entraining agents and pozzolanic materials greatly increase the workability of concrete, but do not affect its strength adversely. Air bubbles act as a sort of ball-bearing between the particles to slide past each other and give easy mobility to the particles.

2.3.2 Measurement of Workability of Fresh Concrete

There are different methods of measuring the workability of fresh concrete. Each of them measures only a particular aspect of it, so much so, there is really no unique test, which measures the workability of concrete in its totality. Although, new methods are being developed everyday, IS 516 envisages the following methods:

1. Slump cone test,
2. Compacting factor test,
3. Flow test,
4. Vee-Bee Consistency test,
5. Split tensile test.

1. Slump Cone Test: Slump test is the most commonly used method of measuring the consistency of concrete, which can be employed either in the laboratory or at the work site. It is not a suitable method for very wet or very dry concrete. It does not measure all factors contributing to the workability. However, it is used conveniently as a control test, and gives an indication of the uniformity of concrete from batch to batch. Additional information on workability and quality of concrete can be obtained by observing the manner in which the concrete slumps.

The apparatus for conducting the slump test essentially consists of a metallic mould in the form of a frustum of a cone having the internal dimensions as under:

    Bottom diameter   :   20 cm
    Top diameter   :   10 cm
    Height   :   30 cm

The thickness of the metallic sheet for the mould should not be less than 1.6 mm. Suitable guides are provided for lifting the mould vertically.

Fig. 2.3 shows the details of the slump cone apparatus. The internal surface of the mould is thoroughly cleaned and freed from superfluous moisture, and any old set concrete before commencing the test. The mould is placed on a smooth, horizontal, rigid and non-absorbant surface. The mould is then filled in the four layers, each approximately $1/4^{th}$ of the height and tamped 25 times by the tamping rod, taking care to distribute the strokes evenly over the cross-section. After the top layer has been rodded, the concrete is struck off level with a trowel and tamping rod. The mould is removed immediately from the concrete, by raising it carefully in a vertical position. This allows the concrete to subside. This subsidence is referred to as slump of concrete.

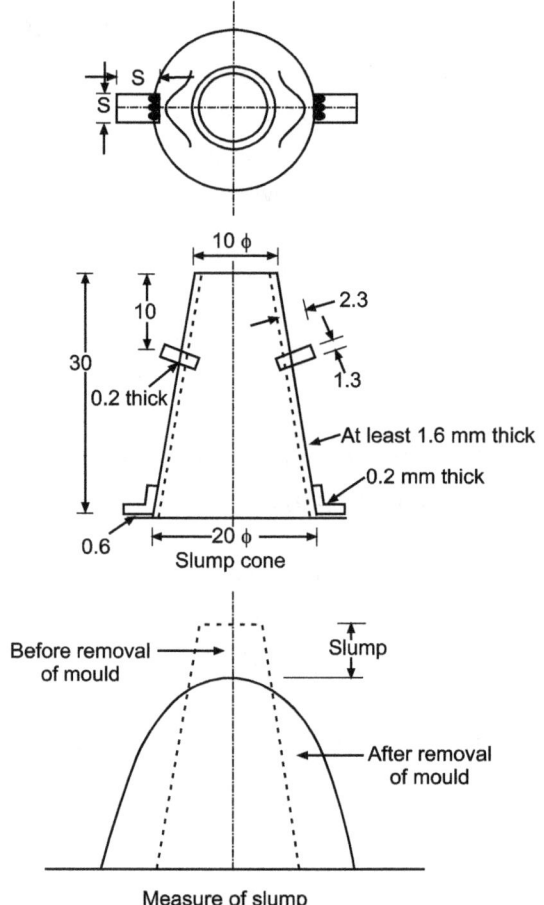

Measure of slump
Fig. 2.3: Sump Cone Test

The difference in level between the height of the mould and that of the highest part of the subsided concrete is measured. This difference in height in mm is known as **Slump of Concrete**.

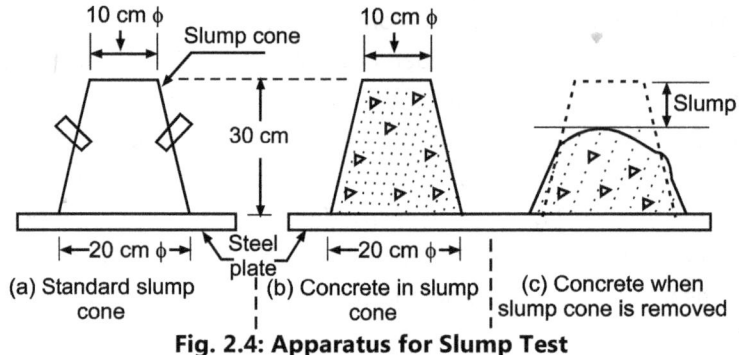

Fig. 2.4: Apparatus for Slump Test

The pattern of slump is shown in the Fig. 2.4. It indicates the characteristics of concrete in addition to slump value. If the concrete slumps evenly, it is called *true slump*. If one half of the cone slides down, it is called *shear slump*. In case of a shear slump, the slump value is measured as the difference in height between the height of the mould and the average value of the subsidence. Shean slump also indicates that the concrete is non-cohesive, and shows the characteristic of segregation. If the concrete breaks and spreads in all directions it is called collapse slump.

It is seen that the slump test gives fairly good consistent results for a plastic mix. This test is not sensitive for a stiff mix. In case of dry mix, no variation can be detected between mixes of different workability. In the case of rich mixes, the value is often satisfactory, their slump being sensitive to variations in workability. However, in a lean mix with tendency of harshness, a true slump can easily change to shear slump. In such case, the tests should be repeated.

Nominal values of slump for different degrees of workability are shown below:

Degree of Workability	Slump in mm	Compaction	Use for which concrete is suitable
(i) Very low	0-25	0.78	Roads vibrated by power operated machines. If slump is nearer to 25 mm concrete may be compacted by hand operated machines.
(ii) Low	25-50	0.85	Roads vibrated by hand operated machines. For slump value near to upper limit, hand compaction may be done.
(iii) Medium	50-100	0.92	Mass concrete foundation without vibration. Lightly reinforced section with vibration. When the slump is nearer to 25 mm, concrete may be compacted by hand operated machines. Used in roads vibrated by power operated machines.
(iv) High	100-175	0.95	When the slump is nearer to 50 mm, concrete may be compacted by hand operated machines. Used in roads vibrated by power operated machines.

Despite many limitations, the slump test is very useful on the site to check day-to-day or hour-to-hour variation, in the quality of the mix. An increase in the slump may mean, for instance, that the moisture content of the aggregate has suddenly increased or there has been a sudden change in the grading of aggregate. The slump test gives warning to correct the causes for the change of slump value. This test is very popular for its simplicity.

Importance of slump test:

The slump test is used for measuring the consistency of concrete which can be employed either in laboratory or a site of work. It is used conveniently as a control test and gives an indication of uniformity of concrete from batch to batch. Additional information on workability and quality of concrete can be obtained by observing the manner in which the concrete slumps.

Advantages of slump test:

(i) It is used to give workability of concrete mix in laboratory and in field both.

(ii) It gives true value of workability for normal mix and lean mix.

Limitations of slump test:

(i) It cannot be considered as reliable for stiff concrete mix.

(ii) If true slump is not measured accurately, the test is unreliable.

2. Compaction Factor Test: Compaction factor test measures the workability in an indirect manner, i.e. the amount of compacting onlined for a given amount of work. This test has been held to be more accurate than the slump test, specially for concrete mixes of medium and low workability.

Its use has been popular in laboratories. For concrete of very low workability, which cannot be fully compacted for comparison, the compaction test is not suitable.

This test works on the principle of determining the degree of compaction, achieved by the standard amount of work done, by allowing the concrete to fall through a standard height. The degree of compaction, called the compacting factor, is measured by the density ratio, i.e. the ratio of density actually achieved in the test to the density of the same concrete fully compacted.

∴ The compacting factor is,

$$= \frac{\text{Weight of partially compacted concrete}}{\text{Weight of fully compacted concrete}}$$

Compacting Factor Apparatus: The sample of concrete to be tested is placed in the upper hopper upto the brim. The trap door is opened so that the concrete falls into the cylinder. Now, the trap door of the lower hopper is opened and the concrete is allowed to fall into the cylinder. The excess concrete remaining above the top level of the cylinder is then cut-off with the help of planer blades supplied, is known as "weight of partially compacted concrete". The cylinder is emptied and then refilled with the concrete from the same sample in layers, approximately 5 cm deep. The layers are heavily rammed or preferably vibrated so as to obtain full compaction. The top surface of the fully compacted concrete is then carefully struck-off with the top of the cylinder and weighed to the nearest 10 gms. This weight is known as "weight of fully compacted concrete".

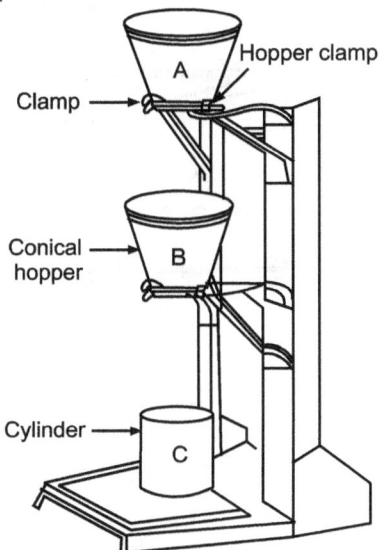

Fig. 2.5: Compacting Factor Apparatus

3. Flow Test: The flow test measures the spread or a flow of concrete, subjected to jolting its greatest value in relation to segregation. It gives a good assessment of the consistency of stiff, rich, cohesive mixes.

However, it is not normally performed in the field. It should be noted that this test does not measure workability, as the concretes having the same flow may differ in consistency in this workability.

In this test, a standard mass of concrete is subjected to jolting. The spread or the flow of the concrete is measured, and thus, the flow is related to workability. Fig. 2.6 shows the details of the apparatus used. It can be seen that the apparatus consists of a flow table, about 76 mm in diameter, over which eccentric circles are marked. A mould made from smooth metal casting in the form of a frustum of a cone is used.

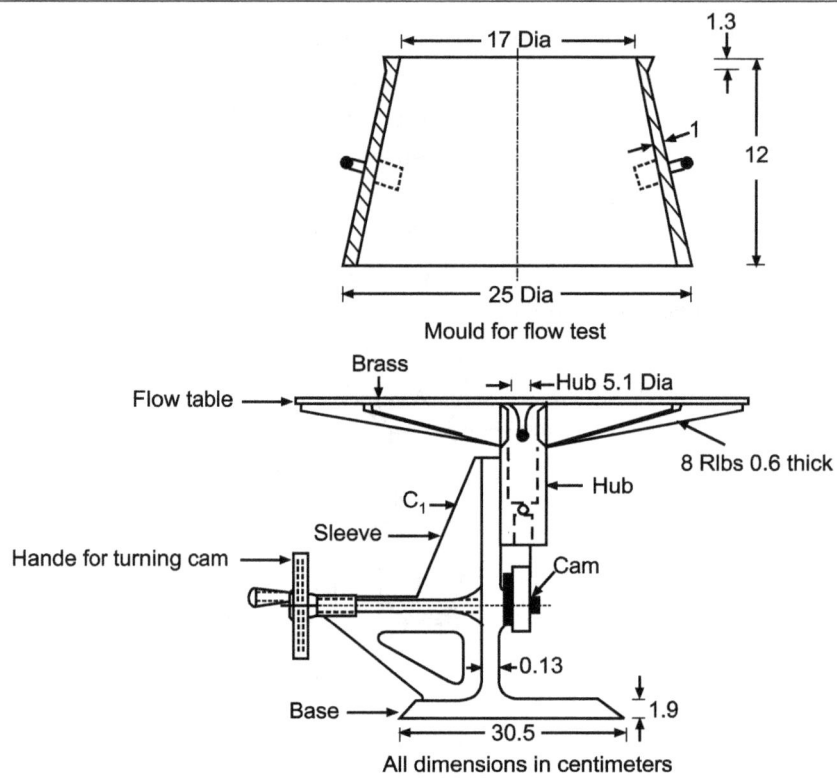

Fig. 2.6: Flow Test

The table top is cleaned of all gritty materials and is wetted. The mould is kept on the centre of the table, firmly held and is filled in two layers. Each layer is rodded 25 times with a tamping rod 1.6 cm in diameter and 61 cm long, round at the lower tamping end. After the top layer is rodded evenly, the excess of concrete which has overflowed the mould is removed. The mould is lifted vertically upwards and the concrete stands on its own without support. The table is then raised and dropped from a height of 12.5 mm, 15 times in about 15 seconds. The diameter of the spread concrete is measured in about 6 directions nearest to 5 mm and the average spread is noted. The flow of the concrete is the percentage increased in the average diameter of the spread concrete over the base diameter of the mould.

$$\text{Flow per cent} = \frac{\text{Spread diameter in cm} - 25}{25} \times 100$$

This value could range from 0 to 150 per cent.

4. Vee-Bee Consistency Test: This is a good laboratory test to measure indirectly the workability of concrete. This test consists of a electrical vibrator, a metal pot, a sheet metal cone, a standard iron rod, funnel, glass plate etc. The apparatus is shown in Fig. 2.7.

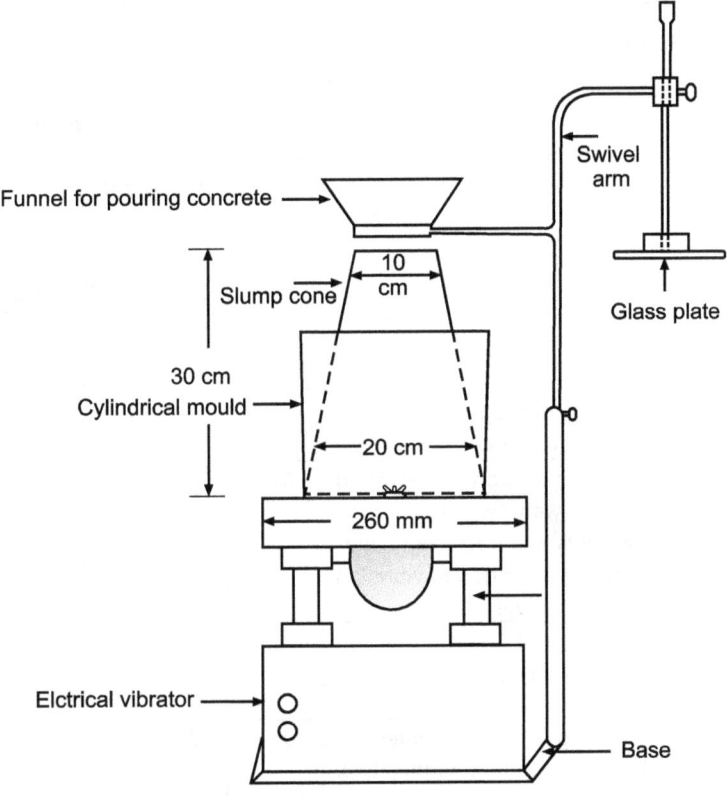

Fig. 2.7: Vee-Bee Consistometer

The slump test as described earlier is performed by placing the slump cone on the cylindrical pot of the consistometer instead the sheet metal. A glass disc attached to the swivel arm is turned and placed on the top of the concrete in the pot. The electrical vibrator is then switched On and simultaneously a stop-watch is started. The vibration is continued till such time, as the conical shape of the concrete disappears and the concrete assumes a cylindrical shape. This can be judged by observing the glass disc from the top. Immediately after the concrete fully assumes a cylindrical shape, the stop-watch is switched Off. The time taken for the shape of the concrete to change from the slump cone shape to cylindrical shape, in seconds, is known as Vee-Bee degree. This method is very suitable for every dry concrete whose slump value cannot be measured by Slump test.

Workability for Different Conditions:

Table 2.3: Suggested Values of Workability of Fresh Concrete for Different Placing Conditions

Degree of Workability	Placing Condition	Values of Workability			
		Compacting factor, size of aggregate			Vee-Bee time, slump for 20 mm aggregate
		10 mm	20 mm	40 mm	
1. High (flowing)	Hand compaction of heavily reinforced sections.	0.95	0.95	0.95	125-150 mm slump
2. Medium (plastic)	Concreting the lightly reinforced section by hand or vibration of heavily reinforced sections.	0.88	0.90	0.92	5-2 sec Vee-Bee time, 25-75 mm slump
3. Low (stiff plastic)	Concreting of lightly reinforced sections with vibration; road pavements and slabs with hand-operated vibrators; and vibration of mass concrete.	0.82	0.84	0.85	10-5 sec Vee-Bee time, 5-50 mm slump
4. Very low (stiff)	Concreting of shallow section with vibrations.	0.75	0.78	0.80	20-10 sec Vee-Bee time, 0-25 mm slump
5. Extremely low (very stiff)	Concreting by intensive vibrations with centrifugation, vibropressing etc.	0.65	0.69	0.80	30-20 sec Vee-Bee time.

2.3.3 Segregation, Bleeding and Harshness

1. Segregation: It can be defined as 'the separation of the constituent materials of concrete'. A good concrete is one in which all the ingredients are thoroughly and properly mixed to make a homogeneous mixture. If a sample of concrete exhibits a tendency for separation, then the sample is said to be having the tendency for segregation. Such concrete is weak and possesses undesirable properties in the hardened concrete due to lack of homogeneity. Due to considerable differences in the sizes and specific gravities in the constituent materials of concrete, it is natural that the materials show a tendency to fall apart. Segregation is of three types. Firstly, the coarse aggregates separating out from the rest of the matrix, secondly, the paste separating out from the coarse aggregate, and thirdly, water separating out from the rest of the material. A well-made concrete is that concrete which is made taking into consideration various parameters such as grading, size, shape, surface texture, optimum quantity of water etc. Such concrete will not show any tendency for segregation.

Segregation occurs in the given conditions:
   (i) Badly proportioned mix causes matrix not to bind with aggregates.
   (ii) Dropping of concrete from heights will result in segregation.
   (iii) When concrete is discharged from a badly designed mixture, it shows segregation.
   (iv) Conveyance of concrete by conveyer belt, long distance hawl by dumper, long lift by skip hoist are the other situations promoting segregation.
   (v) Excessive vibration also causes segregation.
   (vi) The immediate working on the concrete without any time interval is likely to press the coarse aggregate down which results in the movement of excess of paste to the surface.

Therefore, segregation can be removed by correctly proportioning the mix, by proper handling, transporting, placing, compacting and finishing.

Precautions for freedom from segregation:
Following points should be kept in mind in order to eliminate or minimise segregation
   (a) The concrete mix should be properly designed.
   (b) The water/cement ratio should be kept constant.
   (c) The height of free fall of concrete should not exceed 3.0 m in any case.
   (d) The concrete operation should be supervised strictly.
   (e) The concrete should be placed from the final position as near as possible.
   (f) The concrete should be remixed till it attains uniform colour.
   (g) The air entraining agents should be used for reducing segregation as these reduce the quantity of mixing water.
   (h) The water or sand content or, both should be altered for preventing segregation.
   (i) Formwork for concrete should be proper to avoid leakage.

2. Bleeding: 'It is a particular form of segregation in which some of the water from the concrete comes out to the surface of the concrete'. The bleeding is observed in a highly wet mix, badly proportioned and insufficiently mixed concrete. Due to bleeding, water comes-up and accumulates at the surface. When the surface is worked-up with the trowel and floats, the aggregates go down and the cement and water come upto the top surface. This formation of cement paste at the surface is known as '*Laitance*'. This Laitance produces dust in summer and mud in rainy season. If Laitance is formed on a particular lift, a plane of weakness will form and the bond with the next lift will be poor. This can be avoided by removing the Laitance fully before the next lift is poured. Bleeding rate increases with the time upto about one hour or so and thereafter rate decreases till final setting. Bleeding is an inherent phenomenon in concrete and can be reduced by proper proportioning and uniform mixing.

The bleeding is not completely harmful, if the rate of evaporation of water from the surface is equal to or more than the rate of bleeding. It is the delayed bleeding that causes undue harm to the concrete, when the concrete has lost its plasticity. Controlled re-vibration may be of some use to overcome the bad effects of bleeding.

Precautions for freedom from bleeding:

Following points should be kept in mind in order to reduce bleeding

(a) The concrete mix should be designed properly and carefully.

(b) Size of the aggregate should be kept as small as possible.

(c) The richer concrete should be used.

(d) Excessive vibration should not be used.

(e) If possible fines such as fly ash or pozzolana may be added to concrete.

(f) Finely ground and with low alkali content cement may be used.

(g) The air entraining agents should be used to prevent bleeding.

Difference between Segregation and Bleeding:

Segregation	Bleeding
1. The separation of coarse aggregate from the mix is called segregation of concrete.	1. The appearance of water on the surface of the compacted concrete is bleeding.
2. It is due to less percentage of cement in the mix.	2. It is due to less percentage of fine aggregate in the concrete mix.
3. It is due to improper design mix.	3. It is due to the use of excess of water.
4. It makes the concrete of poor strength.	4. It makes the surface of concrete dusty, porous and weak.

3. Harshness: Concrete is said to be harsh when, it does not give a smooth surface with a certain amount of trowelling. It indicates that the cement mortar is not sufficient to fill the voids of the coarse aggregate. The harshness is also due to the presence of excessive proportion of one particle size in an aggregate grading. This interferes with smooth finish. To avoid harshness, adequate proportion of fine aggregate to coarse aggregate must be ensured. If the grading is poor, excess particle size should be sieved, eliminated and then the aggregate is used.

But, in some situations harsh concrete is preferred for its more strength and high density. If correct amount of vibrations are used harsh concrete will turn into very dense, strong and durable concrete.

4. Cohesiveness: Lack of segregation is called 'Cohesiveness'. Minimum segregation means concrete with maximum cohesiveness.

2.3.4 Honey Combing

After compaction and formwork is removed (sides and bottom of structural elements) some holes, i.e. porous structure, observed on the surface of concrete, that porous face or surface is known as *honey combing*. This occurs due to insufficient compaction or due to leakage of cement grout from the shuttering during the concreting operations.

Following precautions should be taken during concreting to avoid honey-combing

(a) The compaction or tampering should be sufficiently done at heavy reinforced structure.

(b) The gaps in the formwork should be filled with cement or polythene bags to avoid leakage.

(c) Finely ground cement, sand may be used to form a standard paste of cement.

(d) Segregation and bleeding should be avoided.

[B] HARDENED CONCRETE

Introduction

The principal properties of hardened concrete which are of practical importance are those concerning its strength; stress-strain characteristics; shrinkage and creep deformation; response to temperature variation; permeability and durability. Of these, the strength of concrete assumes a greater significance because the strength is related to the structure of hardened cement paste and gives an overall picture of the quality of concrete. The strength of concrete at a given age under given curing conditions is assumed to depend mainly on water-cement ratio and degree of compaction. Abram's water-cement law in this connection is well-known. Probably it is more correct to relate the strength of concrete to the concentration of the solid products of hydration of cement in the space available for these products, and the Power's gel/space ratio versus strength is more relevant in these studies. The voids present in concrete mass have been found to influence greatly the strength of concrete.

2.4 Properties of Hardened Concrete

In hardened state the following are the properties of concrete
(1) Strength,
(2) Durability,
(3) Impermeability,
(4) Dimensional changes, and
(5) Fire resistance.

(1) Strength: 'The ability of concrete to resist force is called its *strength*'. The hardened concrete should, therefore, have sufficient strength to bear the load for which it is designed. The strength of hardened concrete mainly depends upon the water/cement ratio, quality of cement, degree of compaction and curing.

The strength is further classified as:
(a) Compressive strength.
(b) Flexural strength.
(c) Tensile strength.
(d) Bond strength.
(e) Shear strength.

(a) Compressive strength: The most important property of concrete is its high strength, and therefore, it is used to resist compressive stresses. The strength of the concrete generally means compressive strength and measured in N/mm^2. Compressive strength is influenced by a number of factors, in addition to the water/cement ratio and degree of compaction, which are given below.
(i) Type of cement and its quality,
(ii) Texture of aggregates,
(iii) Curing.
(iv) Temperature at which the concrete is hardened, and
(v) Time of hardening.

(b) Flexural strength: When concrete is subjected to bending, tensile and compressive strength are developed. The most common plain concrete structure, subjected to flexure, is a highway pavement. The strength of concrete for pavement is evaluated by means of bending test on beam specimens. Flexural strength is expressed in terms of 'Modulus of rupture' which is the maximum tensile or compressive stress at rupture.

It is computed from the formula $\dfrac{f}{y} = \dfrac{M}{I}$.

The value of modulus of rupture ranges from 11 to 23 per cent of the compressive strength and an average value of 15 per cent is generally adopted. The use of angular aggregate results in relatively high flexural strength as compared to compressive strength.

(c) Tensile strength: Concrete has low tensile strength. It generally varies from 8 to 12% of the compressive strength. Concrete is not normally required to resist tensile forces because of its poor tensile properties. Tension is, however, of great importance in regard to cracking caused by chemical activity, drying, shrinkage and lowering of temperature. In the design of reinforced concrete members, it is assumed that tensile stresses are taken up by reinforcement and not by the concrete.

(d) Bond strength: 'The measure of adhesion between concrete and steel, when steel is embedded in concrete', is called *bond strength*. It is more for vertical bars than horizontal bars. The bond strength can be increased by using deformed bars instead of plain bars in the concrete mix, and decreasing the water/cement ratio. Generally, hooks are provided in steel reinforcements to increase this strength.

(e) Shear strength: Shearing of concrete is always accompanied by tension and compression due to bending. Shear strength is about half the compressive strength. Concrete fails in shear strength due to diagonal tension.

Following table indicates permissible stresses for concrete with various mixes:

Table 2.4: Permissible Stresses in Concrete

Permissible stresses in N/mm^2

Sr. No.	Concrete Mix	Permissible stresses in N/mm^2					
		Compression		Tension		Bond	
		Bending	Direct	Bending	Shear	Average	Local
1.	1: 2: 4	5	4	0.5	0.5	0.6	1
2.	1: 1: 2	8	6	0.8	0.8	0.9	1.5
3.	1: 1: $\frac{1}{2}$: 3	7	5	0.7	0.7	0.8	1.3

2. Durability: 'The capacity to resist the forces of disintegration owing to natural causes, such as temperature changes, variations in moisture content, action of water containing chemicals and weather' is called *durability of concrete*.

Durability depends upon the quality of materials used for the concrete construction. It also depends upon the methods which are adopted for mixing, placing, compacting and curing the concrete.

The durability is controlled by using:

(a) Optimum water/cement ratio,

(b) Sound cement,

(c) Durable aggregates,

(d) Dense grading of aggregates,

(e) Careful hatching and mixing,

(f) Careful plaining,

(g) Thorough and uniform compaction,

(h) Long periods of curing.

Generally speaking, the life of concrete is limited by the disintegrating methods of:

(a) Weathering by the action of rain and frost.

(b) Weathering by the expansion and contraction, resulting from alternate drying and wetting.

(c) Chemical attack by industrial chemicals and wastes, sewage, animal and vegetable oils, fats, sea water etc.

(d) Wear by abrasion from foot.

(e) Wear by vehicular traffic and wind-borne particles.

3. Impermeability: The resistance provided by concrete to the passage of water through it, is called *impermeability*.

Impermeable concrete is obtained by selecting aggregates having minimum voids, using a concrete mix of low water/cement ratio, sufficient and uniform compaction and proper curing. Concrete has a tendency to be porous due to the presence of voids formed during and after planning. For obtaining workable mix, more water is used than required to a chemical combination with the cement, as such it occupies space and later on, it evaporates and leaves behind air voids. In the second case, as the chemical reaction proceeds, there is a continual decrease in the volume in the cement and water than the fresh paste.

In order to make the concrete impermeable, the surface should be covered by special gasoline-proof members, plastic films etc.

4. Elastic properties of concrete: 'The elastic properties of concrete are the properties which exhibit concrete as an elastic material'.

(a) Elasticity,

(b) Shrinkage,

(c) Creep, and

(d) Thermal expansion.

(a) Elasticity: Concrete is not truly an elastic material, but it behaves as an elastic material within the range of usual working stresses. The *modulus of elasticity* of concrete may be defined as 'the change of stress with respect to elastic strain' and is determined from the equation:

$$\text{Modulus of Elasticity, } E_c = \frac{\text{Unit stress}}{\text{Unit strain}}$$

It is a measure of the stiffness of the concrete structure.

The factors which increase the strength of concrete also increase its modulus of elasticity although to a lesser degree, lower water/cement ratios, richer mixtures, lower air contents, longer curing periods and the greater ages improve the modulus of elasticity of concrete. The type and grading of aggregates also affect the modulus of elasticity.

(b) Shrinkage: In its plastic stage, concrete shrinks due to absorption of water by the aggregate, and bleeding of the free water to the top of the surface. This water, dries rapidly at the surface and causes shrinkage. Cracks develop due to shrinkage. At this stage, the concrete being plastic, no stresses are produced due to shrinkage.

Shrinkage also occurs during chemical process of hydration of the cement. The chemical combination of cement and water results in the reduction of volume, and shrinkage takes place. If the concrete can freely shrink, it will not adversely affect the structure, but if it is retained, tensile stresses will be developed causing cracks.

Shrinkage of concrete is increased by water consistencies, greater water/cement ratios and high cement content. The shrinkage cannot be completely eliminated. It can, however, be reduced by the use of saturated aggregates, low cement content, properly designed mixes, moist and cool conditions of casting and shallow lifts on placing. Use of tight and nonabsorbent formwork will also reduce shrinkage. The action of contraction and expansion of concrete on drying and wetting is known as moisture movement. For water retaining structure, great care is to be taken to avoid development to shrinkage cracks.

Factors Affecting Shrinkage:
1. **Water/Cement ratio:** Shrinkage of concrete is increased with greater water/cement ratios.
2. **Cement content:** Greater cement content increases shrinkage.
3. **Temperature:** If the temperature of concrete is above the freezing point, cool concreting gives better ultimate strength and durability and less shrinkage.
4. **Curing:** Proper curing reduces shrinkage.
5. Relative humidity in the atmosphere affects the shrinkage, i.e. shrinkage will be less when humidity will be more.
6. Rapid drying causes more shrinkage.
7. Water saturated aggregates, properly designed concrete, moist and cool conditions of placing reduce the shrinkage.

(c) Creep: When some load is applied on a structure, deformation exists but this deformation ceases when this load is removed. If this load is applied for longer period, and deformation continues to take place and does not cease, when the load is removed, then this deformation is known as creep. In short, 'the permanent strain induced in concrete due to sustained load over a long period of time' is called creep. It is also known as plastic flow or time yield. It is more than elastic deformation. Circumstances tell the liking and disliking of creep. It is undesirable in pre-stressed concrete structure, whereas desirable in R.C.C. columns and in continuous beams, because it tries to adjust stresses in highly stressed and less stressed portions. While designing, this factor must be taken into consideration, otherwise the structure will fall. Creep may be due to viscus flow of cement/water paste or flow of water out of the cement resulting in the closure of internal voids.

Factors Affecting Creep:
(i) **Mixing proportion:** W/C ratio is the main factor affecting creep. Creep increases with increases in W/C ratio i.e. poor mix proportion increases the creep. So creep can be said to be inversely proportional to strength.
(ii) **Quality of aggregate:** If aggregate used is of good quality, creep decreases.
(iii) **Age of concrete:** Upto the time concrete achieves complete strength, creep decreases. But after that due to sustained load, creep goes on increasing.

(5) Thermal expansion: Concrete expands and contracts with variations to temperature. The average value of co-efficient of thermal expansion of concrete is $3 \times 10^{-6}/°C$, approximately same as that of steel. If the expansion and contraction of concrete is restricted, then stresses will be formed in the concrete. This expansion depends upon the types of aggregate used, if there are silicons such as quartz, then it will be highest and if calcareous aggregate, such as limestone, is used, then it will be at a minimum. In big structure, it is controlled by providing an expansion joint.

(6) Fire resistance: When concrete is subjected to high temperatures, aggregate and steel expands. The cementitious material, on heating, loses its water of crystallisation and thus shrinks. Aggregate and steel go on expanding. This causes the concrete to crack and crumble. From this point of view, quartz which has a large coefficient of expansion, should be avoided as an aggregate.

Broken bricks are more fire resisting and broken stone is better than gravel in this respect.

Steel loses its strength at high temperature. To protect it, proper cover to concrete should be provided. As the structure will be subjected to unequal expansion due to bad conductivity of concrete, the difference in expansion of steel and its surrounding concrete will be greatly minimized, if the steel is not exposed to heat directly. Usually, 2.5 to 4 cm of cover is considered to be enough. Refractory concrete can be made with high alumina cement and fire-clay brick aggregates. It can stand a temperature of 1600°C.

2.5 Microcracking

Very fine cracks occurs at the interface between coarse aggregate and cement paste even prior to application of load on concrete. The cracks remain stable upto about 30 per cent or more of the ultimate load and then begin to increase in length, number and width. At 70 to 90 per cent of ultimate strength cracks open through the mortar and forms a continuous crack pattern. This is the fast crack propagation stage and, if load is sustained, failure may take place with time.

2.5.1 How Microcracks Occurs?

Concrete is two phase material i.e. paste phase and aggregate phase. But at the microscopic level in the vicinity of large aggregate particles considered as third phase i.e. transition zone, which represents interfacial region between the particles of coarse aggregate and hardened paste. Transition zone is generally plane of weakness. The quality of paste in the transition zone is of poorer quality. Firstly due to internal bleeding, water accumulate below elongated flaky and large pieces of aggregate which reduces bond strength between paste and aggregate. Secondly, the size and concentration of crystalline compounds such as calcium hydroxide and ettringite are also longer in transition zone.

Due to drying and shrinkage or temperature variation, the transition zone develops even before a structure is loaded. When structure is loaded and at high stress levels, these microcracks propogates and bigger cracks are formed resulting in failure of bond.

2.6 Stress-Strain Relation

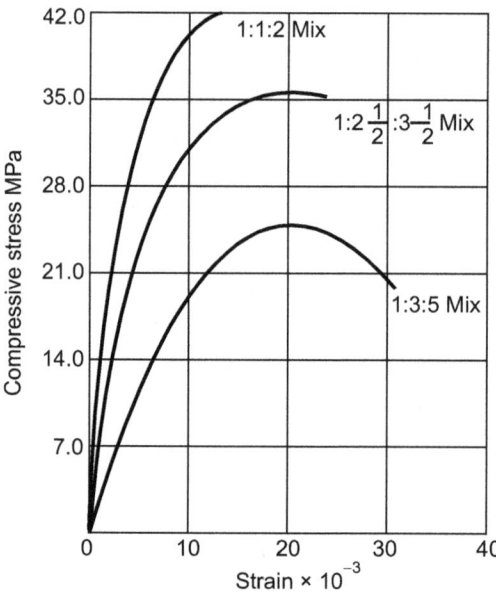

Fig. 2.8: Stress-Strain Curves for Different Mixes

A typical stress-strain curve of concrete is shown in Fig. 2.8. The relation is fairly linear in the initial stage but subsequently become non-linear reaching a maximum value and then a descending portion is obtained before concrete finally fails. The curve is generally obtained by testing a cube or cylinder under compression and measuring the deformations by means of dial gauges and load corresponding to each deformation is recorded. Then dial gauge reading divided by gauge length will give strain and load applied divided by cross-sectional area gives stress. These stress and strains are plotted on the graph to get the stress-strain relationship.

2.7 Testing of Concrete

Testing of concrete plays an important role in controlling and confirming the quality of concrete works. Systematic testing of raw materials, fresh concrete and hardened concrete are inseparable part of any quality control programme for concrete, which helps to achieve higher efficiency of the material used and greater assurance of the performance of the concrete with regard to both strength and durability.

2.7.1 Significance of Testing

One of the purposes of testing concrete is to confirm that the concrete used at site has developed the required strength. As the hardening of concrete takes time, one will not come to know the actual strength of concrete for some time. This is an inherent disadvantage in conventional test. But, if strength of concrete is to be known at an early period, accelerated strength test can be carried out to predict 28 days' strength. But, mostly, when correct materials are used and careful steps are taken at every stage of the work, concrete normally gives the required strength. The tests also have a deterring effect on those responsible for construction works. The results of the test on hardened concrete, even if they are known late, help to reveal the quality of concrete and enable adjustment to be made in the production of further concretes. Tests are made by casting cubes or cylinder from the representative concrete or cores cut from the actual concrete. It is to be remembered that the standard compression test specimen gives a measure of the potential strength of the concrete, and not of the strength of the concrete in structure.

2.7.2 Determination of Compressive Strength of Concrete Cubes

Compression test is carried to determine the compressive strength of concrete cubes or concrete cylinders. It is the most common test conducted on hardened concrete, partly because it is on easy test to perform and partly because most of the desirable characteristic properties of concrete are qualitatively related to its compressive strength.

The compression test is carried out on cube specimen of the size $15 \times 15 \times 15$ cm or cylinder of height 30 cm and diameter 15 cm. Concrete ingredients are filled into the mould in three layers and each layer is compacted by tamping rod not less than 25 blows or by using vibrators. Same specimens are placed in water for curing at temperature $27° \pm 2°$ C. The cube moulds are tested after 3 days, 7 days (168 Hrs) and 28 days (672 Hrs). The days/Hrs, being measured from the time the water is added to the dry ingredients.

The failure load divided by cross-sectional area i.e. 225 cm^2 gives the ultimate compressive strength of the cubes. When the cubes are tested at 3, 7 and 28 days curing rapid hardening concrete shows about 90% strength gain in the first 7 days and remaining in the days thereafter. The test results are co-related by testing 2 and 3 specimens at each curing period.

The strength of the concrete depends on number of variables; they include:
1. Water/Cement ratio,
2. Fineness of cement,
3. Curing time,
4. Age of concrete,
5. Strength of aggregate,
6. Size of aggregate,
7. Grading, texture, and shape of the aggregate, and
8. Temperature of curing.

Approximate relation of strength of concrete with water/cement ratio is given by:

$$\text{Strength} = k \left[\frac{C}{(W + C + A)} \right]^2$$

where A, C and W are absolute volumes of air, cement and water, and k is a constant depending upon the characteristics of the materials, particularly cement.

Relative strength of the concrete with age of concrete with respect to that of 28 days curing is given in table 2.5 on a qualitative basis. The designer can give an appropriate correction to the strength of concrete when he is certain about the time of actual application of the load.

Table 2.5: Relative Strength of Concrete at Different Ages

Period after casting	Age factor
7 days	0.65
28 days	1.0
3 months	1.10 to 1.15
6 months	1.15 to 1.20
12 months	1.20 to 1.25

2.8 Creep

We have seen that the relation between stress and strain for concrete is a function of time. The gradual increase in strain with time under load is due to creep. Creep can thus be defined as "the increase in strain under a sustained stress". All materials undergoes creep under some condition of loading to a greater extent. But concrete creeps significantly at all stresses and for a long time. Creep in concrete is associated with gel structure of cement paste.

When a concrete is subjected to loading, the deformation of concrete member takes place. The deformation of member increases with time even if load is kept constant. This phenomenon is called as creep of concrete, or plastic flow, plastic yield or plastic deformation.

The creep may be due to viscous flow of the cement paste, closure of internal voids and crystalline flow in aggregates, but it is believed that the major portion is caused by seepage of colloidal water from the gel that is formed by hydration of cement. The rate of expulsion of the colloidal water is a function of the applied compressive load and of the friction in the capillary channels. The greater the force, the steeper the pressure gradient with resulting increase in rate of expulsion of moisture and deformation.

Creep occurs both in compressive and tensile loading and it is assumed that the magnitude of creep is same in both the cases. If a loaded concrete member is kept in a atmosphere subjected to shrinkage, member will undergo in deformation from three different causes viz. elastic deformation, drying shrinkage and creep deformation as shown in Fig. 2.9. The creep magnitude can be calculated by knowing the magnitude of deformation due to shrinkage and elastic deformation and deducting the sum of these two deformations from the total deformation gives the *magnitude of creep*.

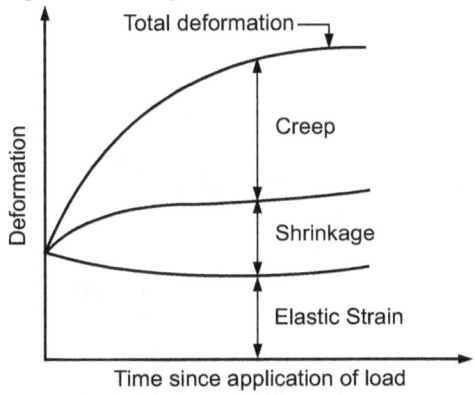

Fig. 2.9: Time-Dependent Deformation in Concrete Subjected to a Sustained Load

If a sustained load is removed, the strain decreases immediately by an amount equal to the elastic strain at the given age, generally lower than the elastic strain on loading. This instantaneous recovery is followed by a gradual decrease in strain called *creep recovery* (Fig. 2.10). The shape of the creep recovery curve is rather like that of the creep curve, but the recovery approaches its maximum value much more rapidly. The reversal of creep is not complete, and creep is not a simply reversible phenomenon, so that any sustained application of load, even only over a period of a day, results in residual deformation.

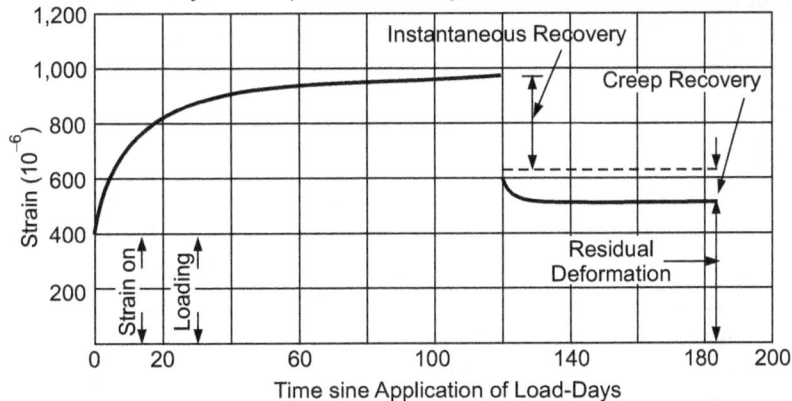

Fig. 2.10: Creep and Recovery of a Mortar Specimen Stored in Air at a Relative Humidity of 95 per cent, Subjected to a Stress of 15 MPa and Then Unloaded

2.8.1 Factors Affecting Creep

(i) **Influence of aggregate:** Aggregate influence the creep of concrete through restraining effect on the magnitude of creep. Greater the maximum size of aggregate graded uniformly from fine to coarse, the less is the creep of concrete. The modulus of elasticity of aggregate also influence the creep. Higher the modulus of elasticity lesser is the creep. Light weight aggregate shows higher creep than normal weight aggregate.

(ii) **Water-cement ratio:** A higher water-cement ratio increases the size of pores in the paste structure. This makes the water to escape easily and under a sustained load, the absorbed water may be expelled readily and this causes a high rate of creep. Broadly speaking all the factors affecting water cement ratio affects the creep.

(iii) **Influence of age:** Age of the concrete at the time of loading effect the creep. As we know the quality of gel improves with time. Such gels creeps less, whereas young gels under load creeps more because they are not so stronger.

(iv) **Type of cement:** The type of cement affects the creep as it influence the strength of concrete at the time of application of load. In fact, the portland cement and high alumina cement lead to same creep. Under drying conditions, portland blast furnace cement results in higher creep than the usual type of portland cement. For the same strength, concrete with portland pozzolana cement may exhibit less creep, as initially there is less cement paste present. Fineness of cement affects the strength development at early ages and thus influences creep. The creep is inversely proportional to the strength of concrete at the time of application of load.

(v) **Relative humidity of air:** One of the most important factor affecting the creep is the relative humidity of air surrounding the concrete. We can say that, for a given concrete, creep is higher at lower relative humidity.

(vi) **Size of specimen:** Creep has been found to decrease with an increase in the size of the specimen. This is due to the reduced seepage, as the path travelled by the expelled water is greater with a resulting increase in frictional resistance to the flow of water from the interior.

2.9 Shrinkage

Volume change is one of the objectionable property of concrete which affect the long term strength and durability. Due to the volume change the cracks are developed in the concrete. The volume change is mainly due to thermal property of aggregate and concrete, alkali aggregate reaction, sulphate action etc. One of the objectionable defect in concrete is the presence of cracks, particularly in floors and pavements.

The important factor which contribute to the cracks in floor and pavement is due to shrinkage. It is difficult to make concrete which does not shrink or crack. *Shrinkage* can be defined as "volume change of concrete due to loss of moisture at different stages due to different reasons."

Shrinkage can be classified in the following ways:

(a) Plastic shrinkage.
(b) Drying shrinkage.
(c) Autogeneous shrinkage.
(d) Carbonation shrinkage.

(a) Plastic Shrinkage: Plastic shrinkage occurs soon after the concrete is placed or when the concrete is in plastic state. The reason of plastic shrinkage is loss of water from the surface of concrete due to evaporation or by absorption by aggregates or subgrade. The loss of water results in reduction of volume.

In case of floor and pavements where the large surface area is exposed to drying as compared to depth, the drying of concrete is very fast. In such cases, due to exposed surface area to hot sun and drying wind result is plastic shrinkage.

Sometimes if concrete surface is not subjected to drying but made with high water-cement ratio, large quantity of water bleeds and rise to the surface. When this water dries, the surface of concrete gets cracked. This type of effect may occur due to the excess vibration or yielding of formwork.

The shrinkage can be reduced by controlling the loss of water from the surface of concrete. This can be done by proper curing or by covering the surface of concrete by polyethylene sheeting immediately after placing the concrete or by working at night.

(b) Drying Shrinkage: The hydration is the continuous process, the drying shrinkage is also a continuous process when concrete is subjected to drying condition. Drying shrinkage of concrete is similar to drying of timber. The loss of free water from concrete does not cause any volume change. But the loss of water held in gel pores causes the volume change. The shrinkage may be defined as, "volume change that takes place after the concrete has set and hardened". Windrawal of water from concrete stored in unsaturated air voids causes shrinkage, a part of this shrinkage can be recovered on immersion of concrete in water.

(c) Autogeneous Shrinkage: In a sealed concrete where no moisture movement to or from the paste is permitted when temperature is constant some shrinkage may occur, known as autogeneous shrinkage. This occurs in the interior of large concrete mass. This type of shrinkage is of least importance and hence not applicable in the practice.

(d) Carbonation Shrinkage: The CO_2 present in atmosphere reacts with $Ca(OH)_2$ present in cement in the presence of moisture forming $CaCO_3$. Carbonation penetrates beyond the exposed surface of concrete only very slowly. Carbonation is accompanied by increase in weight and shrinkage. Carbonation also results in increased strength and reduced permeability. The magnitude of carbonation shrinkage is very small and hence it is not of much significance.

2.9.1 Factors Affecting Shrinkage

The factors which affects the creep also affects the shrinkage. The factors which influence the shrinkage are listed below.

(a) **Water-cement ratio:** Shrinkage increases with increase in water-cement ratio.
(b) **Cement content:** The shrinkage increases with cement content.
(c) **Relative humidity:** The shrinkage increases with decrease in humidity and the immersion of concrete in water causes expansion.
(d) **Type of aggregate:** Aggregates which exhibit moisture movement and low modulus of elasticity causes large shrinkage. Increase in maximum size causes restraining effect hence decreases shrinkage.
(e) **Size and shape of specimen:** Shrinkage decreases with increase in size of specimen.
(f) **Type of cement:** Shrinkage is somewhat more in rapid hardening cement than other types.

These are the some of the major factors affecting the shrinkage. Shrinkage of concrete results in cracks in concrete which can not be eliminated but can be reduced by reducing the shrinkage. The part of the shrinkage may be recovered by immersing the concrete in water. The effect of drying and wetting on shrinkage is shown in Fig. 2.11.

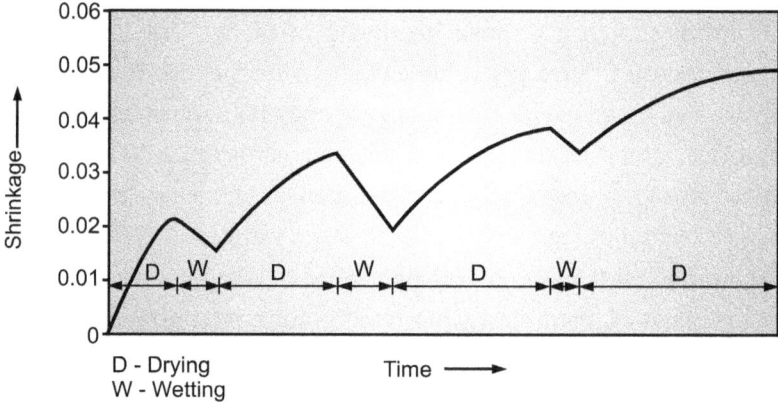

Fig. 2.11: Diagram of Effect of Drying and Wetting on Shrinkage

2.10 Quality Control during Concreting

Quality in general terms is totality of features and characteristics of a product or service that bear on its ability to satisfy the stated or implied needs. The stated or implied needs are those derived by balanced excellence and equity within the sustainable regime and in the given socio-techno-economic scenario. The quality management has evolved over the period through:

- Policing quality – acceptance and Rejection through inspection and assessment by user.
- Judging quality – confidence building through third party judgement.
- Fostering quality – ensuring quality of the final product by attending to quality at all intermediary stages such as in Certification Marking Schemes.

Concrete, generally manufactured at the site, is likely to have variability of performance from batch to batch and also within the batch. The magnitude of this variation depends on several factors, such as the variation in the quality of constituent materials, variation in mix proportions due to batching process, variations in the quality of batching and mixing equipment available, the quality of overall workmanship and supervision at the site, and variation due to sampling and testing of concrete specimens.

The above variations are inevitable during production to varying degrees. For example, the cements from different batches or sources may exhibit different strengths. The grading and shape of aggregates even from the same source varies widely. Considerable variations occur partly due to the quality of the plant available and partly due to the efficiency of operation. Some of the variations in test results are due to variations in sampling, making, curing and testing the specimen even when carried out in terms of relevant specifications.

The quality control of concrete is thus to reduce this variation and to produce concrete of uniform quality consistent with specified minimum performance requirements which can be achieved by good workmanship and maintenance of the plant at peak efficiency.

The concrete industry strives at making 'quality', a way of life and a way of management through Quality Systems Approach covering all aspects of ISO 9000 series.

Exercise

1. State advantages and disadvantages of slump test.
2. State importance of concrete.
3. Explain process diagram concrete.
4. Define the following term:
   (i) Concrete
   (ii) Workability
5. State the properties of concrete.

6. State the factors influencing workability and durability separately.
7. Explain the difference between bleeding and segregation and state measures to be taken to avoid each.
8. Explain the effect of water-cement ratio on strength of concrete. Show the relation between water-cement ratio and compressive strength by graph.
9. Define the term water-cement ratio and its importance.
10. Explain the Vee Bee consistometer test related to workability.
11. Write a brief note on creep of concrete.
12. (a) Define the workability of concrete. State the various methods for measurement of workability of concrete mix in laboratory. Explain any one with sketch.
    (b) Enlist factors affecting strength of concrete.

Unit 3

ADMIXTURES, TYPES OF CONCRETE AND SPECIAL CONCRETE

[A] ADMIXTURES

3.1 Introduction

A material other than cement, water and aggregate that is used as an ingredient of concrete and added to batch before or during mixing is called as *admixture*. Admixtures are used in concrete to improve a certain property of concrete. The properties which are commonly modified by adding admixture are rate of hydration, setting time, workability, dispersion and air entrainment. Generally the quantity of admixture added is small.

3.2 Functions of Admixtures

1. Admixtures are used to accelerate the rate of hydration.
2. Used to reduce the initial setting time.
3. Used to increase the strength of concrete.
4. Used to improve the workability.
5. Reduces the heat of hydration.
6. Helps in improving the durability of concrete.
7. Help in controlling shrinkage, creep, and swelling of concrete.
8. Increases the impermeability of concrete.
9. Improves the pumpability of concrete.
10. Used to increase the bond between old and new concrete layers.
11. Prevents the corrosion of concrete.
12. Increases the resistance to chemical attack.
13. Used to produce cellular concrete.
14. Used to produce coloured concrete or mortar.
15. Used to produce concrete of fungicidal, germicidal and insecticidal properties.

3.3 Classification of Admixtures

Admixtures are classified as follows:

1. Plasticizers (water reducer): Reduce water requirement and to increase workability (high range water reducer).

2. Superplasticizers: Improved version of plasticizer.
3. Accelerators: Accelerate the harding process, so used for urgent repair work.
4. Retarders: Slows down the chemical process of hydration, so used in Hot weather.
5. Grouting admixtures.
6. Air entraining admixtures: Produce air bubble hence increase the fluidity of concrete.
7. Air detraining admixtures: Remove excess air bubble.
8. Gas forming admixtures: Reduce gas bubble for light weight concrete.
9. Expansion producing admixtures.
10. Waterproofing admixtures: Improve workability, reduce water, make dense and impervious concrete.
11. Corrosion inhabiting admixtures: Prevent corrosion of reinforcement.
12. Fungicidal, germicidal and insecticidal admixture.
13. Bonding admixture: Increase bond strength between old and new concrete.
14. Pozzolanic or mineral admixture: More resistant to action of salt.
15. Colouring admixture: Add pigment to obtained coloured concrete.
16. Workability admixtures: Improve workability of concrete.

3.3.1 Platicizers

As we have discussed earlier concrete requires different workabilities in different situations. The workability of concrete can be increased either by making changes in the quantities of ingredient or by adding excess water. But by adding excess water only fluidity of concrete is increased not the workability and another disadvantage of excess water is loss of homogeneity, affect the strength and durability of concrete, increase in tendency of segregation and bleeding etc.

Now-a-days we are having plasticizers and superplasticizers which can be used to improve the workability without using the extra water. These are also called as *water reducers*. In practice, now-a-days use of plasticizers and superplasticizers is increased all over the world for reinforced concrete works and even for mass concreting work to reduce the water requirement and to increase the workability of concrete. Due to the use of superplasticizers the water-cement ratio is reduced for given workability, which naturally increases the strength of concrete and durability of concrete. The quantity of plasticizers used in concrete is about 0.1% to 0.4% by weight of cement. For these doses for constant workability the reduction in water requirement is about 5% to 15%. At the same time the increase in workability at same water-cement ratio may be about 30 mm to 150 mm slump. This naturally increases the strength.

As discussed above, the plasticizers are mainly used to fluidise the mix and improve the workability. The mechanism due to which this happens is dispersion. The portland cement has tendency to flocculate in wet concrete. Some amount of water get entrapped in the flocs. When the plasticizers are used they get absorbed on the cement particles and creates particle to particle repulsive force. Due to which particles are deflocculated or dispersed, which releases water entrapped into flocs and make it available to fluidify the mix.

The basic products used as plasticizers are:
1. Anionic surfactants – Lingosulphonates, salts of sulphonates, hydrocarbons.
2. Non-ionic surfactants – Polyglycol esters, acid of hydroxylated carboxylic acids.
3. Carbohydrates etc.

3.3.2 Superplasticizers

These are improved version of plasticizers also called as high range water reducers. By using superplasticizers the reduction of water requirement for same workability is about 30% whereas it was 15% in case of plasticizers. The practical application of superplasticizers is for production of flowing, self levelling, self compacting and high strength and high performance concrete. The mechanism of action of superplasticizer is more or less same as plasticizers. By using superplasticizers it is possible to use water-cement ratio as low as 0.25 or even lower than this, to obtain the high strength concrete. Along with the increased strength with lower water cement ratio, it also permits a reduction of cement content.

The products used as superplasticizers are:
1. Modified lingosulphonates.
2. Sulphonated melamine – Formaldehyde.
3. Sulphonated napthalene – Formaldehyde.
4. Acrylic polymer based.
5. Cross linked acrilic polymer.
6. Multicarboxylatethers etc.

3.3.3 Accelerators

These are the admixtures which are added to concrete to accelerate the hardening process or early strength of the concrete. These are generally used to permit earlier removal of formwork, to reduce the required period for curing. These are used commonly in the emergency repair work and in cold weather concreting where it compensate the retarding effect due to low temperature. The products which are used as accelerator are:
1. Calcium chloride.
2. Soluble carbonates.
3. Silicates, fluosilicates and
4. Organic compounds such as triethenolamine.

Calcium chloride is not used now-a-days because the recent studies shows that these are harmful to reinforced concrete and prestressed concrete but may be used for plain cement concrete. Now-a-days some of the accelerators produced are powerful which sets the concrete stone hard within five minutes or less. These are very useful for underwater construction, repair works of water constructions and basements. These may be used in the concreting at low temperature.

3.3.4 Retarders

These are the admixtures which slows down the chemical process of hydrations so that concrete will remain plastic and workable for longer time. These are very useful in case of hot weather concreting to overcome the accelerated hydration process. These are also used in mass concreting to avoid the cold joints. The products which can be used as retarders are:

1. Sugar.
2. Carbohydrate derivatives.
3. Soluble zinc salts.
4. Soluble borates.
5. Calcium sulphate.
6. Lingo sulphonic acids and their salts.
7. Hydroxylated carboxylic acids etc.

Sometimes concrete may have to be placed in difficult condition and delay may occur in transporting and placing. In RMC, the concrete is to be transported for longer distance to the site and takes considerable time. In all above cases, setting time requires to be retarded by using retarders, so that concrete remain in plastic state when finally placed and compacted. Retarders may be used on the surface of formwork so that it prevents the hardening of matrix at the interface of the concrete and formwork, whereas the rest of the concrete gets hardened.

Gypsum may be used as retarders under adequate inspection and control, otherwise addition of excess amount may cause undesirable expansion and indefinite delay in the setting of concrete. Some of the retarders also reduce the water requirement of the mixture, making further reduction possible in the water-cement ratio. These admixtures increase the compressive strength and also durability under freezing and thawing.

3.3.5 Grouting Admixtures

Grouting under different conditions requires different qualities of grout mixes. In some cases grouting mixture required to set earlier and in some cases grouting mixtures required to flow for longer period so that it can flow into cavities and fine cracks. There are many admixtures which can be used as grouting mixtures such as accelerators, retarders, gas forming agents, workability agents and plasticizers which satisfies the requirements of grouting mixtures.

Accelerators are used where early setting or plugging effect is required. Plasticizers and superplasticizers are one of the ingradient of the grout mixture for effective fluidity.

3.3.6 Air Entraining Admixtures

These admixtures when used in concrete, forms millions of air bubbles which will act as flexible ball bearings and will modify the property of plastic concrete without altering the setting or rate of hardening property of concrete.

The type of air entraining agents used to produce the air entraining concrete are:
1. Natural wood resins.
2. Animal and vegetable fats and oils.
3. Alkali salts or sulphated and sulphonated organic compounds.
4. Water soluble soaps of resin acids.
5. Hydrogen peroxide, aluminium powder etc.

Use of air entraining agent increases the resistance of concrete to freezing and thawing, increases the workability, reduces the tendancy of concrete to segregate and bleeding and laitance, decreases the permeability, increases the resistance to chemical attack. Different air entraining agents produces different amount of air bubbles. The amount of air entertainment increases with the mixing time upto certain limit and thereafter reduces. The air entrainment decreases with increase in temperature of concrete. The action of air entraining agent in concrete is that, when these are mixed in concrete it reduces the friction between the particles (as shown in Fig. 3.1) hence increases the fluidity of concrete. Air entrainers while improving the plasticity and durability of concrete, may have an adverse effect on strength of concrete. Air entraining agents also find very useful application in making cellular concrete and light-weight aggregate concrete.

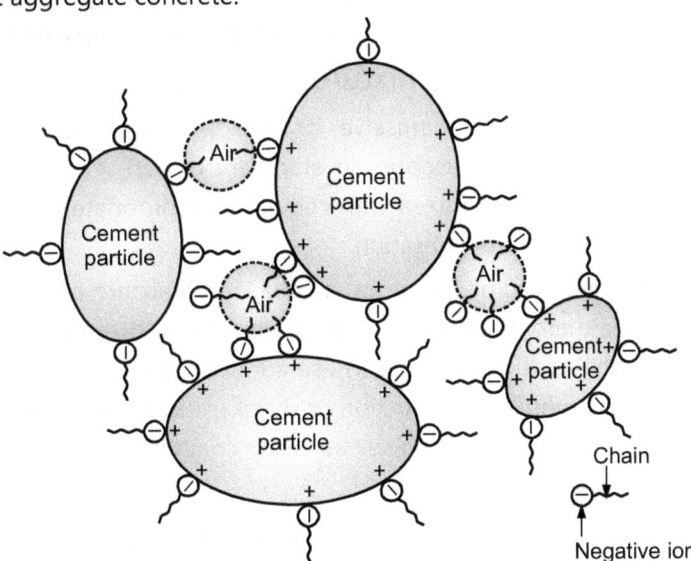

Fig. 3.1: Structure of Air-entrained of Concrete

3.3.7 Air Detraining Agents

Sometimes aggregates releases gases into or excessive air entrainment, in plastic concrete. To overcome these excess air entrainment it is necessary to use an admixtures which are capable of dissipating the excess of air or other gases. The compounds which can be used as air detraining agents are tributyl phosphate, water insoluble alcohol and silicones. These helps in removing the part of the air entrained from the concrete mixture.

3.3.8 Gas Forming Admixtures

A gas forming agent is a chemical admixture such as aluminium powder, which reacts with hydroxides and produces small bubbles of hydrogen gas throughout the matrix. The quantity of gas formation depends on the amount of aluminium powder, fineness, composition of cement, temperature and mix proportion. The quantity generally added is about 0.005 to 0.02% by weight of cement. But when light weight concrete is produced the large quantity may be used. The action of gas formation when properly controlled, causes a slight expansion of plastic concrete or mortar and thus reduces or eliminates the voids caused by normal settlement that occur during the placement of concrete. This may also increases the bond to reinforcing bars and improve the effectiveness of grout in filling joints. The zinc, magnesium powders and hydrogen peroxide are also used as gas forming agents. Larger amounts of powders increases the expansion appreciably resulting in light-weight, low-strength concrete. Some times hydrogen peroxide and bleaching powder can be used in combination to produce oxygen gas instead of hydrogen bubbles in concrete.

3.3.9 Expansion Producing Admixtures

These admixtures either expand themselves or react with other constituents of concrete with resulting expansion. These are used in development of non-shrinking cement in which expansion producing compound is mixed with cement in appropriate proportion to get the desired expansion or shrinkage compensation.

The products which are used as expansion producing admixture are granulated iron and anhydrous sulpoaluminate etc. The expansion produced due to use of these admixtures may be about the same as the drying shrinkage. These admixtures are employed in laying heavy machine foundations, patching and production of shrinkage compensating concrete which is free from shrinkage cracks, and producing self stressing concrete.

3.3.10 Water Proofing Admixtures

The important requirement of concrete is that it must be impervious to water under two conditions, firstly, when subjected to pressure on one side, secondly absorption of water by capillary action. Water proofing admixtures are available in powder, paste or liquid form and may consist of pore filling or water repellent materials. The materials which are used in pore filling class are silicate of soda, aluminium, zinc sulphate and calcium chloride. In addition to pore filling these materials also accelerate the setting time of concrete and thus render the concrete more impervious at early age. The other materials which are chemically inactive pore filling materials such as chalk, fullers, earth and talc may be used. These improves the workability and facilitate the reduction of water for given workability and to make dense and impervious concrete.

Some materials such as soda, calcium soaps, potash soap, resin, vegetable oils, fats, waxes and coal tar residue are used as a water repellent materials in admixtures. Air entraining agents may be considered in this type as it increases the plasticity of concrete and therefore help to place concrete uniformly. They also reduce bleeding by holding the water in films around the air bubbles, thus reducing permeability.

3.3.11 Corrosion Inhibiting Admixtures

The problem of corrosion of reinforcement in concrete is universal. Compounds such as sodium benzoate, sodium nitrate can be used to prevent the corrosion of reinforcement. Two per cent of sodium benzoate is used in mixing water or a 10% benzoate cement slurry is used to paint the reinforcement or both may be used to prevent the corrosion. Sodium nitrate and calcium nitrate are also found effective corrosion preventive compounds.

3.3.12 Fungicidal, Germicidal and Insecticidal Admixture

Certain materials like polyhalogenated phenols, dieledren emulsions and copper compounds when grounded with cement or added as admixtures impart fungicidal, germicidal or insecticidal property to the hardened concrete or mortar.

3.3.13 Bonding Admixture

When fresh concrete is placed on the concrete already set or partially set, the bonding between these two layer will be weak. The bonding admixtures are therefore used in cement or mortar grout for application to an old concrete surface just prior to patching with mortar or concrete. The bonding admixtures are water emulsions of several organic materials. Their function is to increase the bond strength between old and new concrete. The commonly used products are rubber, synthetic rubber or any organic polymer such as polyvinyl chloride, polyvenyl acetate etc. There are two types of bonding admixture, first in which the bonding is accomplished by a metallic aggregate and in other, synthetic latex emulsions are used. The quantity used of these admixtures is about 5 to 20% by mass of cement.

3.3.14 Pozzolanic or Mineral Admixtures

Pozzolanic materials are siliceous materials, which themselves does not possess cementitious value, but meet with calcium hydroxide in presence of water to form compound of low solubility having cementitious properties. The action is termed as pozzolanic action.

Pozzolanic materials are of two types, first natural pozzolans such as clay or shale, opaline cherts, diatonaceous earths, volcanic stuff and pumicites and second, artificial pozzolans such as flyash, blast furnace slag, silica fume, rice husk ash, metakaoline, surkhi etc.

The pozzolanic materials can be used as partial replacement of portland cement. The quantity of material replaced may be between 10 to 35%. By using pozzolanic materials in the concrete, concrete may be more permeable but more resistant to the action of salt, sulphate or acids. The gain of strength is somewhat slower than the normal concrete. Pozzolana when used in concrete improves the workability, and resistance of chemical attack. It also lowers the heat of hydration and thermal shrinkage. Some pozzolans reduces the expansion caused by the alkali-aggregate reaction. Pozzolanic materials may be used as some replacement of cement resulting reduced cost.

IS 456-2000 permits the use of pozzolanas (clause 5.2) like flyash, silica fume, rice husk ash, metakaoline, ground granulated blast furnace slag (GGBS) (i.e. flyash confirming to grade I of IS: 3812 and GGBS confirming to IS 12089).

Flyash: Flyash conforming to grade I of IS 3812 may be used as part replacement of OPC provided uniform blending with cement is ensured. Flyash is the residue from the combustion of powdered coal collected by the mechanical or electrostatic separators from the fuel gases of thermal power plants. Flyash mainly consist of spherical glassy particles ranging from 1 to 150 microns in diameter. Now-a-days the use of flyash is increased to produce high strength and high performance concrete. The use of flyash as concrete admixture has not only technical advantages but it contributes also to the environmental pollution control. In our country we are producing about 75 million tons of flyash per year, the disposal of which is serious problem.

Flyash can be used in two ways in the concrete one, grind the certain per cent of fly ash with cement clinker in factory to produce portland pozzolana cement and second use the flyash as admixture on site at the time of making concrete.

The flyash produced at different factories has different chemical properties, therefore it is not available in ready to use condition. The chemical requirements of fly ash as per IS 3812 is given in Table 3.1.

Table 3.1: Chemical Requirements (IS: 3812-1981)

Sr. No.	Characteristics	Requirement
(1)	(2)	(3)
(i)	Silicon dioxide (SiO_2) plus aluminium oxide (Al_2O_3) plus iron oxide (Fe_2O_3) per cent by mass, (Min)	70.0
(ii)	Silicon dioxide (SiO_2), per cent by mass, (Min)	35.0
(iii)	Magnesium oxide (MgO), per cent by mass, (Max)	5.0
(iv)	Total sulphur as sulphur trioxide (SO_3), per cent by mass (Max)	2.75
(v)	Available alkalis, as sodium oxide (Na_2O), per cent by mass, (Max) (See Note 1)	1.5
(vi)	Loss on ignition, per cent by mass, (Max)	12.0

Note 1: Applicable only when reactive aggregates are used in concrete and are specially requested by the purchaser.

Note 2: For determination of available alkalis, IS: 4032-1968 'Method of chemical analysis of hydraulic cement' shall be referred to.

Silica Fume: Silica fume (very fine non-crystalline silicon dioxide) is a by-product of the manufacture of silicon, ferrosilicon or the like, iron quartz and carbon in electric arc furnace. It is usually used in proportion of 5 to 10% of the cement content of mix. Silica fume is essentially silicon dioxide in non-crystalline form. The silica fume are very much finer than the cement particles. The average diameter of the particle is about 0.1 micron i.e. about 100 times smaller than average cement particles.

Silica fume does not contribute to the strength, but use of it being a very fine pozzolanic material creates dense packing and pore filling of cement paste. By using silica fume it is possible to produce a concrete of about 60 to 90 MPa compressive strength.

Rice Husk Ash (RHA): Rice husk ash is produced by burning rice husk and contain large proportion of silica. To achieve amorphous state, rice husk may be burnt at controlled temperature. RHA exhibit high pozzolanic characteristics and contribute to high strength and high impermeability of concrete. Each ton of paddy produces about 40 kg of RHA.

Metakaoline: Metakoaline is obtained by calcination of pure or refined kaolintic clay at a temperature between 650°C and 850°C, followed by grinding to achieve a fineness of 700 to 900 m²/kg. The resulting material has high pozzolanic characteristics. IS: 456-2000 suggest that metakaoline having fineness 700-920 m²/kg specific surface area may be used as pozzolanic material in concrete.

Ground Granulated Blast Furnace Slag (GGBS): GGBS is a non-metallic product consist of silicates, and aluminates of calcium and other bases. The molten slag is rapidly chilled by quenching in water to form a glassy sand like grains, further these grains are ground to fineness less than 45 microns. IS: 456-2000 suggests, GGBS obtained by grinding granulated blast furnace slag confirming to IS 12089 may be used as part replacement of OPC provided uniform blending with cement is ensured.

The chemical composition of GGBS is similar to that of cement clinkers. When the GGBS is used as a replacement of cement the water requirement reduces to obtain the same slump. It also reduces the heat of hydration. Refinement of pore structure is obtained by using GGBS in concrete. The main advantage of use of GGBS is reduction in permeability and increased resistance to chemical attack. Therefore GGBS is best applicable in the marine structure or concreting in saline environment.

3.3.15 Colouring Admixtures

Certain pigments are sometime added to the concrete to obtain coloured concrete. The basic requirements of these pigments are, it should not affect the properties of concrete such as setting time, compressive strength etc. Various metallic oxides and mineral pigments are used.

The pigments are thoroughly mixed or intergrounded in cement or they may be mixed in dry concrete mixture before adding water.

3.3.16 Workability Admixtures

The admixtures which are used to improve the workability of concrete are known as *workability admixtures*. The different types of admixtures discussed earlier can be used as workability admixtures, such as retarders, platicizers, superplasticizers and air entraining agents. The details of these type of admixtures are given in previous sections of this topic.

3.4 Effects of Various Properties of Concrete

Concrete consists of cement, sand, aggregate and water. Anything other than these if added in concrete either before or during mixing to alter the properties to our desired requirement are termed as admixtures. The use of admixtures offers certain beneficial effects to concrete like improved workability, acceleration or retardation of setting time, reduce water cement ratio, and so on.

There are two basic types of admixtures available: chemical and mineral. Admixtures like flyash, silicate fume, slag comes in the category of mineral admixtures. They are added to concrete to enhance the workability, improve resistance to thermal cracking and alkali-aggregate reaction and to enable reduction in cement content.

Flyash is fine residue left after combustion of ground or powdered coal. They are all generally finer than cement and consist mainly of glassy-spherical particles as well as residues of hematite and magnetite, char and some crystalline phases formed during cooling. The use of flyash in concrete makes the mix economical, and improves the workability, reduces segregation, bleeding and reduced heat of hydration but also provides ecological benefits.

Silica fume, which is also known as microsilica. It is obtained as a byproduct during the production of silicon and ferrosilicon alloys. The particle size of silica fume is 100 times smaller than cement particles i.e. its fine as cigarette smoke. Its a highly effective pozzolanic material, which improves the properties of concrete such as improved compressive strength, bond strength, abrasion resistance, dense concrete that results in protection of reinforcement against corrosion.

Chemical admixtures are added to concrete in very small amounts mainly for air entrainment, reduction of water or cement content, plasticizing of fresh concrete mixtures or to control the setting time of concrete. These admixtures can be broadly catagorised as superplasticizers, accelerators, retarders, water reducers and air entraining admixtures.

Superplasticizers are added to reduce the water requirement by 15 to 20% without affecting the workability leading to a high strength and dense concrete. Superplasticizers are liner polymers containing sulfonic acid groups attached to the polymer at regular intervals. The commercial formulation can be sulfonated melamine-formaldehyde condensates, sulfonated naphthalene formaldehyde condensates, and modified lignosulfonates, polycar-boxylate derivatives. The main purpose of superplasticizers is to produce a flowing concrete with very high slump 175 to 200 mm which can be used effectively in densely reinforced structures, the increased slump of concrete depends upon dosage, type and time of superplasticizers (it's better to add it before concrete is placed.), water cement ratio, nature and amount of cement.

Accelerators are added to reduce the setting time of concrete thus helping early removal of forms and are also used in cold weather concreting. Calcium chloride is the most commonly used accelerator for concreting. The use of calcium chloride in reinforced concrete can promote corrosion activity of steel reinforcement. As people are getting aware so there is a growing interest in using chloride free accelerator.

Retarders are added to increase the setting time by slowing down the hydration of cement. They are preferred in places of high temperature concreting. Retarders consist of organic and inorganic agents. Organic retarders include unrefined calcium, sodium and ammonia salts lignosulfonic acids, hydrocarboxylic acids and carbohydrates. Inorganic retardants include oxides of lead, zinc, phosphate and magnesium salts. Most retarders also act as water reducers. They are called water-reducing retarders. Thus resulting in greater compressive strength due to low water cement ratio.

Water reducing admixtures are added to concrete to achieve certain workability (slump) at low water cement ratio. A concrete with specified strength at lower cement content thus saving on the cement. Water reducers are mostly used in hot weather concreting and to aid pumping. Water reducer plasticizers are hygroscopic powder, which can entrain air into concrete.

Air entraining admixtures entrain small air bubbles in concrete. These air bubbles act as rollers thus improving the workability and are also very effective in freeze-thaw cycles as they provide a cushioning effect on the expanding water in the concreting in cold climate.

Air entraining admixtures are compatible with most admixtures, care should be taken to prevent them from coming in contact during mixing.

Generally, the effectiveness of both the types of plasticisers are dependent on the ambient temperature condition and thus in summer the amount of plasticiser to be used to cater for the same degree of increase in plasticity can be more than the quantity to be used in winter.

Change in normal setting time within some fixed requirement also makes the production dependent on others chemicals and as such plasticisers with different nomenclatures are available in the market.

CICO Technologies Limited, an Indian ISO 9001: 2000 Company with 75 years backing produces a range of plasticising admixtures for concrete.

A number of RMC companies are using CICO admixtures. some modifications are required at the time of trials. modification in the Plasticisers can fulfill the requirements of any particular client.

Transparent Concrete

The reinvention of concrete seems to be a goal for architects and material scientists alike. The light transmitting concrete from Hungarian architect Aron Losoncziwas the first example we saw, but now Italian company Italcementi Group has created their own version of translucent cement that combines the best qualities of cement walls and transparent windows. The material, called i.light, was created specifically for the Italian pavilion at the

2010 World Expo in Shanghai. The walls of the pavilion felt solid and looked solid from an angle, but when viewed straight-on they looked rather like windows that were able to let in light.

Italcementi's creation was made with a proprietary mixture of cement and admixtures that bonds with a thermoplastic polymer resin. The resin is injected into tiny holes that span the width of each cement panel, resulting in approximately 20 percent transparency. The transparency can be changed by modifying the amount of resin in the panels.

Previous transparent cement creations involved using fiber optic cables to transmit light, which is an effective method but very expensive. The method used to produce i.light is much less expensive and lets in natural light from more angles. It is not yet available commercially, having been developed just for the World Expo.

[B] TYPES OF CONCRETE

3.5 Light Weight Concrete

Light-weight concrete is a concrete, which has a density much lower than that of ordinary concrete. The densities as low as 400 kg/m^3 compared to 2400 kg/m^3 of ordinary concrete, have been achieved by any of the following ways.

1. Porous, light-weight aggregates of low specific gravity are used instead of ordinary aggregates, whose specific gravity is around 2.6. Such a concrete is being generally called as light-weight aggregate concrete.
2. Large size voids can be produced in the concrete mass intentionally. Such a concrete is called aerated or cellular or foamed or gap concrete.
3. Fine aggregates can be eliminated from the mix thus producing a large number of voids. Such concrete is called no-fines concrete. The terms no-fines indicates that the concrete is composed of cement and coarse aggregate (commonly 10 or 20 mm grading) only.

3.5.1 Advantages of Light-Weight Concretes

Advantages of using light-weight concretes are:
1. The dead-weight of the structures is reduced resulting in smaller sections.
2. The form work is to withstand lower pressures during vibration than in the case in the ordinary concrete.
3. There is a better thermal insulation than ordinary concrete.
4. Light-weight concretes are very economical for non-load bearing walls.
5. Light-weight concretes can easily take and hold nails, can be easily cut and provide a good key to plaster, thus making it advantageous for precast concrete products.

Light-weight concrete has become more popular in recent years owing to the tremendous advantages it offers over the conventional concrete. Modern technology and a better understanding of the concrete has also helped much in the promotion and use of light-weight concrete. A particular type of light-weight concrete is called structural light-weight concrete is the one which is comparatively lighter than conventional concrete but at the same time strong enough to be used for structural purposes. It, therefore, combines the advantages of normal weight concrete and discards the disadvantages of normal weight concrete. This type of concrete will have great future in the years to come.

3.5.2 Light-Weight Aggregate

The light-weight aggregates having bulk density upto 1200 kg/m^3 are used to manufacture the structural concrete for reduction of the self-weight of the structure. These aggregates can be either natural, such as diotomite, pumice, volcanic cinder etc. or manufactured, such as bloated clay or foamed blast-furnace-slag. In addition to reduction in the weight, the concrete produced by using light-weight aggregate provides better thermal insulation and improve fire resistance.

The main requirement of the light-weight aggregate is its low density; some specifications limit the bulk density to 1200 kg/m^3 for fine aggregate and approximately 1000 kg/m^3 for coarse aggregates for the use in concrete. Because of high water absorption, the workable concrete mixes become stiff within a few minutes of mixing, thus requiring the wetting of the aggregates before mixing in the mixer. In the mixing operation, the required water and aggregate are usually premixed prior to the addition of cement. Approximately, 6 litres of extra water are needed per cubic metre of light-weight aggregate concrete to enhance the workability by 25 mm. To produce satisfactory strength of concrete, the cement content may be 350 kg/m^3 or more. Due to the increased permeability and rapid carbonation of concrete, the cover to the reinforcement using light-weight aggregate in concrete should be increased. The other characteristics of concrete using light-weight aggregates are coarse surface texture due to reduced workability, lower tensile strength, lower modulus of elasticity (50 to 75 per cent of that of normal concrete) and higher creep and shrinkage. However, the ratio of creep strain to the elastic strain is the same for both the light-weight and normal-weight concretes.

Light-weight aggregates can be classified into two categories namely natural light-weight aggregates and artificial light-weight aggregate.

Table 3.2

Natural light-weight aggregates	Artificial light-weight aggregates
1. Pumice	1. Artificial cinders
2. Diatomite	2. Coke breeze
3. Scoria	3. Foamed slag
4. Volcanic cinders	4. Bloated clay
5. Sawdust	5. Sintered flyash
6. Rice husk	6. Thermocole beads
	7. Expanded shales and slate
	8. Vermiculite

IS : 9142 – 1979 covers the specifications for artificial light-weight aggregates for concrete masonary units.

3.6 Polymer Concrete

Polymer concrete composites are obtained by the combined processing of polymeric materials with some or all of the ingredients of the cement concrete composites. Depending on the process by which the polymeric materials are incorporated, polymer concrete can be classified as follows:

3.6.1 Types of Polymer Concrete

Following types of polymer concrete are being developed presently. They are:

(a) Polymer impregnated concrete (PIC).

(b) Polymer cement concrete (PCC).

(c) Polymer concrete (PC).

When portland cement concrete is impregnated with selected polymers like methylmethacrylate, styrene, acrylonitrile, t-butyl styrene and polymerized by using radiation, application of heat or by chemical initiation, the resulting composite product is polymer impregnated concrete. The polymer impregnation of concrete can be either partial or total. The partial impregnation improves the durability and chemical resistance. On the other hand, total impregnation improves structural properties considerably.

Polymer cement concrete is a composite obtained by incorporating a polymeric material into concrete during the mixing stage. Such plastic mixture is cast in moulds, cured, dried and polymerised. The monomers that are used in polymer cement concrete are:
 (a) Polyster-styrene
 (b) Epoxy-styrene
 (c) Furons
 (d) Vinylidene chloride

3.6.2 Polymer Concrete

Concrete is porous, this porosity is due to air-voids, water voids or due to the inherent porosity of gel structure itself. On account of the porosity, the strength of concrete is naturally reduced. It is conceived by many research workers that reduction of porosity results in increase of strength of concrete. Therefore, process like vibration, pressure application etc. have been practised mainly to reduce porosity. For this, the addition of polymer and subsequent polymerization is the latest technique adopted to reduce the inherent porosity of the concrete, to improve the strength and other properties of concrete.

Polymer concrete is a composite wherein the polymer replaces the cement-water matrix in the cement concrete. The polymer concretes are manufactured in a manner similar to cement concrete. Monomers are added to the graded aggregate and the mixture is thoroughly mixed by hand or machine. The thoroughly mixed polymer concrete material is cast in moulds of wood, steel or aluminium etc., to the required shape or form. Mould releasing agents can be added for easy demoulding. This is then polymerized either at room temperature or at an elevated temperature. The polymer phase binds the aggregate to give a strong concrete. Polymerisation can be achieved by any of the following methods:
 (i) Thermal-catalytic reaction.
 (ii) Catalyst-promotor reaction or
 (iii) Radiation.

In first method, only the catalyst is added to the monomer and polymerisation is initiated by decomposing the catalyst by application of elevated temperatures of upto 90°C. Typical catalyst used for different monomer systems include benzoyl peroxide, methyl-ethyl-ketone peroxide etc.

In the second method, a constituent called promoter or accelerator is also added, which decomposes the catalyst or accelerates the reaction, at the ambient temperature itself. Typical promoters include nepthanate, dimethyl-p-toluidine, ferric chloride etc.

Gamma radiation is applied in the radiation polymerisation method.

Depending on the method of polymerisation and the other conditions, polymerisation takes place within a period ranging from a few minutes to a few hours.

Polymer concretes can be reinforced with steel, nylon, polypropylene or glass fibres in a manner similar to cement concrete. Polymer concretes have good potential as repair material and for overlaps. Polymer concrete can be used for rapid repair of damaged airfields, pavements and industrial structures. It can also be used for treating the sluice ways and stilling basic of the dam. Polymer concrete pipes have been used for the transportations of a variety of chemicals, for carrying effluents and waste water etc. Polymer concretes posses good electrical properties and can be used for high voltage insulator application. Electrical structures such as poles for electrical transmission lines have been manufactured from polymer concrete.

3.7 Fibre Reinforced Concrete

Concrete is presently the most widely used construction material. Because of its speciality of being cast in any desirable shape, it has replaced stone and brick masonry. Inspite of all this, it has some serious deficiencies which for its remarkable qualities of flexibility, resilience and ability to redistribute stress, would have prevented its use as a building material. Plain concrete is inherently weak in tension and has limited ductility and little resistance to cracking. Microcracks are inherently present in concrete and because of its low tensile strength, the cracks propagate with the application of load, leading to brittle fracture of concrete. The low tensile strength of concrete is being compensated for in several ways and this has been achieved by the use of reinforcing bars and also by applying prestressing techniques. Though these methods provide tensile strength to concrete, they do not increase the inherent tensile strength of concrete itself. These deficiencies have led researchers to investigate and develop a material which could perform better in areas where conventional concrete has several limitations. One such development has been two phase composite material i.e. fibre reinforced concrete, in which cement based matrix is reinforced with ordered or random distribution of fibres of specific geometry.

Fibre reinforced concrete can be defined as "a composite material consisting of mixtures of cement mortar or concrete and discontinuous, discrete, uniformly dispersed suitable fibres".

3.7.1 Types of Fibre

Fibre is a small piece of reinforcing material possessing characteristic properties. They can be circular or flat. The fibre is often described by a convenient parameter called "aspect ratio". The aspect ratio of the fibre is the ratio of its length to its diameter. Typical aspect ratio ranges from 30 to 150.

Fibre can be broadly classified into two categories namely naturally occuring fibres and artificial fibres.

Naturally occuring fibres are produced in almost all countries. Their processing requires very low degree of industrialization. The energy requirements and cost for their production is also very low. Further random mixing of fibres in cement or cement concrete requires semi-skilled personnel in construction work. This makes locally available natural fibres a very attractive material for improving and reducing the cost of cement concrete.

The natural fibres are basically of four types:

1. Bast or stem fibres (e.g. Jute, Flax, Hemp, Kneaf)
2. Leaf fibres (e.g. Sisal, Henequeen)
3. Fruit fibres (e.g. Coir)
4. Wood fibres (e.g. Bamboo, Reeds etc.)

The use of natural fibres as reinforcing medium not only in the cement matrices but also in soil cement construction, provides a wide flexibility in its use. This is mainly due to use of locally available material and least dependence for its production on industry. The relative cheapness of natural fibres points the direction of their development in large scale as a building material in conjunction with cement concrete for housing and many other cost effective construction.

However, their low elastic modulus, high water absorption, susceptibility to fungal and insect attack, alkali attack from the cement concrete are the disadvantages of using natural fibres.

Artificial fibres are steel, glass, carbon, polypropylene, nylon, polyester, polyethylene.

Steel fibre is one of the most commonly used fibre. Generally, round fibres are used. The diameter vary from 0.25 to 0.75 mm. The steel fibre is likely to get rusted and lose some of its strengths. But investigations have shown that the rusting of the fibres takes place only at the surface. Use of steel fibre makes significant improvements in flexural, impact and fatigue strength of concrete. It has been extensively used in various types of structures, particularly for overlays of roads, airfield pavements and bridge decks.

Polypropylene and nylon fibres are found to be suitable to increase the impact strength. They posses very high tensile strength, but their low modulus of elasticity and higher elongation do not contribute to the flexural strength.

Glass fibre is a recent introduction in making fibre concrete. It has very high tensile strength (10200 to 40800 kg/sq.cm.). Glass fibre which is originally used in conjunction with cement was found to be effected by alkaline condition of cement. Therefore, alkali-resistant glass fibre by trade name "CEM-FIL" has been developed and used. The alkali resistant fibre reinforced concrete show considerable improvement in durability when compared to the conventional E-glass fibre.

Carbon fibre possess very high tensile strength (21120 to 28150 kg/sq.cm.) and young's modulus. It has been reported that cement composite made with carbon fibre as reinforcement will have very high modulus of elasticity and flexural strength. The limited studies have shown good durability.

In another way, fibre can be classified into two basic categories, those having a higher modulus of elasticity than concrete matrix (**called hard intrusion**) and those with lower elastic modulus (**called soft intrusion**). Steel, carbon and glass have higher modulus of elastic modulli than cement mortar matrix and polypropylene. Nylon and vegetable fibres (For example, jute, coir, bamboo etc.) are low modulus fibres. High modulus fibres improve both flexural and impact resistance simultaneously. Whereas low modulus fibres improve impact resistance of concrete but do not contribute much to flexural strength.

3.7.2 Factors Affecting Properties of Fibre Reinforced Concrete

Fibre reinforced concrete is the composite material containing fibres in cement matrix in an orderly manner or randomly distributed manner. Its properties would obviously, depend upon the efficient transfer of stress between matrix and the fibres, which is largely dependent on the type of fibre, fibre geometry, fibre content, orientation and distribution of the fibres, mixing and compaction techniques and concrete and shape and size of the aggregate. These factors are briefly discussed below.

3.7.3 Relative Fibre-Matrix Stiffness

For efficient stress transfer to the fibre, the elastic modulus of the matrix must be lower than that of the fibre. Low modulus fibres, such as natural fibres, nylon and polypropylene, are not likely to give much strength improvement. High modulus fibres such as metallic fibres (For example, steel), glass or crystalline inorganic fibres (For example, asbestos) normally lead to strong composites. High strength high modulus fibres impart characteristics of strength and stiffness to the composite, where low modulus high elongation fibres are capable of large energy absorption characteristics and impart a greater degree or toughness and resistance to impact and explosive loading. The former also contribute to these dynamic properties but to a lesser extent.

3.7.4 Fibre-Matrix Interfacial Bond

The interfacial bond between the matrix and the fibre determines the effectiveness of stress transfer from the matrix to the fibre.

A good bond is essential for improving tensile strength of the composite. The interfacial bond could be improved by larger area of contact, improving the frictional properties and degree of gripping and by treating the steel fibres with sodium hydroxide or acetone.

3.7.5 Fibre-Matrix Strain Compatibility

Associated with the relative fibre-matrix stiffness, the interfacial bond is the need for strain compatibility between the fibre and the matrix. With cement-based matrices, the cracking and often the ultimate strain is of the order of 250 to 500×10^{-4} m/m and since most fibres have far greater extensibility, bond failure occurs early and hinders the efficient use of fibre reinforcement. The low cracking strain of the cement matrix also implies that reinforcement of the matrix can be achieved at fairly low volume fractions of the fibre.

3.7.6 Volume of Fibres

The strength of the composite largely depends on the quantity of fibre used in it. Fig. 3.2 and Fig. 3.3 shows the effect of volume on the toughness and strength. It can be seen from Fig. 3.3, that increase in the volume of fibres, increase approximately, linearly, the tensile strength and the toughness of the composite. Use of higher percentage of fibre is likely to cause segregation and harshness of concrete and mortar.

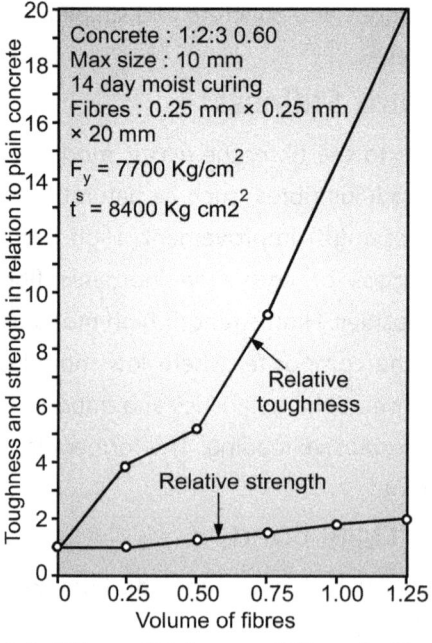

Fig. 3.2: Effect of Volume of Fibres in Flexure

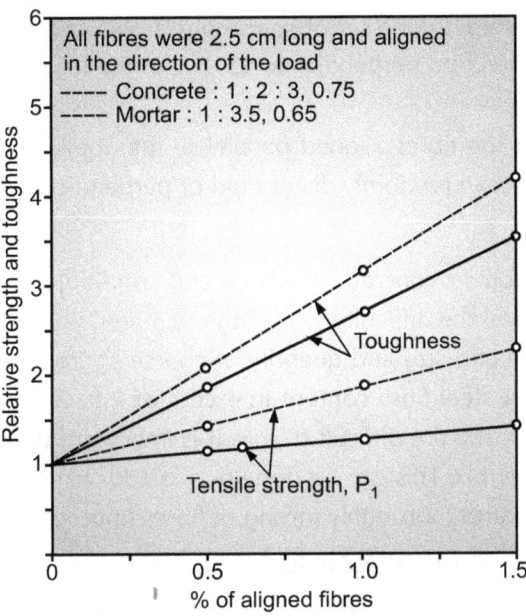

Fig. 3.3: Effect of Volume of Fibres in Tension

3.7.7 Aspect Ratio of the Fibre

Another important factor which influences the properties and behaviour of the composite is the aspect ratio of the fibre. It has been reported that upto aspect ratio of 75, increase in the aspect ratio increase the ultimate strength of the concrete linearly. Beyond 75, relative strength and toughness is reduced. Table 3.2 shows the effect of aspect ratio on strength and toughness.

Table 3.2

Types of concrete	Aspect ratio	Relative strength	Relative toughness
Plain concrete	0	1.00	1.0
With	25	1.50	2.0
Randomly	50	1.60	8.0
Dispersed	75	1.70	10.5
Fibres	100	1.50	8.5

3.7.8 Orientation of Fibres

One of the differences between conventional reinforcement and fibre reinforcement is that in conventional reinforcement, bars are oriented in the direction desired while fibres are randomly oriented. To see the effect of randomness, mortar specimens reinforced with 0.5 %

volume of fibres were tested. In one set of specimens, fibres were aligned in the direction of load, in another in the direction perpendicular to that of the load, and in the third randomly distributed.

It was observed that the fibres aligned parallel to the applied load offered more tensile strength and toughness than randomly distributed or perpendicular fibres.

3.7.9 Mixing

Mixing of fibre reinforced concrete needs careful conditions to avoid balling of fibres, segregation, and in general the difficulty to mixing the materials uniformly. Increase in aspect ratio, volume percentage and size and quantity of coarse aggregate intensify the difficulties and balling tendencies. A steel fibre content in excess of 2 to 3 per cent by volume and an aspect ratio of more than 100 are difficult to mix. It is important that the fibres are dispersed uniformly throughout the mix. This can be done by the addition of fibres before the water is added. Therefore, proper and thoroughly mixing of fibres improve the strength of composite.

3.7.10 Applications of Fibre Reinforced Concrete

The applications of fibre reinforced concrete depends upon the techniques and design approach. Its application can be broadly classified in two heads i.e. cast-in-situ structures and precast products. Due to the superior properties like increased tensile and bending strengths, improved ductility, resistance to cracking, high impact strength and toughness, and high energy absorption capacity, fibre reinforced concrete has found special application in airport pavements, highway pavements, bridge deck overlays, industrial floor and pavements, pile shells, cladding panels, floating unit for marines and tunnel linings.

3.8 Ready-Mixed Concrete

The present practice in our country in case of small jobs is to collect the various constituents for concreting at the site of construction and then mixing the concrete either by hand or by using small mixers. Instead, concrete can be mixed at a central batching plant and delivery at the site by a suitable means of transportation. Such concrete is called "Ready-mixed concrete or premixed concrete". At present two-thirds of the concrete used in America is only ready-mixed concrete. For smaller jobs, the ready-mixed concrete has replaced the conventional method of mixing at site completely.

Ready-mixed concrete can be divided into three types viz.,
1. The plant mixed concrete
2. The transit mixed concrete, and
3. The shrink mixed concrete.

In the plant mixed type, the concrete is mixed in a central batching plant and is transported in special agitator trucks. In the transit mixed type, the mixing is done in the agitator trucks during the transit or even partly at delivery site. In this case, the speed of rotation of concrete is 2 to 6 r.p.m. during agitation and 6 to 16 r.p.m. during mixing at site.

If the concrete is mixed partly in the plant and partly during transit, the concrete is called the *shrink-mixed concrete*.

The agitator truck consists of an ordinary chassis over which is mounted a long horizontal or inclined steel drum, called the cannister, which contains the concrete. A small diesel engine interposed between the drum and the cabin rotates either the drum or a set of paddles inside the drum. There will be a water tank over the engine, which provides sufficient water for mixing the concrete as well as for washing the drum after discharge. In hot weather, the drum shall be capable of being closed tightly to prevent escape of moisture. In case, air entraining is resorted, the concrete can also be transported in open drum trucks, equipped with several rotating paddles, travelling in vertical planes. This means of transport is cheaper than transportation by agitator trucks but cause segregation of ordinary concretes. Rehandling of concrete at site may eliminate some segregation. Hence, agitator trucks are being preferred at present.

The operational area of a ready-mixed concrete plant is governed by what is called as *'the time of haul'*, which is the period which can be safely allowed for the concrete to be placed in forms from the time of adding water without any loss of strength and consistency of concrete. The safe time of haul is the lower value of (i) 90 minutes or (ii) the time taken for 300 revolutions of the drum. The mixing operation shall begin within 30 minutes after the cement has been inter-mixed with the aggregates. The slump after a time of haul of 90 minutes is reduced by 40 mm for concretes with an original slump of 100 to 120 mm and slump is reduced to zero after 6 hours. The time of haul of 90 minutes was found to result in a strength reduction of 5 per cent only. The loss of slump at the end of 90 minutes does not affect the placeability of concrete in any way. If for any particular mix, the loss of slump is found to affect the ease of placing of concrete, the concrete can be retempered by addition of a little water at the site or restore the slump. The reduction in strength due to retempering will be very small, smaller than that would be predicted under the normal strength versus water-cement ratio law.

Ready-mixed concrete offers all the advantages, inherently available in large, centralised batching plants. Hence, in ready-mixed concrete, the ratio of average strength required to the minimum specified strength (usually called the control factor in the mix design), can be reduced. This evidently implies less consumption of cement per unit strength of concrete. Further economy is obtained by avoiding wastage of materials or losses of materials, which is unavoidable when small quantities of concrete are mixed at site. Concreting can proceed faster at the site than when job mixing is relied upon. The technical personnel at the site can concentrate better on the placing of concrete, the compaction and other aspects, since they are relieved of supervision of preparation of concrete. Ready-mixed concrete is a boon for the construction industry in city areas. The many problems such as congested roads and lack of storage space or working space and nuisance of dust and noise can be effectively solved. For repair work of pavements in cities, the quantity of concrete required at each site is small. Hence, for such repairs ready-mixed concrete can be a definite advantage. Ready-mixed concrete facilitates the consumer to straightway start concreting. When once he has ordered the particular quality of concrete and the amount he needs, with the ready-mixed concrete plant, he need not worry about the quantity and procurement of material or quality of concrete. Special concretes can be more freely specified in the designs as the ready-mixed concrete plant offers the flexibility of production due to laboratory facilities and the excellent supervision available at a central mixing plant.

However, proper programming of the requirements and proper communication between the field staff and the plant is essential. Location of the ready-mixed plant at the raw material source and river banks or rail heads will be advantageous and economical. The plant should be so located that the prospective consumers in the vicinity can be reached within the stipulated time of haul of 90 minutes. Taking a speed of 40 km/hr. according to Indian conditions, the effective zone of operation will be within a radius of about 60 km.

3.9 Self Compacting Concrete

Quality of concrete depend upon the various factors. Compaction of concrete is one of the major factor which affect the quality of concrete. If compaction is not complete, it will lead to loss in strength and also affect performance of the structure. The compaction becomes difficult when percentage of reinforcement is high which does not allow insertion of vibrator at some places. Self compacting concrete was therefore developed to overcome the problems mentioned above.

Self compacting concrete is defined as "a concrete which is capable to compact itself by its own self-weight under gravity without any external efforts like vibration of compaction". The mix is therefore required to have ability of passing, ability of filling and ability of being stable.

3.9.1 Type of Self Compacting Concrete

While developing self compacting concrete, it was defined that this concrete should be so designed that it would level itself and further it would deform itself by its self-weight. This would ensure ideal fair faced exposed surface without air entrapment and another major consideration was to avoid compaction and external vibration. The major difficulty which was faced in the development of self-compacting concrete, was on account of contradictory factors that the concrete should be fully flowable but without bleeding or segregation. It is therefore, required that the cement and mortar of self compacting concrete should have higher viscosity to ensure flowability while maintaining no sedimentation of bigger aggregates.

To meet the concrete performance requirements, the following three types of self-compacting concrete are available:
1. Power type self compacting concrete.
2. Viscosity agent type self compacting concrete.
3. Combination type self compacting concrete.

Power type self compacting concrete is proportional to achieve required self-compactability by adjusting water-powder ratio and to provide adequate segregation resistance. Superplasticizers and air entrapping admixtures gives the required deformability.

Viscosity type self compacting concrete is proportional to provide self-compaction by the use of viscosity modifying admixture. Also segregation resistance is also considered while proportioning. Superplasticizers and air entraining admixtures are used for obtaining the desired deformability.

Combination type self compacting concrete is achieved mainly by regulating the water-powder ratio. A viscosity modifying admixture is added in this to reduce the quality fluctuations of the fresh concrete due to the vibration of the surface moisture content of the aggregates and their graduations during the production. This facilitates the production control of concrete.

3.9.2 Materials Used in Self Compacting Concrete

Following are the ingredients in self-compacting concrete:

(i) Cement, (ii) Aggregate and sand, (iii) Water, (iv) Superplasticizer, (v) Viscosity modifying, (vi) Fines or powder material.

3.9.3 Advantages of Self Compacting Concrete

1. It allows more amount of free fall and also more horizontal distance upto which concrete can flow without segregation.
2. It gives better surface finish, as percentage of fines is more. Durability increases as dense packing leads to relatively impermeable concrete.
3. Skilled personal like vibrator operator and mason for finishing is not required. This leads to reduced labour component and thereby reduction in safety hazards.
4. More innovative structures can be designed because SCC can flow through any shape of form work.

5. Economical, where source of supplementary material is nearby and also economical on account of reduced labour component for vibration and finishing work.
6. Cover the reinforcement effectively by aggregates fully soaked in concrete matrix.
7. No entrapped air is possible.

3.9.4 Disadvantages of Self Compacting Concrete
1. Some self compacting concrete mixes may gain strength slowly. It is due to presence of higher proportion of fines i.e., fly ash, micro silica etc.
2. More changes of increased plastics shrinkage cracking.
3. Therefore attention on curing is important particularly on large, flat exposed areas.

3.9.5 Applications
1. For the concreting of two anchorages of Akashi-Kaikyo bridge. The volume of cast concrete in two anchorages is amounted to 299,000 m^3. For this, the concrete was mixed at the batcher plant beside the site and was then pumped out of the plant. It was transported 200 m through pipes to the casting site, where the pipes were arranged in row 3 to 5 m apart. In the final analysis, the use of SCC shortened the anchorage construction period by 20% from 2.5 to 2 years.
2. Self compacting concrete was used for the wall of large LNG tank belonging to Osaka gas company.

    The construction period of structure decreased from 22 months to 18 months and number of workers were reduced from 150 to 50.
3. Self compacting concrete is used in the construction of a pre-cast slab element used in Gujarat school project.
4. Self compacting concrete is used in the construction of art and culture centre of Meudon in France.
5. Self compacting concrete is also used in the construction of commercial centre in Ferrara (Itlay).

3.10 High Performance Concrete

High performance concrete (HPC) is the latest development in concrete. It is not just high strength concrete and has replaced high strength concrete developed in early 1980's. High performance concrete can be defined as "a concrete made with appropriate materials (superplasticizer, retarder, flyash, blast furnace slag and silica fume) combined accordingly to a selected mix design and properly mixed, transported, placed, consolidated and cured to give excellent performance in same properties of concrete, such as high compressive strength, high density, low permeability and good resistance to certain form of attack".

The American Concrete Institute (ACI) defines high-performance concrete as "concrete meeting special combinations of performance and uniformity requirements that cannot always be achieved routinely". When using conventional constituents and normal mixing, placing and curing practices. A commentary to the definition states that a high-performance concrete is one in which certain characteristics are developed for a particular application and environment. Examples of characteristics that may be considered critical for an application are:

1. Ease of placement.
2. Compaction without segregation.
3. Early age strength.
4. Long-term mechanical properties.
5. Permeability.
6. Density.
7. Heat of hydration.
8. Toughness.
9. Volume stability.
10. Long life in service environments.

Because many characteristics of high-performance concrete are interrelated, a change in one usually results in changes in one or more of the other characteristics. Variations in the chemical and physical properties of cementitious materials and chemical admixtures need to be carefully mentioned. Most high performance concretes have a high cementitious content and a water cementitious material ratio of 0.40 or less. However, the proportions of the individual constituents vary depending on local preferences and local materials, mix proportions developed in one part of the country do not necessarily work in a different location. Therefore, for the successful production of high-performance concrete, a greater degree of quality control is required.

HPC concrete is a key element in virtually all large construction projects from all office and residential building to bridges, tunnel and roadways.

3.11 Ferrocement Concrete

It is well known that conventional reinforced concrete members are too heavy, brittle, cannot be satisfactorily repaired if damaged, develop cracks and reinforcements are liable to be corroded. The above disadvantages of normal concrete make it inefficient for certain types of work.

Ferrocement is a relatively new material consisting of wire meshes and cement mortar. It consists of closely spaced wire meshes which are impregnated with rich cement mortar mix. Actually, the reinforcement used in ferrocement is of two types; viz., skelton steel and wire mesh. This skelton steel frame is made conforming exactly to the geometry and shape of structure and is used for holding the wire meshes in position and shape of structure. The skelton steel comprises relatively large diameter (about 3 to 8 mm) and spaced typically at 70 mm to 100 mm. The wire mesh is usually of 0.5 to 1.0 mm diameter wire at 5 to 10 mm spacing and cement mortar is of cement sand ratio of 1 : 2 to 1 : 3 with water-cement ratio of 0.4 to 0.45. The ferrocement elements are usually of the order of 20 to 30 mm. The steel content varies between 300 to 500 kg per cubic metre of mortar. The basic idea behind this material is that concrete can undergo large strains in the neighbourhood of the reinforcement and the magnitude of strains depends on the distribution and subdivision of reinforcement throughout the mass of concrete.

Ferrocement is widely accepted in U.K., Newzealand and U.S. as a boat building material. It has also found various other engineering applications. The main advantages are simplicity of its construction, lesser dead weight of the elements due to their small thickness, its high tensile strength, less crack widths compared to conventional concrete, easy reparability, non-corrosive nature and easier mouldability to any desired shape. There is also saving in basic materials i.e. cement and steel. This material is more suitable to structures like shells, hanging roofs, silos, water tank and pipelines. Ferrocement is found to be a suitable material for casting curved benches for parks, garden and open-air cinema theatre.

[C] SPECIAL CONCRETE

3.12 Concrete or Foamed Concrete or Cellular Concrete

Aerated concrete is made by introducing air or gas into a slurry composed of Portland : cement or lime and finely crushed siliceous filler so that when the mix sets and hardens, a uniformly cellular structure is formed. Though it is called aerated concrete it is really not a concrete in the correct sense of the word. As described above, it is a mixture of water, cement and finely crushed sand. Aerated concrete is also referred to as gas concrete, foam concrete, cellular concrete. In India we have at present a few factories manufacturing aerated concrete. A common product of aerated concrete in India is Siporex.

There are several ways in which aerated concrete can be manufactured:

(a) By the formation of gas by chemical reaction within the mass during liquid or plastic state.

(b) By mixing preformed stable foam with the slurry.

(c) By using finely powdered metal (usually aluminium powder) with the slurry and made to react with the calcium hydroxide liberated during the hydration process, to give out large quantity of hydrogen gas. This hydrogen gas when contained in the slurry mix, gives the cellular structure.

Powdered zinc may also be added in place of aluminium powder. Hydrogen peroxide and bleaching powder have also been used instead of metal powder. But this practice is not widely followed at present.

In the second method preformed, stable foam is mixed with cement and crushed sand slurry thus causing the cellular structure when this gets set and hardened. As a minor modification some foam-giving agents are also mixed and thoroughly churned or beaten (in the same manner as that of preparing foam with the white of egg) to obtain foam effect in the concrete. In a similar way, air entrained agent in large quantity can also be used and mixed thoroughly to introduce cellular aerated structure in the concrete. However, this method cannot be employed for decreasing the density of the concrete beyond a certain point and as such, the use of air entrainment is not often practised for making aerated concrete.

Gasification method is of the most widely adopted methods using aluminium powder or such other similar material. This method is adopted in the large scale manufacture of aerated concrete in the factory wherein the whole process is mechanised and the product is subjected to high pressure steam curing i.e., in other words, the products are autoclaved. Such products will suffer neither retrogression of strength nor dimensional instability

The practice of using preformed foam with slurry is limited to small scale production and in situ work where small change in the dimensional stability can be tolerated. But the advantage is that any density desired at site can be made in this method.

3.13 Properties

Use of foam concrete has gained popularity not only because of the low density but also because of other properties mainly the thermal insulation property. Aerated concrete is made in the density range from 300 kg/m^3 to about 800 kg/m^3. Lower density grades are used for insulation purposes, while medium density grades are used for the manufacture of building blocks or load bearing walls and comparatively higher density grades are used in the manufacture of prefabricated structural members in conjunction with steel reinforcement.

3.14 Pre-stressed Concrete

The member of concrete in which internal stresses are intentionally induced in a planned manner such that the stresses resulting from the super imposed loads get countered to a desired degree is called a prestressed concrete member.

The main principle of prestressing a concrete member consists of inducing sufficient compressive stress in concrete before a member is subjected to loads, in the zones which develop tensile stress due to applied load. The pre-induced compressive stress in concrete neutralizes the tensile stress developed due to external loads. Hence, zone ultimately will be free from any stress. In a pre-stressed member, the entire cross-section becomes effective for resisting bending and danger of cracking is minimized or avoided.

Prestressed concrete is suitably employed for the members subjected to axial tension and in which cracks should be eliminated. These are also extensively used for various bending members, such as roof slabs, domes, runways and railway sleepers.

Advantages:
(i) It is possible to take full advantage of high compressive strength of concrete and high tensile strength of steel used.
(ii) Because of higher strength, prestressed concrete can be safely recommended for structures having longer spans and which are subjected to heavy loads, impact and vibrations. For example, bridges, high rises, huge constructions etc.
(iii) Prestressing eliminates the cracks in concrete under all stages of loading. The entire concrete section, therefore, becomes effective, whereas in R.C.C., only the portion of the section above its neutral axis carries compressive stress.
(iv) Prestressed concrete requires only $1/3^{rd}$ of the concrete required for R.C.C. but of superior quality. Also, the amount of steel required is only $1/4^{th}$ of R.C.C. Thus, there is always a considerable savings in material cost in the case of prestressed concrete.
(v) Reduced dead weight of the superstructure also saves the cost of foundation as the prestressed concrete members are comparatively smaller in section.
(vi) There is considerable savings in cost of shuttering and centering in large structures, because prestressed concrete members are manufactured in factories.
(vii) There is considerable savings in stirrups, since the shear in prestressed concrete members is reduced by inclination of tendons and the diagonal tension is further minimised by the presence of pre-stress.
(vii) In the pre-stressed concrete structures, deflection of beams is considerably reduced.

Limitations:
(i) As in prestressing concrete, higher cost, stronger material and more labour are required, the use of prestressed concrete is generally limited to members which have long spans and carry heavy loads.
(ii) Skilled personnel for expert supervision are required.
(iii) Special machinery for application is required.

[D]
3.15 Under Water Concreting

Special precautions need be taken whenever the concrete is to be placed under water. In regard to the quality of concrete, the recommendations of the portland cement association are as follows:

"The concrete should be plastic and cohesive but should have good flowability. This requires a fairly high slump, usually 150 to 180 mm. A richer mix than generally used for placing under normal conditions is required, usually the cement requirement is not less than eight bags per cubic metre of concrete. The proportions of fine and coarse aggregates should be adjusted to produce desired workability within a somewhat higher proportion of fine aggregate than used for normal conditions. The fine aggregate proportion can often be from 45 to 50 per cent of the total aggregate, depending on the grading. It is also important that the aggregate contain sufficient fine material passing the 300 and 150 micron sieves to produce a plastic and cohesive mixture. The fine aggregate should meet the minimum requirements and somewhat higher percentage of fines would be better in many cases. For most works, coarse aggregate should be graded upto 20 mm or 40 mm."

In addition, the coarse aggregate should not contain loam or any other material which may cause laitance while being worked. The form work constructed in water should be sufficiently water-tight to prevent loss of mortar. If necessary, coffer dams are to be constructed to reduce the velocity of flow of water through the concreting zone.

The following are the principle techniques which have been used for placing concrete under water:
1. Placing in dewatered caissons or coffer dams,
2. tremie method,
3. bucket placing,
4. placing in bags,
5. prepacked concrete.

The placing in detwatered cassions or coffer dams follows the normal in the dry practice.

Tremie Method:

A tremie is a watertight pipe, generally 250 mm in diameter, having a funnel-shaped hopper at its upper end and a loose plug at the bottom or discharge end. The valve at the discharged end is used to de-water the tremic and control the distribution of the concrete.

The concrete is poured into the tremic pipe, lowered into the position through a hopper at the top untill it is filled. The pipe is then raised slightly and the concrete flows outwards. The tremic pipe is to be kept full at any time, to prevent entry of water into it. Continuous placement of large quantities of concrete can be achieved with a tremic pipe.

The risk of segregation and non-uniform stiffening can be minimised by maintaining the surface of concrete in the forms as level as possible and by providing a continuous and rapid flow of concrete.

Bucket Placing:

The buckets are usually fitted with drop-bottom or bottom-roller gates which open freely outward, when tripped. The bucket is completely filled with concrete and covered with a canvas cloth or a gunny sack to prevent the disturbance of concrete as the bucket is lowered into water. The bucket is lowered by a crane upto the bottom surface of concrete and then opened either by divers or by a suitable arrangement from the top. After discharge, the bucket is slowly raised clear of the concrete.

This method has the advantage that the concreting can be carried at considerable depths and permits the use of slightly stiffer concrete than does tremic method. The main disadvantage of the bucket method is the difficulty in keeping the top surface of the placed concrete reasonably level.

Placing in Bags:

The properly filled bags are lowered into water and placed carefully in a header-and-stretcher fashion as in brick masonry construction with the help of divers.

The method has advantages in that, in many cases, no form work is necessary and comparatively lean mixes may be used provided sufficiently plasticity is retained. On the other hand, as the accurate positioning of the bags in place can be only accomplished by the divers, the work is consequently slow and labourious. Voids between adjacent bags are difficult to fill, there is little bonding other than that achieved by mechanical interlock between bags. This method is suitable only for placing the concrete in rather shallow water.

3.16 Concreting in Extreme Weather Conditions

3.16.1 Cold Weather Concreting

In cold countries, concreting has to be done sometimes at temperatures below the freezing point. Any concreting operation done at temperature below 5°C is termed as *cold weather concreting*. Most code do not advocate concreting to be done at an atmospheric temperature below 5°C without special precautions. Due to low temperature, the problems are mainly due to the slower development of concrete strength; the concrete in the plastic stage can be damaged if it is exposed to low temperature and subsequent damage may occur due to alternate freezing and throwing when the concrete becomes harden. The effects of cold weather concreting may be summarized as follows:

1. **Delayed Setting:** At low temperatures the development of concrete strength is retarded as compared with the strength development at normal temperatures. The setting period necessary before removal of form work is thus increased. Although the initial strength of concrete is lower, the ultimate strength will not be severely affected provided the concrete has been prevented from freezing during its early life.

2. **Early Freezing of Concrete:** When plastic concrete is exposed to freezing temperature, it may suffer permanent damage. If the concrete is allowed to freeze before a certain prehardening period, it may suffer irreparable loss in its properties so much so that even one cycle of freezing and throwing during the prehardening period may reduce compressive strength of 50% of what would be expected from normal temperature concrete. The prehardening period depends upon the type of cement and environmental conditions. It may be specified in terms of time required to attain a compressive strength of the order of 3.5 to 7.0 N/mm^2, alternatively it can be specified in terms of period varying from 24 hours to even three days depending upon the degree of saturation and water-cement ratio.

3. **Stress Due to Temperature Differential:** A large temperature differential within the concrete member may promote cracking and has a harmful effect on durability. Such situations are likely to occur in cold weather at the time of removal of form work.

Recommended Practice and Precautions:

As per IS: (Part II) – 1981, the following measures should be taken:

1. **Temperature Control of Ingredients:** The temperature at the time of setting of concrete can be raised by heating the ingredients of the concrete mix. It would be easier to heat the mixing water. The temperature of water should not exceed 65°C, as the flash set of cement will occur when the hot water and cement come in content in the mixers. Therefore, the heated water should come in direct contact with the aggregate, and not the cement, first. The aggregates are heated by passing stream through pipes embedded in aggregate storage bins.

    Another precaution taken along with the heating of ingredients is to construct a temporary shelter around the construction site. The air inside is heated by electric or steam heating or central heating with circulating water. The temperature of the ingredients should be so decided that the resulting concrete sets at a temperature of 10° to 20°C. Higher temperatures of fresh concrete may cause reduced workability.

2. **Proportioning of Concrete Ingredients:** The important factors for cold-weather concreting is the attainment of suitable temperature for fresh concrete. It would be preferable to use high alumina cement for concreting during frost conditions.

The main advantage being the higher heat of hydration generated during the first 24 hours. During this period, sufficient strength (about 10 to 15 N/mm^2) is developed, to make the concrete safe against the action of frost. No accelerator should be used if high alumina cement is used.

Air-entraining agents are generally recommended for use in cold weather. Air-entertainment increases the resistance of the hardened concrete to freezing and throwing and at the same time, improves the workability of fresh concrete.

Accelerators, especially, calcium chloride, speed up hydration of cement, leading to a reduction of period upto which the wet concrete is prone to the action of frost. Further calcium chloride is used beyond 2%, lowers the freezing temperature of mixing water by 1° to 2°C.

3. **Use of Insulating Form Work:** A fair amount of heat is generated during hydration of cement. Such heat can be gainfully conserved by having insulating form work, to maintaining the concrete temperature.

4. **Placement and Curing:** Before placing the concrete, all ice, snow and frost should be completely removed. Care should be taken to see that the surface on which the concrete is to be placed and eminent parts are sufficiently warm. During the period of freezing, water curing is not applicable.

5. **Delayed Removal of Form Work:** Because of slower rate of gain of strength during the cold weather, the form work and props have to be kept in place for a longer time than is usual concreting practice.

The problem of concreting in cold weather can be minimised by adopting precast construction of structures. The precast members are manufactured in the factories where adequate precautions can be taken and concreting can be done at controlled conditions.

3.16.2 Hot Weather Concreting

Any operation of concreting done at atmospheric temperature above 40°C or where the temperature of concrete at the time of placement is expected to be beyond 40°C is termed as hot weather concreting. Concrete is not recommended to be placed at a temperature above 40°C without proper precautions as specified in IS : 7861 (Part - I) – 1975. The effects of hot weather may be discussed as follows:

1. **Accelerated Setting:** A higher temperature results in a more rapid hydration leading to accelerated setting. Thus, reducing the handling time of concrete and also lowering the strength of hardened concrete. The workability of concrete decreases and hence the water demand increases with the increase in the temperature of concrete. The addition of water without proper adjustments in mix proportions adversely affects the ultimate quality of concrete.

2. **Reduction in Strength:** Concrete produced and cured at elevated temperatures generally develops high early strength than normally produced concrete, but the eventual strengths are lower. Because high temperature results in greater evaporation and hence necessitates increase in mixing water, consequently reducing the strength.

3. **Increased Tendency to Cracking:** Rapid evaporation leads to plastic shrinkage cracking, and subsequent cooling of hardened concrete introduces tensile stresses.

4. **Less Time for Finishing:** In hot weather, finishing must be done as early as possible after placing. In certain cases if early finishing is not possible due to faster stiffening and quicker evaporation of water, the quality of finishing will be of poor standard.

5. **Difficulty in Controlling the Air Content:** At higher temperatures it is more difficult to control the air content in air entrained concrete. This adds to the difficulty of controlling workability. For a given amount of air-entraining agent, hot concrete entrains less air than does concrete at normal temperatures.

Recommended Practices and Precautions:

As per IS: 7861 (part I) – 1975, the following measures should be taken.

1. **Temperature Control of Concrete Ingredients:** The temperature of the concrete can be kept down by controlling the temperature of the ingredients. The aggregates may be protected from direct sunrays by erecting temporary sheds. Water can also be sprinkled onto the aggregate before using them in concrete. The mixing water has the greatest effect on lowering the temperature of concrete because the specific heat of water (1.0) is nearly five times that of common aggregate (0.22). Moreover, the temperature of water is easier to control than that of other ingredients. Under certain circumstances, the temperature of water can most economically be controlled by mechanical refrigeration or mixing crushed ice.

2. **Proportioning of Concrete Mix:** The mix should be designed to have minimum cement content consistent with other functional requirements. As far as possible, cements with lower heat of hydration should be preferred to those having greater fineness and heat of hydration. Use of water-reducing or set-retarding admixtures is beneficial. Accelerators should not be used under these conditions.

3. **Production and Delivery:** The temperature of aggregates, water and cement should be maintained at the lowest practical levels so that the temperature of concrete is below 40°C at the time of placement. The period between mixing and delivery should be kept to an absolute minimum by co-ordinating the delivery of concrete with its rate of placement.

4. Placement and Curing of Concrete: The form work, reinforcement and subgrade should be sprinkled with cool water just before the placement of concrete. The area around the work should be kept wet to the extent possible to cool the surrounding air and increase its humidity. Speed of placement and finishing helps minimise problems in hot weather concreting. Immediately after compaction, the concrete should be protected to prevent the evaporation of moisture by means of wet gunny bags etc.

High velocity winds cause higher rate of evaporation, and hence wind breakers should be provided as far as possible. If possible, the concreting can be done during night shifts.

Exercise

1. What are the applications of fibre reinforced concrete in different areas ?
2. What are the factors, which affects the properties of fibre reinforced concrete, explain?
3. What are the special precautions for concreting in cold weather?
4. What is 'high performance concrete'. Explain the role of coarse aggregate. Paste characteristics and interfacial bond between them in high performance concrete.
5. Explain under water concreting.
6. State the advantages of light weight concrete.
7. Write notes on:
   (a) Ready-mix concrete
   (b) Ferrocement
   (c) Ready-mixed concrete
   (d) Light weight concrete
   (e) Underwater concreting
   (f) Polymer concrete

Unit 4
CONCRETE MIX DESIGN

4.1 Introduction

Generally the design engineer specifies in his drawings, the required properties of the hardened concrete at 28 days. The site engineer is then responsible to produce the concrete of the required quality, strength and durability. The proportions of the ingredients of the concrete should be selected such that the concrete of required strength and durability is prepared by using the available materials. This process is generally called as *design of mix*. The design mix concrete is prepared by using the available materials and should involve the maximum overall economy. In special case, it may be designed for any other property, for example, flexural strength. Usually, the concrete mix is designed for its compressive strength.

4.2 Object of Mix Design

1. **Objectives of Mix Design:** Following are the objectives of Mix Design:
    (a) To achieve a specified characteristic compressive strength of 28 days period. (of cube).
    (b) To achieve the specified workability.
    (c) To have sufficient durability.
    (d) To have desired strength in hardened stage.
    (e) To have the economy as much as possible.
    (f) To have satisfactory appearance.
    (g) To comply with certain other specified properties and not to have certain drawbacks such as honey-combing and segregation etc.

2. **Necessity of designing a mix:**
    (a) To get a concrete with proper required strength.
    (b) To get a concrete with sufficient durability, good appearance.
    (c) To get a workable concrete.
    (d) To get an economical concrete.

3. **Factors affecting the concrete mix design**
    (a) Water cement ratio.
    (b) Cement aggregate ratio.
    (c) Gradation of aggregate.
    (d) Consistency.

4. **Methods of Proportioning (Mix Design):** Following are the methods, which are used for proportioning.
   (a) Arbitrary Proportions Method.
   (b) Maximum Density Method.
   (c) Fineness Modulus Method.
   (d) Surface Area Method.
   (e) ACI Committee Method.
   (f) Road No.-4 Method.
   (g) IRC-44 Method.
   (h) High Strength Concrete Mix Design Method.
   (i) Method based on Flexural Strength.
   (j) Indian Standard Method.
   (k) Trial Method.

4.3 Factors Influencing the Choice of Mix Design

The major factors affecting the mix design are:
1. Grade designation
2. Type of cement
3. Maximum nominal size of aggregates
4. Minimum water-cement ratio
5. Workability
6. Durability and
7. Quality control.

1. **Grade designation:** The grade designation gives the characteristics compressive strength requirements of the concrete. As per IS : 456-2000, the characteristics compressive strength is defined as "that value below which not more than 5% of the test results are expected to fall". It is the major factor influencing the mix design. Depending upon the degree of control available at site, the concrete mix has to be designed for a target mean compressive strength which is higher than the minimum specified.

2. **Type of cement:** The type of cement is important mainly through its influence on the rate of development of compressive strength of concrete. The choice of the type of cement depends upon the requirements of performance, where high compressive strength is required. For example, in prestressed concrete railway sleepers, high strength OPC conforming to IS : 8112-1976 will be found suitable. In situations where an early strength development is required, rapid hardening portland cement conforming to IS : 8041-1978 is preferable.

3. **Maximum nominal size of aggregate:** The maximum nominal size of the coarse aggregate is determined by sieve analysis and is designated by the sieve size higher than the largest size on which 15% or more of the aggregate is retained. The maximum nominal size of the aggregate is to be used in concrete as governed by the size of the section and the spacing of the reinforcement. According to IS : 456-2000 and IS : 1343-1980, the maximum nominal size of the aggregate should not be more than $1/4^{th}$ of the minimum thickness of the member, and it should be restricted to 5 mm less than the minimum clear distance between the main bars or 5 mm less than the minimum cover to the reinforcement or 5 mm less than the spacing between the prestoring cables. Within these limits, the nominal maximum size of aggregates may be as large as possible, because larger the maximum size of aggregates smaller is the cement requirement for a particular water-cement ratio. The workability also increases with the increase in maximum size of aggregate. However, the smaller size aggregates provide larger surface area for bonding with the mortar matrix which increases the compressive strength and reduces the stress concentration in the mortar-aggregate interfaces. For the concrete with higher water-cement ratio, the larger maximum size of aggregate may be beneficial whereas for high strengths of concrete, 10 or 20 mm size of aggregate is preferable.

4. **Water-cement ratio:** The strength of a workable concrete mix, depends primarily on the water-cement ratio. The lower the W/C ratio, greater is the compressive strength and vice versa. Fig. 4.1 shows the relationship between target compressive strength at 28 days and water-cement ratio. This is applicable for both ordinary portland cement and portland pozzolana cements.

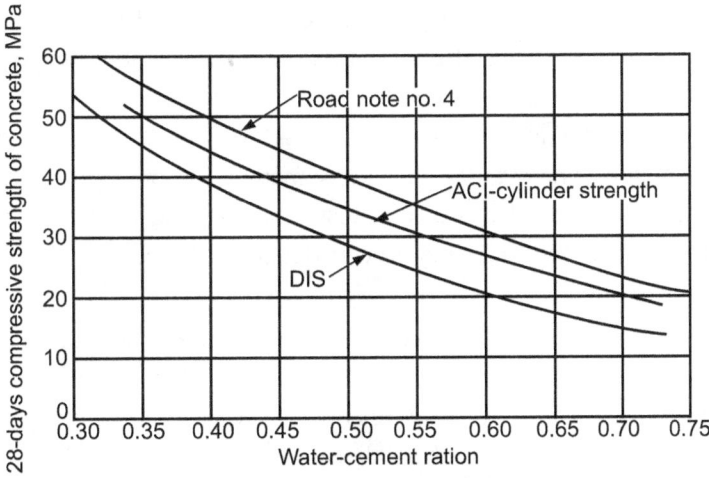

Fig. 4.1: Generalized Relation between Free Water-Cement Ratio and Compressive Strength of Concrete

5. **Workability:** The workability of concrete for satisfactory placing and compaction is controlled by the size and shape of the section to be concrete, the quantity and spacing of reinforcement, and the methods to be employed for transportation of concrete. If section is narrow and having complicated corners, high workability is required. Mix which is not workable for one type of compaction may be workable for other type of compaction because depending upon the compacting equipment used, the workability varies. The requirements of workability affect the W/C ratio requirements and this affect the mix design.

6. **Durability:** It is mainly the resistance of the concrete to weathering, freezing and thawing. High strength concrete is generally more durable than low strength concrete. The requirements of durability are achieved by limitations in terms of minimum cement content, the type of cement and the maximum water-cement ratio.

7. **Quality control:** This is an important factor affecting the mix design. This means control of all the operations, i.e. batching, mixing, placing of the concrete, etc. Variation in strength results from improper mixing, insufficient compaction, irregular curing, the quality of supervision and workmanship. The control of all these variations is important in lowering the difference between the minimum strength and characteristic mean strength of mix and hence reducing the cement content. The factor controlling this difference is the quality control.

4.4 Statistical Quality Control

1. **Concrete quality control:** In the design of reinforced concrete, the strength of concrete is specified by the designer. The design is based on an assumption that the concrete obtained will have strength equal to or greater than the specified strength. The strength of concrete obtained on site will depend on many factors and the results of concrete cubs may show considerable variability. This necessitates such designing of the concrete mix that the concrete will produce an average strength greater than specified. Also the cube test results during work should be checked to control the quality. The following articles deal with the quality of control of concrete by testing the cubes.

2. **Sampling and strength test of cube:** For the work at a site, sampling and strength test of concrete is described in clause IS of IS : 456. Accordingly, samples from fresh concrete shall be taken and cubes shall be made, cured and tested at 28 days. For relatively small and unimportant buildings and works in which quantity of concrete is less than 15 m^3, the strength tests may be waived by the engineer-in-charge at his discretion.

Table 4.1: Optional Test Requirements of Concrete

Grade of concrete	Compressive strength of 15 cm cubes, (min)	Modulus of repture by beam test, (min)	
	at 7 days N/mm²	at 72 + 2h N/mm²	at 7 days N/mm²
M10	7.0	1.2	1.7
M15	10.0	1.5	2.1
M20	13.5	1.7	2.4
M25	17.0	1.9	2.7
M30	20.0	2.1	3.0
M35	23.5	2.3	3.2
M40	27.0	2.5	3.4

In order to get a relatively quicker idea of the quantity of concrete, optional tests on beams for modulus of rupture at 72 ± 2 hours or at 7 days, or compressive strength tests at 7 days may be carried out in addition to 28 days compressive strength tests. For this purpose, the values given in Table 4.1 may be taken for general guidance in the case of concrete made with ordinary portland cement. In all cases, the 28 days compressive strength specified in Table 4.2 shall alone be the criterion for acceptance or rejection of the concrete.

Table 4.2: Grades of Concrete

Group	Grade designation	Specified characteristics of compressive strength of 150 mm cube at 28 days in N/mm²
(1)	(2)	(3)
Ordinary Concrete	M10	10
	M15	15
	M20	20
Standard Concrete	M25	25
	M30	30
	M35	35
	M40	40
	M45	45
	M50	50
	M55	55
High strength Concrete	M60	60
	M65	65
	M70	70
	M75	75
	M80	80

3. **Sampling procedure:** A random sampling procedure shall be adopted to ensure that each concrete batch shall have a reasonable chance of being tested i.e. the sampling should be spread over the entire period of concreting and cover all mixing units.

4. **Frequency:** The minimum frequency of sampling of concrete of each grade shall be in accordance with the following Table 4.3.

Table 4.3

Quantity of concrete in the work, m³	Number of samples
1 – 5	1
6 – 15	2
16 – 30	3
31 – 50	4
51 and above	4 plus one additional sample for each additional 50 m³ or part thereof.

Note: Atleast one sample shall be taken from each shift.

5. **Test-specimen:** Three test specimens shall be made from each sample for testing at 28 days. Additional cubes may be required for various purposes such as to determine the strength of concrete at 7 days or at the time of striking the formwork, or to determine the duration of curing or to check the testing error. Additional cubes may also be required for testing cubes cured by accelerated methods as described in IS : 9013 (Methods of making, curing and determining compressive strength of accelerated-cured concrete test specimens).

6. **Test strength of sample:** The test strength of the sample shall be the average of the strength of three specimens. The individual variation should not be more than ± 15 per cent of the average.

7. **Statistical analysis of test results:** In clause 35.1.2 of IS : 456, it is stated that the design should be based on characteristic values for material strengths and in the loads to be supported. The characteristic values should be based on statistical data if available. When such data are not available, they should be based on experience. It is not possible to express the loads in terms of statistical terms. The loads used, therefore, are those that have given safe designs in the past and are set out in the relevant Indian Standards (mainly IS : 875).

To analyse the test results of material strength like cube strength of concrete, tensile strength of reinforcement etc. the statistical methods are used. The statistical method to decide the cube strength of concrete is briefly set out as follows:

The concrete mass is imagined to be collection of units all of which could be tested; such collection is referred to as *population*. The purpose of testing is to supply the information on the properties of parent population.

Let us consider that we have collected a set of n results or observations such as $x_1, x_2, x_3, ..., x_n$ which shows a scatter. The data are separated into groups by selecting a length of interval of the variable. Find out the number of values of the variable which fall in that group called *frequency*. Represent the group interval as abscissa and the frequency distribution as ordinate to obtain the frequency histogram of the test results. The histogram represents the distribution or dispersion of test results. The area under the histogram represents the total number of results.

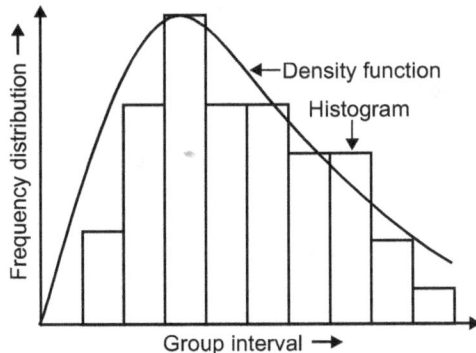

Fig. 4.2: Frequency Histogram and Density Function

8. **Density function:** Referring to Fig. 4.2 where the histogram is drawn, we find that if a large number of cubes were tested, a smooth curve could be drawn through the peaks of rectangles. The curve represents the probability that the random variable takes on any one of its admissible values and is known as density function.

9. **Normal distribution:** To obtain a density function, a histogram is drawn as explained. The results obtained from a histogram give good information regarding the distribution of the sample, but when this is applied to the parent population, it has only limited value. Also, the distribution function obtained experimentally is usually awkward to handle in subsequent manipulations. The difficulty can be overcome by using the readymade distribution curves available in standard statistical tables. The properties of normal distribution curve are also used to assess and control the variability of concrete mix.

Now, one has to find the standard distribution which is suitable to his observed data.

Before applying a standard distribution curve to our results, let us discuss about the standard deviation.

10. **Mean:** Mean is a measure of central tendency or tendency of getting grouped about a central value and defined as:

$$\bar{X} = \frac{\sum X_i}{n}$$

where, $\bar{X}$ = The mean value (sample)
X_i = Individual value of sample
n = Total number of values

11. **Variance:** Variance is the measure of variability. It gives the difference between any single observed data from the mean strength. Also it can be expressed as the square of standard deviation.

12. **Range:** The range is the difference between the largest and the smallest value in a set of observation.

13. **Coefficient of variation:** The variation of the results about the mean can be expressed by coefficient of variation, which is the non-dimensional measure of variation obtained by dividing the standard deviation by the average and is expressed as

$$V = \frac{S}{\bar{X}} \times 100$$

where, V = Coefficient of variation
S = Standard deviation
$\bar{X}$ = The mean value

14. **Standard deviation:** The standard deviation or root mean square (rms) deviation of a set of observations (population) is defined as:

$$S = \sqrt{\frac{\sum (X_i - \bar{X})^2}{n-1}}$$

where, S = Standard deviation
X_i = Individual value of observation
$\bar{X}$ = Mean value of observations
n = Total number of observations

Standard deviation and the coefficient of variation are useful in the design and quality control of concrete. Standard deviation increases with increasing variability. It may be appreciated that the value of S is minimum for very good control and progressively increases as the level of control decreases as indicated in the following table 4.4 (values of coefficient of variation suggested by Himsworth for different degrees of control).

Table 4.4

Type of control	Excellent	Very good	Good	Fair	Poor	Un-controlled
Standard deviation (N/mm²)	2.8	3.5	4.2	5.6	7.0	8.4
Coefficient of variation (per cent)	5	12	15	18	20	25

An important property of standard deviation relating it to the proportions of all the results falling within or outside certain limits, can generally be assumed in the case of concrete work without serious loss of accuracy as long as techniques of random sampling are followed.

Having understood about the standard deviation, let us come back to the distribution curve. This position of the curve along the vertical scale is fixed by the average value. To fulfill this requirement, the standard curve of distribution adopted is normal or Gaussian distribution curve. For concrete cube test results, the assumptions of normal distribution are sufficiently close to reality.

The equation of normal distribution curve is given by

$$Y = \frac{1}{S\sqrt{2\pi}} \cdot e^{-[(X_i - \bar{X})/S^2]}$$

The curve obtained is bell shaped as shown in Fig. 4.3.

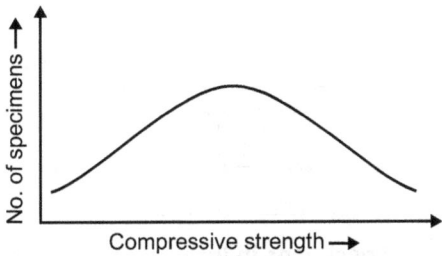

Fig. 4.3: Normal Distribution Curve

It should be noted that the smaller value of standard deviation will result in a curve with dominant peak, whereas a larger value will result in a flatter curve depending upon the level of control exercised in the manufacture of concrete as most of the test results are away from the average (refer to Fig. 4.4).

The normal distribution curve extends to $\pm \alpha$ (infinity) and is symmetrical about the mean. The $\pm \alpha$ indicates extremely low and extremely high results, but in practice the probability of occurrence of such results is low and therefore the normal distribution curve is accepted for our purpose.

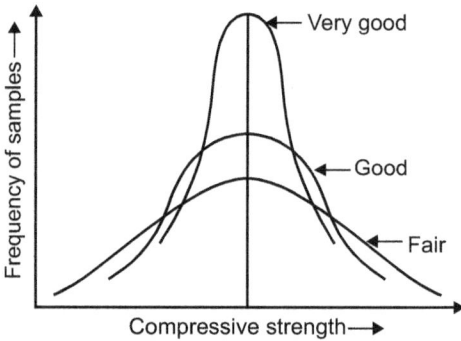

Fig. 4.4: Typical Normal Frequency Curves for Different Levels of Control

The area under the curve between two selected points represents the number of specimens that falls under that strength. We want to express this number as a percentage of total samples. The total samples are infinity for the normal distribution curve. As we deal with the limited number of samples, the area under the curve represents the chance that the strength of an individual sample will lie between given limits. The percentage of specimen considering the total number of samples and normal distribution curves is shown in Fig. 4.5.

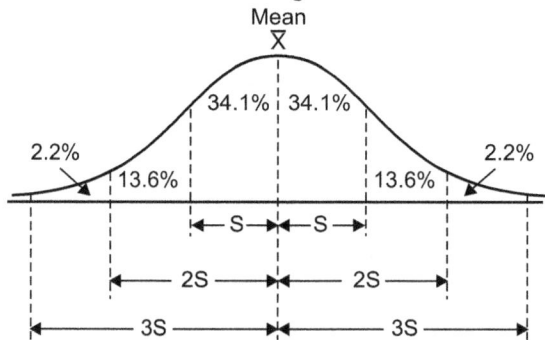

Fig. 4.5: Percentage of Specimens in Intervals of One Standard Deviation – Normal Distribution Curve

From Fig. 4.5, it can be shown that the area under the curve between the abscissa $\bar{X} - S$ and $\bar{X} + S$ is 68.2 % of the total area under the curve i.e. probability of the cube strength of any sample lying between $\bar{X} + S$ is 0.68. Similarly, other probabilities are shown. It is clear that the probability of the cube strength of any sample lying between $\bar{X} + 3S$ is 0.998 and there is only 0.002 probability for a result to fall beyond $\bar{X} \pm 3S$. Thus, for all practical purposes of this graph, variation upto $\pm \alpha$ is immaterial.

It can be shown that 95% of area under this graph lies between − 1.65 S and + α. This means that there is only a 5% probability that a result would fall below $\bar{X}$ − 1.65 S (for material strength) or would fall over $\bar{X}$ + 1.65 S (for loads).

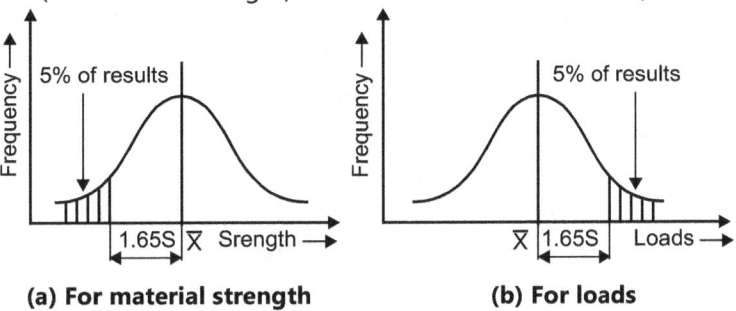

(a) For material strength   (b) For loads

Fig. 4.6: Probability Curves for Characteristics Values

The characteristics strength of material can be defined as

$$f = f_m - 1.65\ S$$

where, f = Characteristics strength of material

f_m = The mean strength

For concrete, the equation can be written as

$$f_{ck} = f_m - 1.65\ S$$

where, f_{ck} is the characteristic strength of concrete.

The above equation shows that not more than 5% of the test results fall below f_{ck}.

Similarly, with regards to loads, the characteristic load F can be defined as:

$$F = F_m + 1.65\ s$$

where, F_m is the mean value of load.

This equation shows that not more than 5% of the loads for given load conditions would exceed F. Infact, as the data are not available for expressing the load in statistical terms, loads that have given safe designs in past shall be used and are set out in relevant Indian Standards.

The statistical methods as adopted IS : 456 for cube test results also after guidance for a mix design. The target mean strength of a mix design should be

$$f_t = f_{ck} + 1.65\ s$$

where, f_t = Target mean strength

S = Standard deviation

15. **Code provisions:** The code provisions of using statistical methods for finding out the concrete strength are set out in clause 9.2.4 and 16 of IS : 456. These are reproduced below and are self-explanatory.

The standard deviation for each grade of concrete shall be calculated separately.

(A) Standard deviation based on test strength of samples:

1. **Number of test results of samples:** The total number of test strength of samples required to constitute an acceptable record for calculation of standard deviation shall not be less than 30. Attempts should be made to obtain the 30 samples, as early as possible, when a mix is used for the first time.
2. **Standard deviation to be brought up-to-date:** The calculation of the standard deviation shall be brought up-to-date after every change of mix design.
3. **In case of significant changes in concrete:** When significant changes are made in the production of concrete batches (for example, changes in the materials used, mix design, equipment or technical control), the standard deviation value shall be separately calculated for such batch of concrete.

(B) Assumed standard deviation:

Where sufficient test results for a particular grade of concrete are not available, the value of standard deviation given in Table 4.13 may be assumed. As soon as the results of samples are available, actual calculated standard deviation shall be used and the mix is designed properly. However, when adequate past records for a similar grade exist and justify to the designer a value of standard deviation different from that shown in Table 4.5. It shall be permissible to use that value.

Table 4.5: Assumed Standard Deviation

Grade of concrete	Assumed standard deviation (N/mm^2)
M10	3.5
M15	
M20	4.0
M25	
M30	5.0
M35	
M40	
M45	
M50	

Note: The above values correspond to the site control having proper storage of cement; weigh batching of all materials; controlled addition of water; regular checking of all materials; aggregate gradings and moisture content; and periodical checking of workability and strength. Where there is deviation from the above table, the values given in the above table shall be increased by 1 N/mm².

(C) Acceptance criteria:

1. **Compressive strength:** The concrete shall be deemed to comply with the strength requirements when both the following conditions are met:

    (a) The mean strength determined from any group of four consecutive test results complies with the appropriate limits in column 2 of Table 4.6.

    (b) Any individual test result complies with the appropriate limits in column 3 of Table 4.6.

2. **Flexural strength:** When both the following conditions are met, the concrete complies with the specified flexural strength.

    (a) The mean strength determined from any group of four consecutive test results exceeds the specified characteristics strength by at least 0.3 N/mm².

    (b) The strength determined from any test result is not less than the specified characteristics strength less than 0.3 N/mm².

Table 4.6: Characteristic Compressive Strength Compliance Requirement

Specified grade	Mean of the group of 4 non-overlapping consecutive test results in N/mm²	Individual test results in N/mm²
(1)	(2)	(3)
M15	≥ f_{ck} + 0.825 X established standard deviation (rounded-off to nearest 0.5 N/mm²) or f_{ck} + 3 N/mm² whichever is greater.	≥ f_{ck} – 3 N/mm²
M20 or above	≥ f_{ck} + 0.825 X established standard deviation (rounded-off to nearest 0.5 N/mm²) or f_{ck} + 4 N/mm², whichever is greater.	≥ f_{ck} – 4 N/mm²

Note: In the absence of established value of standard deviation, the values given in Table 4.6 may be assumed, and attempt should be made to obtain results of 30 samples as early as possible to establish the value of standard deviation.

3. **Quantity of concrete represented by strength test results:** The quality of concrete represented by a group of four consecutive test results shall include the batches from which the first and last samples were taken together with all intervening batches.

   For the individual test result requirements given in column (3) of Table 4.7 or in item (2), only the particular batch from which the sample was taken shall be at risk.

   Where the mean rate of sampling is not specified, the maximum quantity of concrete that four consecutive test results represent shall be limited to 60 m³.

4. If the concrete is deemed not to comply persuant to item (3); the structural adequacy of the parts affected shall be investigated (see, clause 17. IS : 456) and any consequential action as needed shall be taken.

5. Concrete of each grade shall be assessed separately.

6. Concrete is liable to be rejected if it is porous or honeycombed, its placing has been interrupted without providing a proper construction joint, the reinforcement has been displaced beyond the tolerances specified, or construction tolerances have not been met. However, the hardened concrete may be accepted after carrying out suitable remedial measures to the satisfaction of the engineer-in-charge.

Problem 4.1: The following data represents the strength of concrete cubes of the same grade of concrete, prepared and tested in the same conditions. Plot a histogram of distribution of cube strength σ_{cu} in N/mm². Also find out the standard deviation and coefficient of variation of the results. For convenience, the results are arranged in ascending order. Each result given here is an average of three cubes test results taken from same batch.

22.5	23.7	24.2	24.8	25	25.1	25.3	25.5	25.6	25.6
25.7	26.2	26.4	26.6	26.7	26.8	26.9	26.9	27.1	27.2
27.6	27.6	27.7	27.9	28.1	28.7	28.9	29.2	29.8	30.5

Solution: Total frequency = 30

Minimum value = 22.5 N/mm²

Maximum value = 30.5 N/mm²

Select group intervals at 1 N/mm² each and tabulate the frequency distribution as shown below:

Frequency distribution of σ_{cu}

Sr. No.	Class interval σ_{cu}, (N/mm²)	Frequency
1.	22 - 23	1
2.	23 - 24	1
3.	24 - 25	3
4.	25 - 26	6
5.	26 - 27	7
6.	27 - 28	6
7.	28 - 29	3
8.	29 - 30	2
9.	30 - 31	1
		Total = 30

The histogram can be drawn as

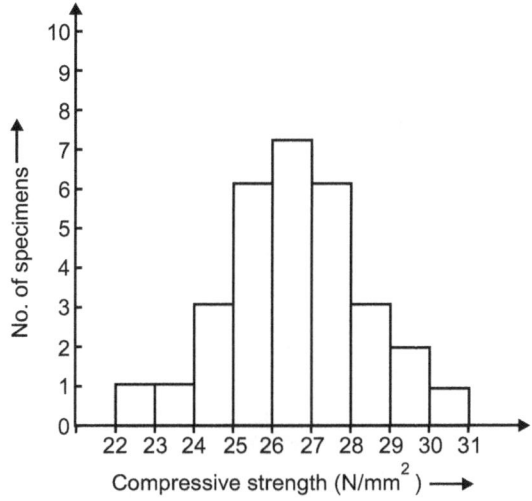

Fig. 4.7

The standard deviation is calculated as;

The mean $\bar{X} = \dfrac{799.8}{30} = 26.66$ N/mm²

Standard deviation (S) $= \sqrt{\dfrac{\sum (X_i - \bar{X})^2}{n-1}} = \sqrt{\dfrac{94.72}{30-1}} = 1.81$ N/mm²

Coefficient of variation $= \dfrac{S}{\bar{X}} \times 100 = \dfrac{1.81}{26.66} \times 100$

Sample No.	Average (X_i)	$\bar{X} - X_i$	$(\bar{X} - X_i)^2$
1.	22.5	4.16	17.31
2.	23.7	2.96	8.76
3.	24.2	2.46	6.05
4.	24.8	1.86	3.46
5.	25.0	1.66	2.76
6.	25.1	1.56	2.43
7.	25.3	1.36	1.85
8.	25.5	1.16	1.35
9.	25.6	1.06	1.12
10.	25.6	1.06	1.12
11.	25.7	0.96	0.92
12.	26.2	0.46	0.21
13.	26.4	0.26	0.07
14.	26.6	0.06	0.00
15.	26.7	0.04	0.02
16.	26.8	− 0.14	0.06
17.	26.9	− 0.24	0.06
18.	26.9	− 0.24	0.19
19.	27.1	− 0.44	0.29
20.	27.2	− 0.54	0.88
21.	27.6	− 0.94	0.88
22.	27.6	− 0.94	1.08
23.	27.7	− 1.04	1.54
24.	27.9	− 1.24	2.07
25.	28.1	− 1.44	4.16
26.	28.7	− 2.04	5.02
27.	28.9	− 2.24	6.45
28.	29.2	− 2.54	9.86
29.	29.8	− 3.14	14.75
30.	30.5	− 3.84	
	Total $\sum X_i = 799.8$		$\sum (\bar{X} - X_i)^2 = 94.72$

Problem 4.2: In a construction where the concreting has been completed in three stages, a series of tests are conducted for a given grade of concrete. The specimens are tested at 28 days in each case and the results are represented in the following table. Establish the standard deviation for the grade of concrete.

\multicolumn{2}{c}{Stage I}	\multicolumn{2}{c}{Stage II}	\multicolumn{2}{c}{Stage III}
Sample number	Concrete strength (N/mm²)	Sample number	Concrete strength (N/mm²)	Sample number	Concrete strength (N/mm²)
1.	28.3	25	27.2	49	35.3
2.	28.1	26	27.6	50	35.1
3.	27.6	27	24.9	51	33.9
4.	26.7	28	26.8	52	33.2
5.	29.2	29	26.4	53	31.3
6.	27.4	30	30.0	54	35.7
7.	26.1	31	29.4	55	34.6
8.	31.2	32	27.1	56	31.3
9.	30.0	33	27.8	57	30.4
10.	25.7	34	30.1	58	32.2
11.	28.6	35	26.8	59	27.3
12.	27.1	36	27.2	60	28.8
13.	28.7	37	27.6	61	31.3
14.	33.6	38	32.7	62	29.0
15.	24.0	39	31.8	63	33.0
16.	30.6	40	30.0	64	32.7
17.	30.5	41	31.3	65	30.8
18.	23.8	42	26.4	66	33.9
19.	29.0	43	37.5	67	28.1
20.	28.0	44	23.3	68	30.1
21.	25.0	45	30.6	69	27.6
22.	29.7	46	26.4	70	29.0
23.	28.1	47	25.3	71	28.8
24.	29.4	48	25.0	72	36.7
				73	29.2
				74	33.4
				75	27.6
				76	29.7
				77	35.0
				78	33.9

The standard deviation of the concrete produced upto the end of **stage I**, i.e. **for samples 1 to 24,**

$$n = 24$$
$$\sum X_i = 676.4$$
$$\bar{X} = \frac{\sum X_i}{n}$$
$$= 28.18 \text{ N/mm}^2$$
$$\sum (X_i - \bar{X})^2 = 120.61$$
$$S = \sqrt{\frac{\sum (X_i - \bar{X})^2}{n-1}}$$
$$= 2.30 \text{ N/mm}^2$$

For stage II (samples 25 to 48):

$$n = 24$$
$$\sum X_i = 679.2$$
$$\bar{X} = 28.30 \text{ N/mm}^2$$
$$\sum (X_i - \bar{X})^2 = 217.64$$
$$S = 3.08 \text{ N/mm}^2$$

For the standard deviation of concrete produced upto the end of second stage,

$$n = 24 + 24 = 48$$
$$\sum X_i = 676.4 + 679.2 = 1355.6$$
$$\bar{X} = \frac{\sum X_i}{n} = 28.24 \text{ N/mm}^2$$
$$\sum (X_i - \bar{X})^2 = 338.42$$
$$S = 2.68 \text{ N/mm}^2$$

For stage III (samples 49 to 78):

$$n = 30$$
$$\sum X_i = 948.9$$
$$\bar{X} = 31.63 \text{ N/mm}^2$$
$$\sum (X_i - \bar{X})^2 = 220.40$$
$$S = 2.76 \text{ N/mm}^2$$

To obtain the standard deviation of the concrete produced to date, it is necessary to combine the standard deviation from different stages.

$$n = 24 + 24 + 30 = 78$$

$$\sum X_i = 2304.5, \quad \bar{X} = 29.55 \text{ N/mm}^2$$

$$\sum (X_i - \bar{X})^2 = 770.77$$

$$\therefore \quad S = \sqrt{\frac{770.77}{77}} = 3.16 \text{ N/mm}^2$$

4.5 Methods of Mix Design

There are many methods of designing a concrete mix. Some of them are:
1. Indian Standard Method (IS Method)
2. Department of Environment Method (DOE Method).

4.5.1 Indian Standard Method (IS Method)

The Indian standard method is based on work done in national laboratories. This method can be applied to both medium strength and high strength concrete. This method is covered in IS 10262: 2009 (concrete mix proportioning – Guidelines).

4.5.1.1 Data for Mix Design

The following data are required for mix proportioning of a particular grade of concrete.
(a) Grade designation
(b) Type of cement
(c) Maximum nominal size of aggregate
(d) Minimum cement content
(e) Maximum water-cement ratio
(f) Workability
(g) Exposure conditions as per Table 4.9 and Table 4.10 of IS 456.
(h) Maximum temperature of concrete at the time of placing.
(i) Method of transporting and placing.
(j) Early age strength requirements, if required.
(k) Type of aggregate.
(l) Maximum cement content and
(m) Whether an admixture shall or shall not be used and the type of admixture and the condition of use.

4.5.1.2 Target Strength for Mix Proportioning

In order that not more than the specified proportion of test results are likely to fall below the characteristic strength, the concrete mix has to be proportioned for higher target mean compressive strength f'_{ck}. The margin over characteristic strength is given by the following relation:

$$f'_{ck} = f_{ck} + 1.65\,S$$

where,
- f'_{ck} = Target mean compressive strength at 28 days in N/mm^2
- f_{ck} = Characteristic compressive strength at 28 days in N/mm^2, and
- S = Standard deviation N/mm^2

[I] Standard Deviation

The standard deviation for each grade of concrete shall be calculated separately.

1. Standard Deviation based on Test Strength of Sample:

(a) **Number of test results of samples:** The total number of test strength of samples required to constitute an acceptable record for calculation of standard deviation shall be not less than 30. Attempts should be made to obtain the 30 samples (taken from site), as early as possible, when a mix is used for the first time.

(b) **In case of significant changes in concrete:** When significant changes are made in the production of concrete bathes (for example changes in the materials used, mix proportioning, equipment or technical control), the standard deviation value shall be separately calculated for such batches of concrete.

(c) **Standard deviation to be brought up-to-date:** The calculation of the standard deviation shall be brought up-to-date after every change of mix proportioning.

2. Assumed Standard Deviation:

Where sufficient test results for a particular grade of concrete are not available, the value of standard deviation given in Table 4.7 may be assumed for the proportioning of mix in the first instance. As soon as the results of samples are available, actual calculated standard deviation shall be used and the mix is proportioned properly. However, when adequate past records for a similar grade exist and justify to the designer a value of standard deviation different from that shown in Table 4.7, it shall be permissible to use that value.

Table 4.7: Assumed Standard Deviation (Clauses 3.2.1.2, A-3 and B-3)

Sr. No. (1)	Grade of Concrete (2)	Assumed Standard Deviation (N/mm^2) (3)
(i) (ii)	M 10, M 15	3.5
(iii) (iv)	M 20, M 25	4.0
(v) (vi) (vii) (viii) (ix) (x)	M 30, M 35, M 40, M 45, M 50, M 55	5.0

Note: The above values correspond to the site control having proper storage of cement, weigh batching of all materials, controlled addition of water, regular checking of all materials, aggregate grading and moisture content, and periodical checking of workability and strength. Where there is deviation from the above values given in the above table shall be increased by 1 N/mm^2.

4.5.1.3 Selection of Mix Proportions

[I] Selection of Water-Cement Ratio:

Different cements, supplementary cementitious materials and aggregates of different maximum size, grading, surface texture, shape and other characteristics may produce concretes of different compressive strength for the same free water-cement ratio. Therefore, the relationship between strength and free-water cement ratio should preferably be established for the materials actually to be used. In the absence of such data, the preliminary free water-cement ratio (by mass) corresponding to the target strength at 28 days may be selected from the established relationship, if available. Otherwise the water-cement ratio given in Table 4.3 of IS 456 for respective environment exposure conditions may be used as starting point.

Table 4.8: Durability Criteria as per IS 456-2000

Exposure	Plain concrete			Reinforced concrete		
	Min. cement	Max. w/c	Min. grade	Min. cement	Max. w/c	Min. grade
Mild	220 kg/m^3	0.60	–	300 kg/m^3	0.55	M 20
Moderate	240 kg/m^3	0.60	M 15	300 kg/m^3	0.50	M 25
Severe	250 kg/m^3	0.50	M 20	320 kg/m^3	0.45	M 30
V. severe	260 kg/m^3	0.45	M 20	340 kg/m^3	0.45	M 35
Extreme	280 kg/m^3	0.40	M 25	360 kg/m^3	0.40	M 40

Adjustments to the minimum cement content for aggregates other than 20 mm nominal maximum size aggregates as per IS 456: 2000.

10 mm	+ 40 kg/cum
20 mm	0
40 mm	–30 kg/cum

The Free Water-Cement Ratio:

The free water-cement ratio selected according to 4.1 should be checked against the limiting water cement ratio for the requirements of durability and the lower of the two values adopted.

[II] Selection of Water Content:

The water content of concrete is influenced by a number of factors, such as aggregate size, aggregate shape, aggregate texture, workability, water-cement ratio, cement and other supplementary cementitious material type of content, chemical admixture and environmental conditions. An increase in aggregates size, a reduction in water-cement ratio and slump and use of rounded aggregate and water reducing admixtures will reduce the water demand. On the other hand increased temperature, cement content, slump, water-cement ratio, aggregate angularity and a decrease in the proportion of the coarse aggregate to fine aggregate will increase water demand.

The quantity of maximum mixing water per unit volume of concrete may be determined from Table 4.9. The water content in Table 4.9 is for angular coarse aggregate and for 25 to 50 mm slump range. The water estimate in Table 4.9 can be reduced by approximately 10 kg for sub-angular aggregates, 20 kg for gravel with some crushed particles and 25 kg for rounded gravel to produce same workability. For the desired workability (other than 25 to 50 mm slump range) the required water content may be established by trial or an increase by about 3% for every additional 25 mm slump or alternatively by use of chemical admixtures conforming to IS9103. This illustrates the need for trial batch testing of local materials as each aggregate source is different and can influence concrete properties differently. Water reducing admixtures or superplasticizing admixtures usually decrease water content by 5 to 10% and 20% and above respectively at appropriate dosages.

Table 4.9: Maximum Water Content per Cubic Metre of Concrete for Nominal Maximum Size of Aggregate (Clauses 4.2, A-5 and B-5)

Sr. No. (1)	Nominal Maximum Size of Aggregate (mm) (2)	Maximum Water Content* (kg) (3)
(i)	10	208
(ii)	20	186
(iii)	40	165

Note: These quantities of mixing water are for use in computing cementitious material contents for trial balance.

---

*Water content corresponding to saturated surface dry aggregate.

[III] Calculation of Cementitious Material Content:

The cement and supplementary cementitious material content per unit volume of concrete may be calculated from the free water-cement ratio and the Quantity of water per unit volume of concrete.

The cementitious material content so calculated shall be checked against the minimum content for the requirements of durability and greater of the two values adopted. The maximum cement content shall be in accordance with IS 456.

[IV] Estimation of Coarse – Aggregate Proportion:

Aggregates of essentially the same nominal maximum size, type and grading will produce concrete of satisfactory workability when a given volume of coarse aggregate per unit volume of total aggregate is used. Approximate values for this aggregate volume are given in Table 4.10 for a water-cement ratio of 0.5, which may be suitably adjusted for other water-cement ratios. It can be seen that for equal workability, the volume of coarse aggregate in a unit volume of concrete is dependent only on its nominal maximum size and grading zone of fine aggregate. Differences in the amount of mortar required for workability with different aggregates, due to differences in particle shape and grading, are compensated automatically by differences in rodded void content.

[i]

For more workable concrete mixes which is sometimes required when placement is by pump or when the concrete is required to be worked around congested reinforcing steel, it may be desirable to reduce the estimated coarse aggregate content determined using Table 4.10, upto 10%. However, caution shall be exercised to assure that the resulting slump, water-cement ratio and strength properties of concrete are consistent with the recommendations of IS 456 and meet project specification requirements as applicable.

Table 4.10: Volume of Coarse Aggregate per Unit Volume of Total Aggregate for Different Zones of Fine Aggregate (Clauses 4.4, A-7 and B-7)

Sr. No.	Nominal maximum size of aggregate (mm)	Volume of coarse aggregate* per unit volume of total aggregate for different zones of fine aggregate			
		Zone IV	Zone III	Zone II	Zone I
(1)	(2)	(3)	(4)	(5)	(6)
(i)	10	0.50	0.48	0.46	0.44
(ii)	20	0.66	0.64	0.62	0.60
(iii)	40	0.75	0.73	0.71	0.69

*Volumes are based on aggregates in saturated surface dry condition.

[V] Combination of different Coarse Aggregate Fractions:

The coarse aggregate used shall confirm to IS 383. Coarse aggregates of different sizes may be combined in suitable proportions so as to result in an overall grading confirming to table 2 of IS 383 for particular nominal maximum size of aggregate.

Table 4.11: Gradation Limits as per IS 383

IS sieve	Zone I	Zone II	Zone III	Zone IV
4.75 mm	90 - 100	90 - 100	90 - 100	90 - 100
2.36 mm	60 - 95	75 - 100	85 - 100	95 - 100
1.18 mm	36 - 70	55 - 90	75 - 100	90 - 100
600 micron	15 - 34	35 - 59	60 - 79	80 - 100
300 micron	5 - 20	8 - 30	12 - 40	15 - 50
150 micron	0 - 10	0 - 10	0 - 10	0 - 15
Remarks	V Coarse	Coarse	Medium	Fine

[VI] Estimation of Fine Aggregate Proportion:

With the completion of procedure given in point (IV), all the ingredients have been estimated except the coarse and fine aggregate content. These quantities are determined by finding out the absolute volume of cementitious material, water and the chemical admixture, by dividing their mass by their respective specific gravity, multiplying by $\frac{1}{1000}$ and subtracting the result of their summation from unit volume. The values so obtained are divided into coarse and fine aggregate fractions by volume in accordance with coarse aggregate proportion already determined in 3.4. The coarse and fine aggregate contents are then determined by multiplying with their respective specific gravities and multiplying by 1000.

CONCRETE TECHNOLOGY (SE - NMU)   CONCRETE MIX DESIGN

4.5.1.4 Trial Mixes

The calculated mix proportions shall be checked by means of trial batches.

Workability of the Trial Mix No. 1 shall be measured. The mix shall be carefully observed for freedom from segregation and bleeding and its finishing properties. If the measured workability of Trial Mix No. 1 is different from the stipulated value, the water and/or admixture content shall be adjusted suitably. With this adjustment, the mix proportion shall be recalculated keeping the free water-cement ratio at the pre-selected value, which will comprise Trial Mix No. 2. In addition, two more trial mixes No. 3 and 4 shall be made with the water content. Same as Trial Mix. No. 2 and varying the free water-cement ratio by ± 10% of the preselected value.

Mix No. 2 to 4 normally provides sufficient information, including the relationship between compressive strength and water-cement ratio, from which the mix proportions for field trials may be arrived at. The concrete for field trials shall be produced by methods of actual concrete production.

Problem 4.3: Design a concrete mix of grade M40 to suit the following data (Illustrated in IS 10262 – 2009).

(A) Stipulations for proportioning:
- (i) Grade designation: M40.
- (ii) Type of cement: OPC 43 grade conforming to IS 8112.
- (iii) Maximum nominal size of aggregate: 20 mm.
- (iv) Minimum cement content 320 kg/m^3.
- (v) Maximum water-cement ratio: 0.45.
- (vi) Workability: 100 mm (slump).
- (vii) Exposure condition: Severe (for reinforced concrete).
- (viii) Method of concrete placing: Pumping
- (ix) Degree of supervision: Good
- (x) Type of aggregate: Crushed angular aggregate
- (xi) Maximum cement content: 450 kg/m^3
- (xii) Chemical admixture type: Superplasticizer

(B) Test Data for materials:
- (i) Cement used: OPC 43 grade confirming to IS 8112
- (ii) Specific gravity of cement: 3.15
- (iii) Chemical admixture: Superplasticizer confirming to IS 9103
- (iv) Specific gravity of
  - (a) Coarse aggregate : 2.74
  - (b) Fine aggregate : 2.74
- (v) Water absorption:
  - (a) Coarse aggregate : 0.5%
  - (b) Find aggregate : 1%

Solution:

Step 1: Target strength for mix proportioning

$$f'_{ck} = f_{ck} + 1.65\, S$$

where, f'_{ck} – Target average strength at 28 days

f_{ck} – Characteristic compressive strength at 28 days

and S – Standard deviation

From table 1, standard deviation, S = 5 N/mm².

Therefore, target strength = 40 + 1.65 × 5

= 48.25 N/mm²

Step 2: Selection of water-cement ratio

Maximum water-cement ratio = 0.45

Based on experience, adopt water-cement ratio as 0.40.

0.40 < 0.45 (hence Ok)

Step 3: Selection of Water content from table 3.

Maximum water content = 186 litre (for 25 mm to 50 mm slump range for 20 mm aggregate)

Estimated water content for 100 mm slump

$$= 186 + \frac{6}{100} \times 186$$

= 197 litre

As superplasticizer is used, the water content can be reduced upto 20% and above. Based on trials with superplasticizer water content reduction of 29% has been achieved.

Hence, the arrived water content = 197 × 0.71

= 140 litre

Step 4: Calculation of cement content

Water-cement ratio = 0.40

$$\text{Cement content} = \frac{140}{0.40}$$

= 350 kg/m³

From Table 2, minimum cement content for 'severe' exposure condition = 320 kg/m³. 350 kg/m³ > 320 kg/m³.

Hence OK.

Step 5: Proportion of volume of coarse aggregate and fine aggregate content.

From Table 4, volume of coarse aggregate corresponding to 20 mm size aggregate and fine aggregate (zone I) for water-cement ratio of 0.5 = 0.60.

In present, water-cement ratio is 0.40. Therefore, volume of coarse aggregate is required to be increased to decrease the fine aggregate content. As the water-cement ratio is lower by 0.10, the proportion of volume of coarse aggregate is increased by 0.02 (at the rate of ± 0.01 for every ± 0.05 change in water-cement ratio). Therefore, corrected proportion of volume of coarse aggregate for the water-cement ratio of 0.40 = 0.62.

For pumpable concrete, these values should be reduced by 10%.

Therefore, volume of coarse aggregate

$$= 0.62 \times 0.9$$
$$= 0.56$$

Volume of fine aggregate content

$$= 1 - 0.56$$
$$= 0.44$$

Step 6: Mix calculations

The mix calculations per unit volume of concrete shall be as follows:

(a) Volume of concrete = 1 m²

(b) Volume of cement = $\dfrac{\text{Mass of cement}}{\text{Specific gravity of cement}} \times \dfrac{1}{1000}$

$$= \dfrac{350}{3.15} \times \dfrac{1}{1000}$$

$$= 0.111 \text{ m}^3$$

(c) Volume of water = $\dfrac{\text{Mass of water}}{\text{Specific gravity of water}} \times \dfrac{1}{1000}$

$$= \dfrac{140}{1} \times \dfrac{1}{1000}$$

$$= 0.140 \text{ m}^3$$

(d) Volume of chemical admixture (superplasticizer @ 2% by mass of cementitious material).

$$= \dfrac{\text{Mass of chemical admixture}}{\text{Specific gravity of admixture}} \times \dfrac{1}{1000}$$

$$= \dfrac{7}{1.145} \times \dfrac{1}{1000}$$

$$= 0.006 \text{ m}^3$$

(e) Volume of all in aggregate = [a − (b + c + d)]
= [1 − (0.111 + 0.140 + 0.006)]
= 0.743 m³

(f) Mass of coarse aggregate = e × Volume of coarse aggregate × Specific gravity of fine aggregate × 1000
= 0.743 × 0.56 × 2.74 × 1000
= 1140 kg

(g) Mass of fine aggregate = e × Volume of fine aggregate × Specific gravity of fine aggregate × 1000
= 0.743 × 0.44 × 2.74 × 1000
= 896 kg

Step 7: Mix proportions for trial No. 1

Cement = 350 kg/m³
Water = 140 kg/m³
Find aggregate = 896 kg/m³
Coarse aggregate = 1140 kg/m³
Chemical admixture = 7 kg/m³
Water-cement ratio = 0.4

Step 8: The slump shall be measured and the water content and dosage of admixture shall be adjusted for achieving the required slump based on trial, if required. The mix proportions shall be reworked for the actual water content and checked for durability requirements.

Step 9: Two more trials having variation of ±10% of water cement ratio in step 8 shall be carried out and a graph between three water-cement ratios and their corresponding strengths shall be plotted to work out the mix proportions for the given target strength for field trials. However, durability requirement shall be met.

Problem 4.4: Design a concrete mix of grade M40 using fly as a part replacement of OPC to suit the following data (Illustrated in IS 10262-2009).

(A) Stipulations for proportioning:
(i) Grade designation: M40
(ii) Type of cement: OPC 43 grade confirming to IS 8112
(iii) Type of mineral admixture: Fly ash confirming to IS 3812 (Part I)
(iv) Maximum nominal size of aggregate: 20 mm.
(v) Minimum cement content: 320 kg/m³.
(vi) Maximum water-cement ratio: 0.45.
(vii) Workability: 100 mm (slump)

(viii) Exposure condition: Severe (for reinforced concrete)
(ix) Method of concrete placing: Pumping
(x) Degree of supervision: Good
(xi) Type of aggregate: Crushed angular aggregate
(xii) Maximum cement (OPC) content: 450 kg/m^3
(xiii) Chemical admixture type: Superplasticizers.

(B) Test Data for materials:
(i) Cement used: OPC 43 grade confirming to IS 8112
(ii) Specific gravity of cement: 3.15
(iii) Fly ash: Confirming to IS 3812 (Part I)
(iv) Specific gravity of fly ash: 2.2.
(v) Chemical admixture: Superplasticizer confirming to IS 9103.
(vi) Specific gravity of:
 (a) Coarse aggregate : 2.74
 (b) Fine aggregate : 2.74
(v) Water absorption:
 (a) Coarse aggregate : 0.5%
 (b) Fine aggregate : 1.0%

Solution:

Step 1: Target strength for mix proportioning

$$f'_{ck} = f_{ck} + 1.65\,S$$

where, f'_{ck} – Target average compressive strength at 28 days

f_{ck} – Characteristics compressive strength at 28 days

and S – Standard deviation

From table 1, standard deviation, $S = 5$ N/mm^2.

Therefore, target strength $= 40 + 1.65 \times 5$
$= 48.25$ N/mm^2

Step 2: Selection of water-cement ratio from Table 2.

Maximum water-cement ratio = 0.45

Based on experience, adopt water-cement ratio as 0.40.

0.40 < 0.45 hence OK

Step 3: Selection of water content from table 3,

Maximum water content for 20 mm aggregate

= 186 litre (for 25 mm to 50 mm slump range)

Estimated water content for 10 mm slump

$$= 186 + \frac{6}{100} \times 186$$

$$= 197 \text{ litre}$$

As superplasticizer is used, the water content can be reduced upto 30%. Based on trials with superplasticizer water content reduction of 29% has been achieved. Hence, the arrived water content

$$= 197 \times 0.71$$

$$= 140 \text{ litres}$$

Step 4: Calculation of cement and fly ash content

Water-cement ratio = 0.40

Cementitious material (cement + fly ash) content

$$= \frac{140}{0.40} = 350 \text{ kg/m}^3$$

From Table 2, minimum cement content for severe exposure conditions = 320 kg/m³. 350 kg/m³ > 320 kg/m³ hence OK.

Now, to proportion a mix containing fly ash the following steps are suggested:
(a) Decide the percentage fly ash to be used based on project requirement and quality of materials.
(b) In certain situations increase in cementitious material content may be warranted. The decision on increase in cementitious material content and its percentage may be based on experience and trial.

Note: This illustrative example is with increase of 10% cementitious material content.

Cementitious material content = 350 × 1.10
= 385 kg/m³
Water content = 140 kg/m³

So   Water-cement ratio = $\frac{140}{385}$

= 0.364

Fly ash @ 30% of cementitious material content

= 385 × 30%
= 115 kg/m³
Cement (OPC) = 385 − 115
= 270 kg/m³
Saving of cement while using fly ash = 350 − 270
= 80 kg/m³ and
Fly ash being utilized = 115 kg/m³

Step 5: Proportion of volume of coarse aggregate and fine aggregate contents.

From Table 4, volume of coarse aggregate corresponding to 20 mm size aggregate and fine aggregate (zone I) for water-cement ratio of 0.50 = 0.60.

In the present case, water-cement ratio is 0.40. Therefore, volume of coarse aggregate is required to be increased to decrease the fine aggregate content. As the water-cement ratio is lowered by 0.10, the proportion of volume of coarse aggregate is increased by 0.02 (at the rate of ± 0.01 for every ± 0.05 change in water-cement ratio). Therefore, corrected proportion of volume of coarse aggregate for the water-cement ratio of 0.40 = 0.62.

For pumpable concrete, these values should be reduced by 10%.
Therefore,

$$\text{Volume of coarse aggregate} = 0.62 \times 0.9$$
$$= 0.56$$
$$\text{Volume of fine aggregate content} = 1 - 0.56$$
$$= 0.44$$

Step 6: Mix calculations

The mix calculations per unit volume of concrete shall be as follows:

(a) Volume of concrete = 1 m³

(b) Volume of cement = $\dfrac{\text{Mass of cement}}{\text{Specific gravity of cement}} \times \dfrac{1}{1000}$

$= \dfrac{270}{3.15} \times \dfrac{1}{1000}$

$= 0.086$ m³

(c) Volume of fly ash = $\dfrac{\text{Mass of fly ash}}{\text{Specific gravity of fly ash}} \times \dfrac{1}{1000}$

$= \dfrac{115}{2.2} \times \dfrac{1}{1000}$

$= 0.052$ m³

(d) Volume of water = $\dfrac{\text{Mass of water}}{\text{Specific gravity of water}} \times \dfrac{1}{1000}$

$= \dfrac{140}{1} \times \dfrac{1}{1000}$

$= 0.140$ m³

(e) Volume of chemical admixture (superplasticizer) @ 20% by mass of cementitious material

$= \dfrac{\text{Mass of admixture}}{\text{Specific gravity of admixture}} \times \dfrac{1}{1000}$

$= \dfrac{7}{1.145} \times \dfrac{1}{1000}$

$= 0.007$ m³

(f) Volume of all in aggregate

$$= [a - (b + c + d + e)]$$
$$= 1 - (0.086 + 0.052 + 0.140 + 0.007)$$
$$= 0.715 \text{ m}^3$$

(g) Mass of coarse aggregate

$$= f \times \text{Volume of coarse aggregate} \times \text{Specific gravity of coarse aggregate} \times 100$$
$$= 0.715 \times 0.56 \times 2.74 \times 1000$$
$$= 1097 \text{ kg}$$

(h) Mass of fine aggregate

$$= f \times \text{Volume of fine aggregate} \times \text{Specific gravity of fine aggregate} \times 1000$$
$$= 0.715 \times 0.44 \times 2.74 \times 1000$$
$$= 862 \text{ kg}$$

Step 7: Mix proportions for Trial No. 1

Cement = 270 kg/m^3
Fly ash = 115 kg/m^3
Water = 140 kg/m^3
Fine aggregate = 862 kg/m^3
Coarse aggregate = 1097 kg/m^3
Chemical admixture = 7.7 kg/m^3
Water-cement ratio = 0.364

Step 8: The slump shall be measured and the water content and dosage of admixture shall be adjusted for achieving the required slump based on trial, if required. The mix proportions shall be reworked for the actual water content and checked for durability requirements.

Step 9: Two more trials having variation of ±10% of water-cement ratio in step 8 shall be carried out and a graph between three water-cement ratios and their corresponding strengths shall be plotted to work out the mix proportions for the given target strength for field trials. However, durability requirement shall be met.

Problem 4.5: A nominal mix of grade M20 is to be adopted on site by using table 4.1. It is decided to use volume batching. Find out the volumetric proportions for the mix. Consider the bulk density of cement, sand and gravel as 1440 kg/m³, 1700 kg/m³ and 1700 kg/m³ respectively.

Solution: First find the proportions by mass,

Cement 1 bag = 50 kg

From table 4.1 total quantity of dry aggregate (fine + coarse) required = 250 kg.

Selecting ratio of fine to coarse aggregate by mass as 1: 2

$$\text{Sand required} = \frac{1}{3} \times 250 = 83.33 \text{ kg}$$

$$\text{Gravel required} = \frac{2}{3} \times 250 = 166.67 \text{ kg}$$

Using water-cement ratio 0.45,

Water required = 0.45 × 50 = 22.5 kg

To convert mass into volume, divide the mass by bulk density.

Then, Water required = 22.5 litres

$$\text{Cement} = 50 \text{ kg} = \frac{50}{1440} = 0.0347 \text{ m}^3$$

$$\text{Sand} = 83.33 \text{ kg} = \frac{83.33}{1700} = 0.0343 \text{ m}^3$$

$$\text{Gravel} = 166.67 \text{ kg} = \frac{166.67}{1700} = 0.0686 \text{ m}^3$$

It may be approximated to proportion 1: 1: 2 (1 cement: 1 sand: 2 gravel by volume) with water cement ratio as 0.45 by mass (22.5 litres of water).

The proportion above is obtained by considering the volume on dry basis. If sand contains moisture, suitable modifications for bulking of sand can be done.

4.5.2 Department of Environment (DOE) Method

This method has only two types of aggregates recognised namely crushed and uncrushed. The water content required to give various levels of workability expressed as slump and vee bee time can be determined for the two types of aggregates, namely crushed and uncrushed with different maximum sizes varying from 10 mm to 40 mm. The degree of workability 'very low', 'low', 'medium' and 'high' have now been referred in terms of specific values of slump and vee bee. Time DOE method of mix design results in expressing the mix proportions in terms of quantities of materials per unit volume of concrete.

This method is applicable to ordinary and rapid hardening portland cements and to sulphate resisting portland cement used with normal weight aggregates or with air cooled slag aggregates but not with light weight aggregates. Three maximum sizes of aggregates are recognised viz., 40, 20 and 10 mm.

The following procedure is adopted for the design of a concrete mix.

1. The target mean strength is calculated based on the characteristic strength, standard deviation and statistical value 'K' which depends upon the accepted proportion of low results and the number of tests.

$$f_t = f_{ck} + K.S$$

where, f_t = Target mean strength

f_{ck} = Characteristic mean strength.

2. From table 4.2, a value is obtained for the compressive strength of a mix made with a free water-cement ratio of 0.5, according to the specified age, the type of cement and the type of aggregate used.

3. This strength value is then plotted on Fig. 4.2 and a curve is drawn from the point and parallel to the printed curves until it intercepts a horizontal line passing through the ordinate representing the target means strength. The corresponding value of the free water-cement ratio can then be read from the abscissa.

4. The free water content, required depending upon the type and maximum size of aggregate to give a concrete of the specified slump or Vee bee is obtained from table 4.3.

5. Knowing the water-cement ratio and water content, the cement content is obtained by -

$$\text{Cement content} = \left(\frac{\text{Free water content}}{\text{Free water-cement ratio}}\right)$$

6. An estimate of the wet density of the fully compacted concrete is obtained from Fig. 4.9, depending upon the free water content and the specific gravity of the combined aggregate. From this estimated density of concrete, the total aggregate content is determined from the following relations:

Total aggregate content = $D - W_c - W_{fw}$

where D = the wet density of concrete (kg/m^3)

W_c = the cement content (kg/m^3)

W_{fw} = the free water content (kg/m^3)

7. The recommended proportion of fine aggregate depending upon the maximum size of aggregate, the workability level and the free water-cement ratio are shown in Fig. 4.10 to 4.12, for sand of different zones 1 to 4; as specified in British code BS: 882 and for maximum size of aggregate of 10 mm, 20 mm and 40 mm. The fine aggregate content is determined as a percentage of the total aggregate from the figures.

Fine aggregate content = (Total aggregate content) × (Proportion of fines)

Coarse aggregate content = (Total aggregate content) − (Fine aggregate content)

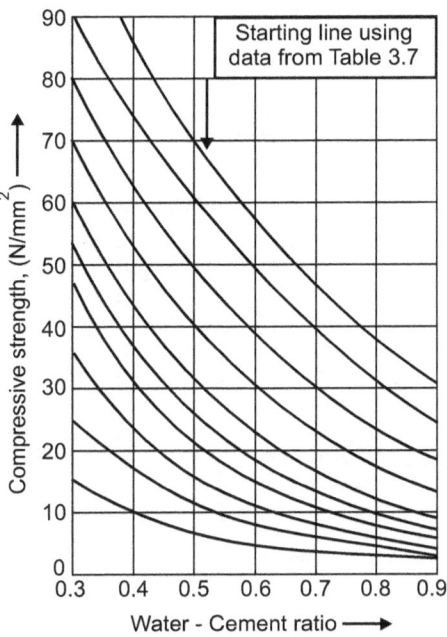

Fig. 4.8: Relationship between Compressive Strength and Water-Cement Ratio

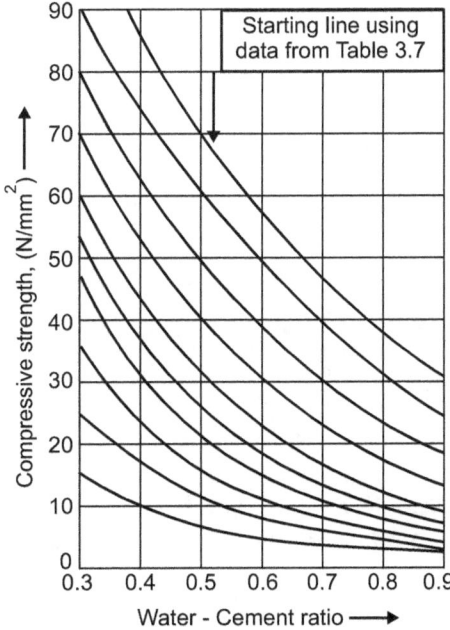

Fig. 4.9: Estimated Wet Density of Fully Compacted Concrete

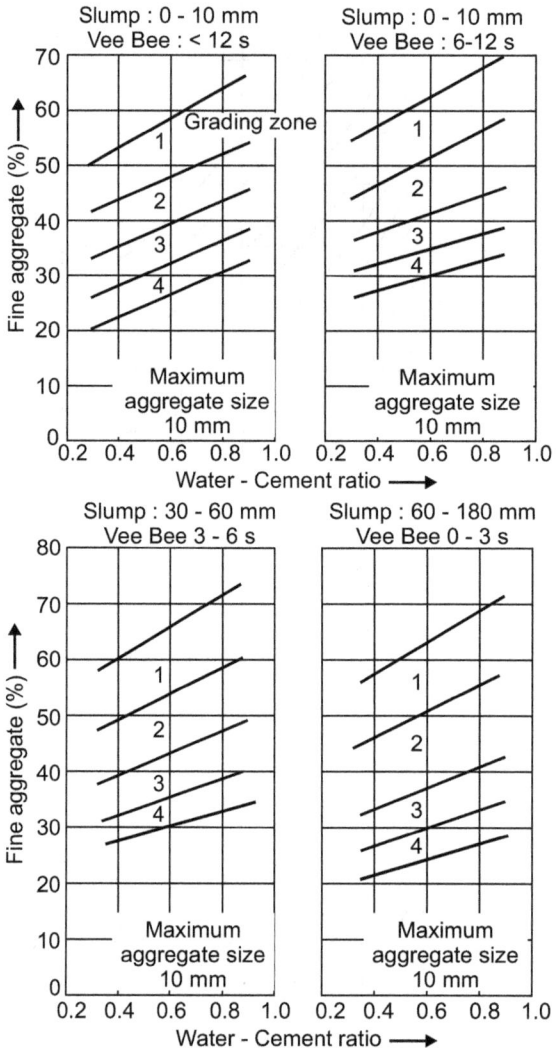

Fig. 4.10: Recommended Weight of Fine Aggregate as a Function of Free Water-Cement ratio for Various Workabilities and Maximum Sizes

Table 4.11: Approximate Compressive Strength of Concrete Mixes Made with Water-Cement Ratio of 0.5

Types of cement	Types of coarse aggregate	Compressive strength (N/mm^2) age (days)			
		3	7	28	91
Ordinary or sulphate resisting portland cement	Uncrushed	18	27	40	48
	Crushed	23	33	47	55
Rapid-hardening portland cement	Uncrushed	25	34	46	53
	Crushed	30	40	53	60

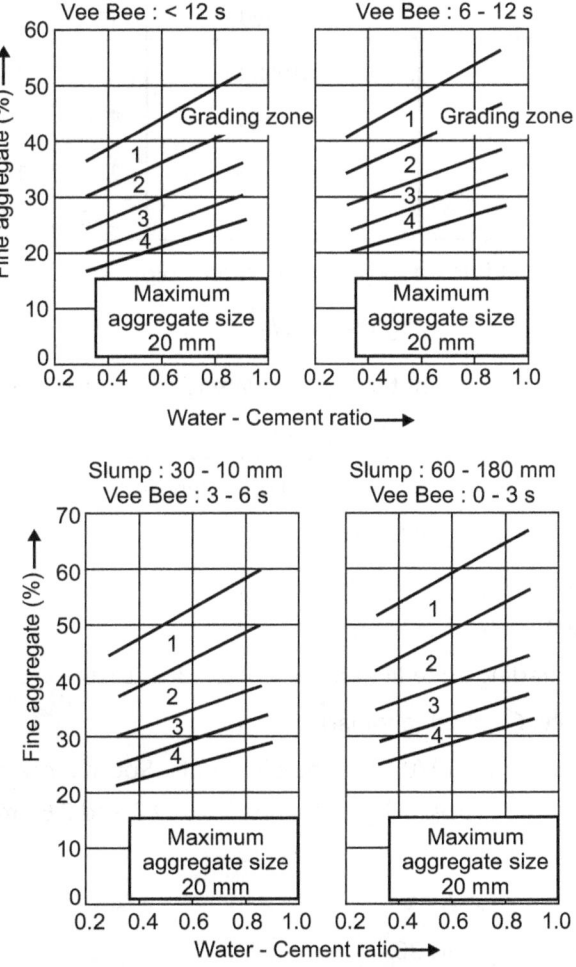

Fig. 4.11: Recommended Weight of Fine Aggregate as a Function of Free Water- Cement Ratio for Various Workabilities and Maximum Sizes

Table 4.12: Approximate Water Content (kg/m³) Required to Give Various Level or Workability

Slump (mm) ...... Vee bee (secs)		0-10 12	10-30 6-12	30-60 3-6	60-180 0-3
Maximum size of aggregate (mm)	Types of aggregate				
10	Uncrushed	150	180	205	225
	Crushed	180	205	230	250
20	Uncrushed	135	160	180	195
	Crushed	170	190	210	225
40	Uncrushed	115	140	160	175
	Crushed	155	175	190	205

Note: When coarse and fine aggregate of different types are used. The water content is estimated by the expression give by $\left(\frac{2}{3} W_f + \frac{1}{3} W_c\right)$

where W_f = Water content appropriate to the type of fine aggregate

W_c = Water content appropriate to the type of coarse aggregate

Problem 4.6: Design a concrete mix of medium strength to suit the following data:

Characteristic cube strength: M-30

Types of cement: Ordinary portland

Fine aggregate: Natural river sand.

Conforming to grading zone III of table 4 of IS : 383-1970.

Coarse aggregate: Crushed (angular)

Conforming to IS : 383-1970 Code requirements. Specific gravities of cement, sand and coarse aggregate (crushed granite) are 3.14, 2.63 and 2.61 respectively.

Type of exposure: Mild

Degree of quantity control: Very good

Vee bee (sees) – 6.12 for M 30.

Design the mix proportions for the above grade of concrete.

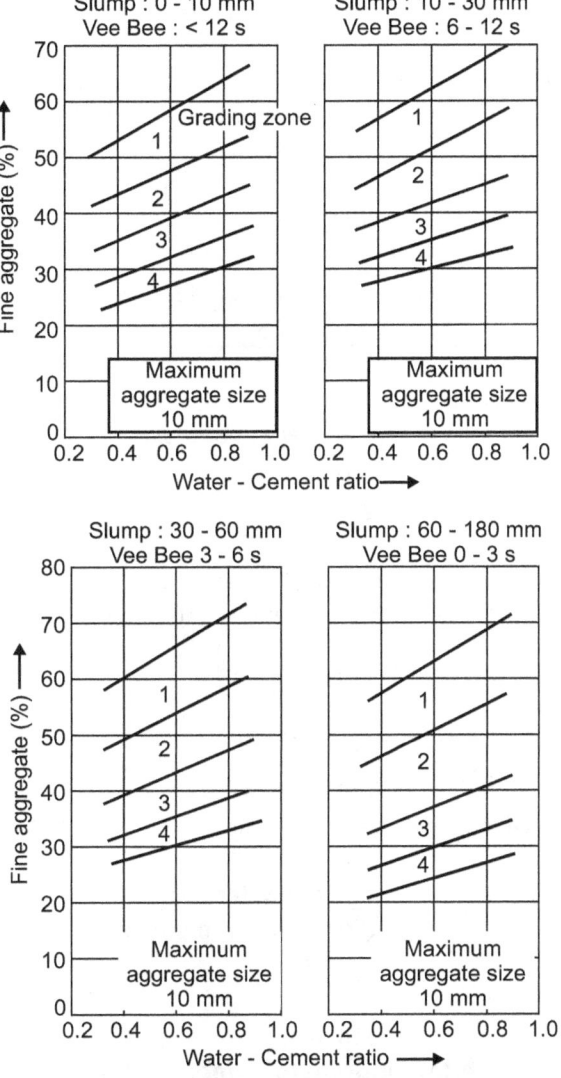

Fig. 4.12: Recommended Weight of Fine Aggregate as a Function of Free Water-Cement Ratio for Various Workabilities and Maximum Size

Solution:

1. **Target mean strength:** Target mean strength is calculated as:

$$f_t = f_{ck} + K.S$$
$$= (30 + 1.65 \times 50)$$
$$= 38.25 \text{ N/mm}^2$$

2. **Selection of free water-cement ratio:** From table 4.11, the approximate 28 days compressive strength of concrete made with a free water-cement ratio 0.5 using ordinary portland cement with crushed type aggregate is 47 N/mm². This strength value is plotted in Fig. 4.8 and a curve is drawn from this point and parallel to the printed curves until it intercepts a horizontal line passing through the ordinate representing the target mean strength. The corresponding value on the abscissa represents the free water-cement ratio. Thus, from Fig. 4.12, the free water-cement ratio obtained for the corresponding target mean strength of M-30 is 0.575.

Mix	Target mean strength N/mm²	Free water-cement ratio
M-30	38.25	0.575

3. **Selection of free water content:** From table 4.12, the approximate free water content (kg/m³), required for
   (a) Uncrushed type of fine (W_f) aggregate of maximum size = 10 mm
      For M-30 grade = 180 kg/m³
   (b) Crushed type of coarse aggregate (W_C) of maximum size = 20 mm
      For M-30 grade = 190 kg/m³
   Since coarse and fine aggregates of different types are used (crushed and uncrushed respectively), the total free water content is estimated using this expression –

$$W_{FW} = \left(\frac{2}{3} W_F + \frac{1}{3} W_C\right)$$

$$= \left(\frac{2}{3} \times 180 + \frac{1}{3} \times 190\right)$$

$$= 183.33 \text{ kg/m}^3$$

4. **Determination of cement content:** The cement content is determined from the relation

$$\text{Cement content} = \left(\frac{\text{Free water content}}{\text{Free water-cement ratio}}\right)$$

$$= \frac{183.33}{0.575}$$

$$= 318.84 \text{ kg/m}^3$$

5. **Determination of total aggregate content:** The total aggregate content is calculated as:

$$T_A = (D - C - W_{FW})$$

where, D = Wet density of concrete (kg/m³)
  C = Cement content (kg/m³)
  W_{FW} = Free water content

From Fig. 4.9, the value of D for M-30 is 2365 kg/m³.
∴ T_A = (2365 − 318.84 − 183.33) = 1863 kg/m³

6. **Selection of fine aggregate content:** From Fig., the proportion of fine aggregate content for M-30; Vee bee is (6 - 12) sec and free water-cement ratio is 0.575 in range of 31 - 38%. Therefore,

   ∴   Average value = 34.5%

   ∴ Fine aggregate content = (Total aggregate content) × (Proportion of fines)

                         = (186.3) × (34.5%)

                         = 643 kg/m^3

7. **Calculation of coarse aggregate content:**

   Coarse aggregate content = (Total aggregate content) – (Fine aggregate content)

                         = (1863) – (643)

                         = 1220 kg/m^3

8. **The various ingredients per m^3 of concrete for M-30:**

   Cement = 318.84 kg

   Fine aggregate = 643 kg

   Coarse aggregate = 1220 kg

   Water = 183.33 kg

9. **Mix proportions of weight:**

   Cement: Fine aggregate: Coarse aggregate: Water = 1 : 2.02 : 3.83 : 0.58.

4.6 Scaffolding and Underpinning

4.6.1 Scaffolding

When the height of construction is more than 1 m, workmen need some platform on which they can stand safely, keep necessary materials of construction, tools such as bricks, mortar, trowel, plumb bob, hammers etc. Temporary platform made out of timber or steel, to facilitate construction, repairs, maintenance or demolition is called as **scaffolding**. As work progresses, height of scaffolding is increased suitably.

4.6.1.1 Types of Scaffolding

Different types of scaffolding commonly used are described below:

(a) Single Scaffolding or Brick Layer's Scaffolding: (Ref. Fig. 4.13 (a)) In this type, only one row of vertical members (mostly of timber, bamboo or hollow steel tubular sections) called as standards are erected at a distance of about 1 m from the wall to be constructed. The standards are spaced at a distance of 1.5 to 3 m c/c. Standards "S" are fastened to ledgers "L" by rope or other means. Ledgers are the horizontal members, parallel to the wall and at right angles to standard. Putlogs "P" are placed on ledgers, at right angles to the walls, one end of which is held firmly in wall and are spaced at 1.2 m to 1.5 m c/c. Planks are placed on the putlogs. Guard boards "G" are placed at working level, whereas toe boards are placed slightly above planks to guard against material. Diagonal braces "D" are placed diagonally, to increase stability of standards against lateral movement. This type of scaffolding is slightly weaker than double scaffolding and is used while laying bricks, hence is known as Brick Layer's scaffolding.

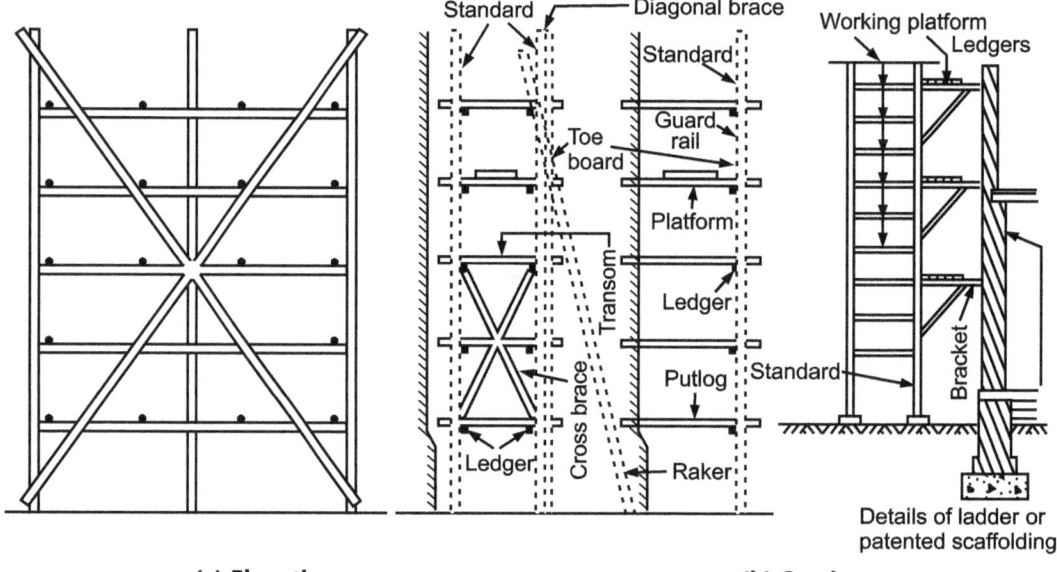

(a) Elevation   (b) Section

Fig. 4.13: Brick Layer's Scaffolding

(b) Double Scaffolding or Mason's Scaffolding: Frame work of this scaffolding is similar to single scaffolding, except that as against one row of standards provided in single scaffolding, *two rows of standards* are provided in Double scaffolding, and hence it is stronger than single scaffolding. It is used by Mason in construction of stone masonry, hence is termed as Mason's Scaffolding. As shown in Fig. 4.13 (b), one row of standards is placed about 20 cm away from wall, and the other row is about 1.2 to 1.5 m away from wall. Putlogs are not required to be embedded in the wall, and are supported on the two rows of ledgers. Thus, this type of scaffolding is independent of wall.

(c) Cantiliver Scaffolding or Needle Scaffolding (Ref. Fig. 4.14): This type of scaffolding is provide under the following conditions:

    (i) Single scaffolding as well as double scaffolding rests at ground level. Such scaffolding may obstruct traffic on busy street.

    (ii) If repairs are to be carried out only in few floors at higher elevation in tall building, then it is uneconomical to provide scaffolding from ground floor.

This type of scaffolding is required to be erected with great care, to avoid damages to other parts of building.

At floor level holes are made @ 0.5 to 1 m interval, through which steel joists called as **'needles'** are inserted and projected outside. To provide necessary reaction for the cantiliver outside struts are provided over these joists, which will butt against upper floor slab. On the projected end of Needle, standards are provided. Thus, needle beams provide necessary support to standards. Ledgers, putlogs, planks etc. are provided similar to those in single scaffolding. The strut ends are secured to the floors by wedges.

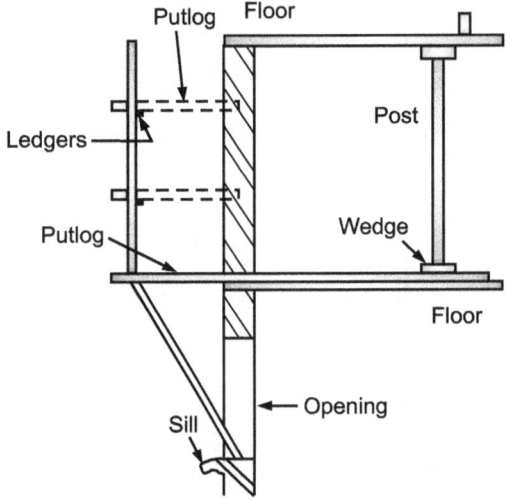

Fig. 4.14: Cantiliver Scaffolding

(d) Suspended Scaffolding: In this type of scaffolding, working platform is suspended from roof (or top of upstream of dam or bridge) by means of ropes or chains. Arrangements are made to raise or lower the platform, so that work can be carried out at desired level. This scaffolding is light in weight and is used to carry occasional maintenance and repairs such as white washing, painting, removing obstacles etc. In this type of scaffolding, standards are not required to be erected. This type of scaffolding does not create any obstruction to traffic etc. at lowerer level.

(e) Steel Scaffolding (Ref. Fig. 4.15): Now-a-days, steel scaffolding is being used in preference to timber scaffolding, as it has the following advantages:

    (i) These are simple to erect, as only few sizes and fasteners are to be dealt with.

    (ii) It can be used to support vertical loads of all types.

    (iii) The scaffolding can be used for form work as well. Hence, its versatility increases.

    (iv) Compared to timber scaffolding it is light, strong, fire resistant, durable and has higher scrap value.

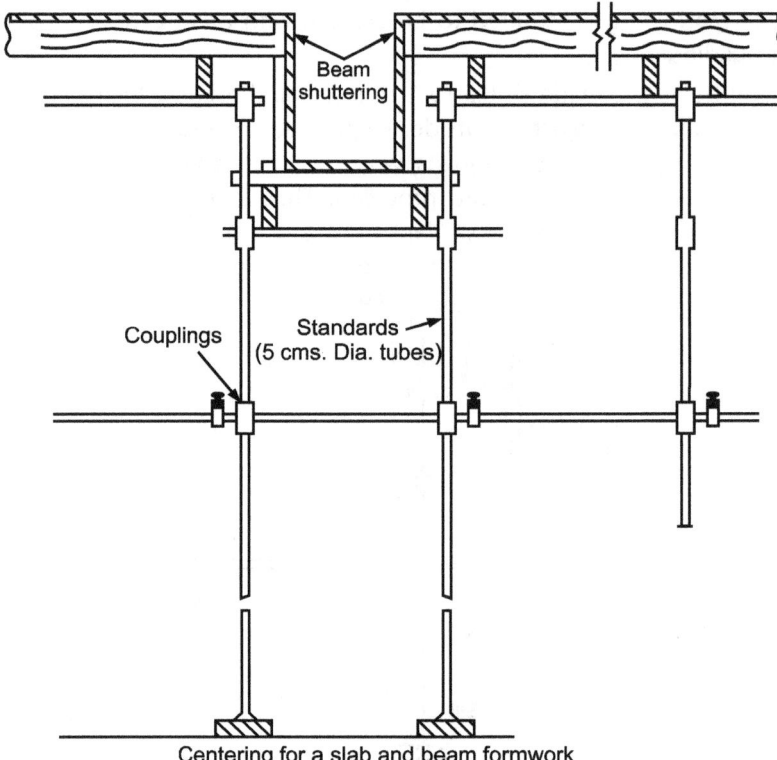

Fig. 4.15: Steel Scaffolding

However, it has the following disadvantages:
(i) Initial investment is high. But in long run it is cheap.
(ii) Small fittings, if lost, becomes difficult to replace. Proper care is required to be taken for storing and handling.
(iii) To guard against corrosion, scaffolding is required to be cleaned, and painted periodically.

Steel tubes used for scaffolding are of 5 mm thickness and are of 40 to 60 mm diameter. Scaffolding can be erected speedily by using special couplings and set screws.

4.6.2 Underpinning

It is a method of providing new foundation below the existing foundation without damaging the stability of existing structure to meet the following requirements :

(i) If deep foundation is to be constructed adjoining to a building having shallow foundation; the shallow foundation may face some problems, and may need strengthening.

(ii) If height of existing building is to be increased, and existing foundation, if unable to bear increased load, may require strengthening.

(iii) If basement is to be provided to the existing building and if depth and strength of existing foundation is insufficient, then existing foundation may need strengthening.

4.6.2.1 Methods of Underpinning

Of the various methods, the following methods are commonly used for underpinning :

(i) Alternate pit method
(ii) Cantilever beam method
(iii) Micropile method.

(a) Alternate Pit Method

(i) Pits of size 1.2 × 1.2 m or 1.5 × 1.5 m and to a depth greater than the depth of existing foundation, are excavated on either side of the existing wall.

(ii) To start with, pits are excavated at mid length of wall; and further pits are excavated in alternate bays spaced at 3 to 4 m c/c.

(iii) Holes are made in the existing wall at desired level, so that, steel joists (RSJ) called as needle beam with bearing plate on the top can be inserted. Bottom and top of the hole is levelled and RSJ with bearing plate is inserted and RSJ is supported at either ends. With this arrangement, load of wall above the needle beam is transferred on needle beam, and no damage will be caused for a short period, if soil below the existing foundation is removed.

(iv) As soon as soil below the foundation is removed it is replaced by new, stronger foundation on an unyielding strata.

(v) Same process is continued in alternate bays; and new foundation is provided using rich cement concrete.

(vi) Later on balance pits are excavated and new foundation is provided in similar manner.

(vii) Needle beams and vertical supports are removed and load is transferred to the new foundation.

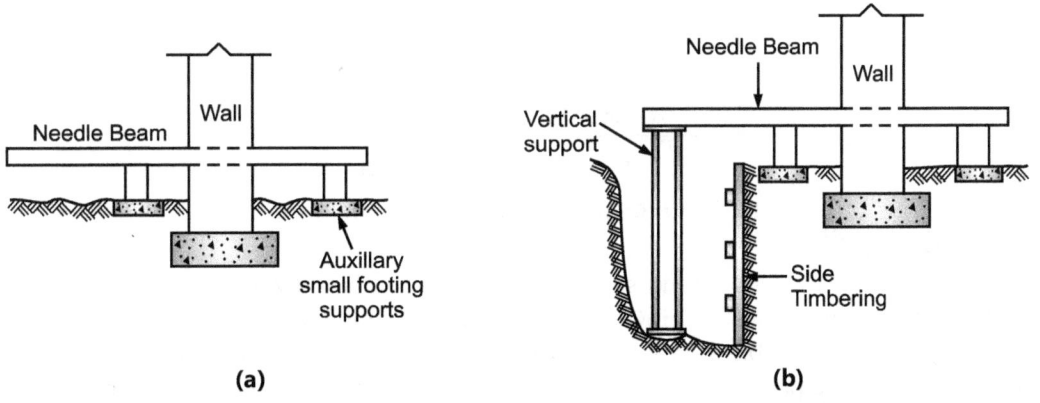

(a) (b)

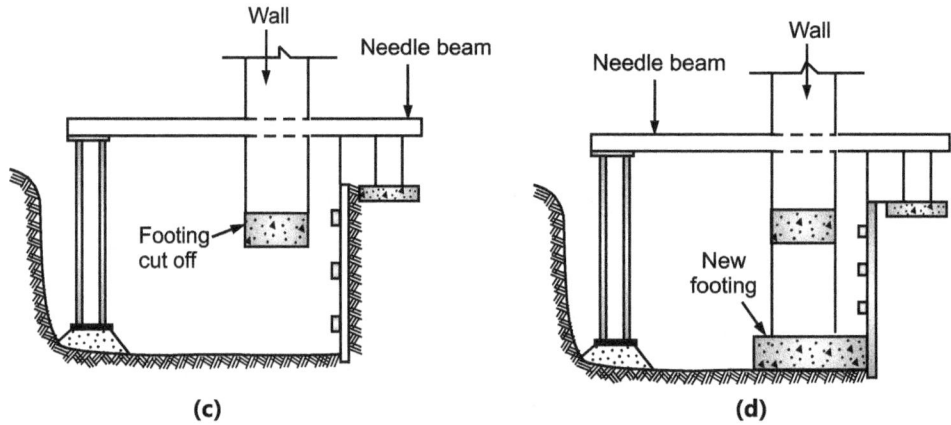

(c) (d)

Fig. 4.16: Alternate pit method

(b) Cantilever Needle Beam Method

If sufficient space is not available to support the needle beams, outside the existing building, then the needle beam is supported on a fulcrum inside building. At the end of needle beam, load is placed on the needle beam. Due to cantilever action, load of the wall is transferred on the needle beam; and soil below existing foundation can be removed without causing any damage to existing building and new stronger foundation can be provided.

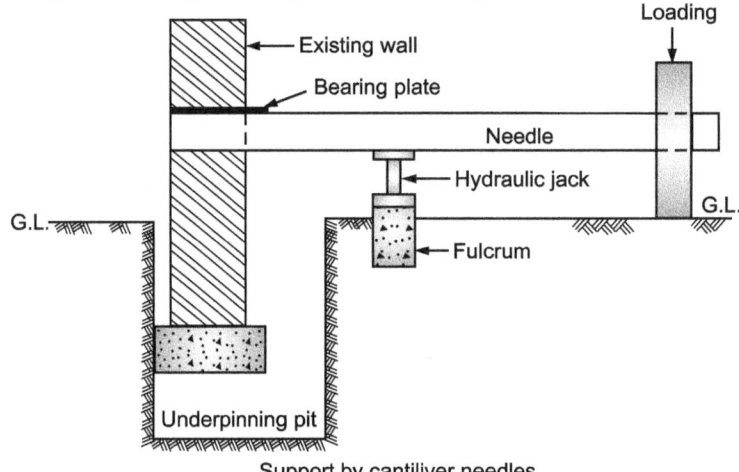

Support by cantiliver needles

Fig. 4.17: Cantilever needle beam method

(c) Pile method

Pit method is used with strong strata at a shallow depth and without any ground water problem pits can be excavated. However, if ground water table is met at shallow depth and unyielding strata is available at greater depth, then bored piles are provided on either side of existing wall; and the piles are interconnected by providing pile cap through existing wall.

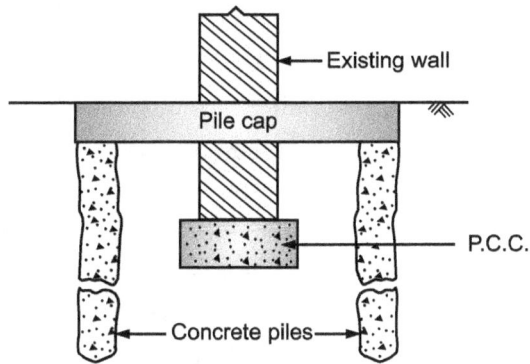

Fig. 4.18: Pile method

4.7 Strutting and Shoring

Term scaffolding is used for the arrangement made to facilitate construction of new walls or repairing and maintenance of old walls, whereas term shoring is used in connection with arrangements made to give support to a damaged wall, so as to prevent it from further damage / collapse.

Shoring is provided to a structure under the following circumstances:

When a structure has become/or is likely to become unsafe due to differential settlement, or negligence of maintenance, bad workmanship, unequal settlement due to excessive de-watering or vibrations in adjoining area.

More skill, care and factor of safety is required while providing shoring. Shores are generally made of timber, but for heavier loads, steel beams are adopted. Shores may also be made of concrete or masonry. Support may be given externally or internally or both externally and internally.

Types of Shoring:

Support to be provided may be (i) Inclined, (ii) Horizontal or (iii) Vertical. Based on the characteristics of the support, shorings are classified as:

(a) Raking or Inclined Shoring

(b) Flying or Horizontal Shoring

(c) Dead or Vertical Shoring.

[a] Raking Shores:

These consist of providing inclined timber called as *raker*, one end of which rests against a defective wall through wall plate and other end rests against *sole plate* which is embedded in ground at an inclination, [preferably at right angles to raker] to distribute load uniformly. Wall plate is a thick wooden plank [of about 30 cm in width] placed against defective wall and is secured to the wall by means of needles. Wall plate is provided to distribute the load. Rakers are inter connected by braces and are tied at bottom by iron dog or hoop iron.

Following precautions should be taken while providing rakers:

(i) In order to maintain equilibrium, the following three forces must meet at a point and form a triangle of forces.

Vertical load from wall, over turning forces from floors or roofs and resisting inclined. *For this purpose, centre line of raker and centre line of wall must meet at floor level.*

(ii) Higher the inclination of raker, lesser will be its horizontal component. i.e. its resistance to outward movement of wall reduces. Hence, inclination of top raker should not be more than 75°.

(iii) Rakers should not be fixed by providing wedges as it is likely to damage the building.

(iv) There is greater uncertainty about magnitude of destabilising forces. Hence, higher factor of safety should be provided.

(v) Provisions made in local bye laws, etc. should be taken into account.

R.C.C. shore in the form of R.C.C. frame may be used to resist unstable tall retaining wall. Similarly, R.C.C. shore connected to pile cap on top of raker pile can resist destabilising forces effectively.

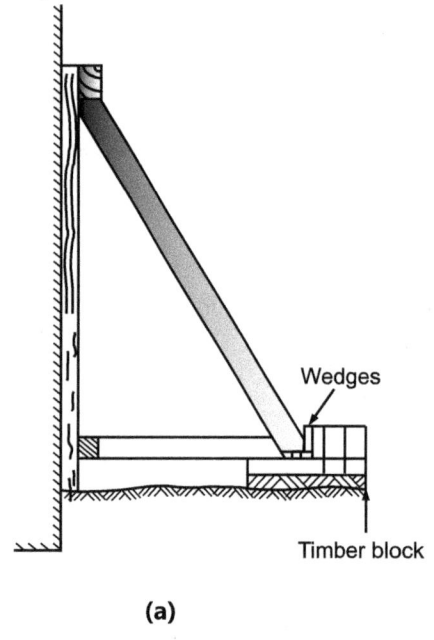

(a)

Timber block

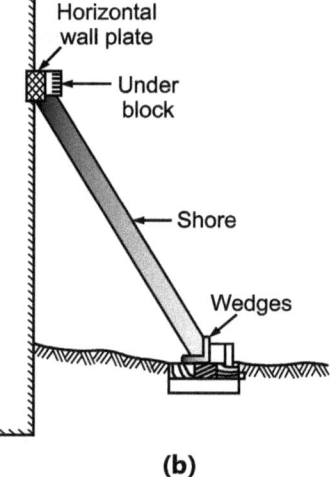

(b)

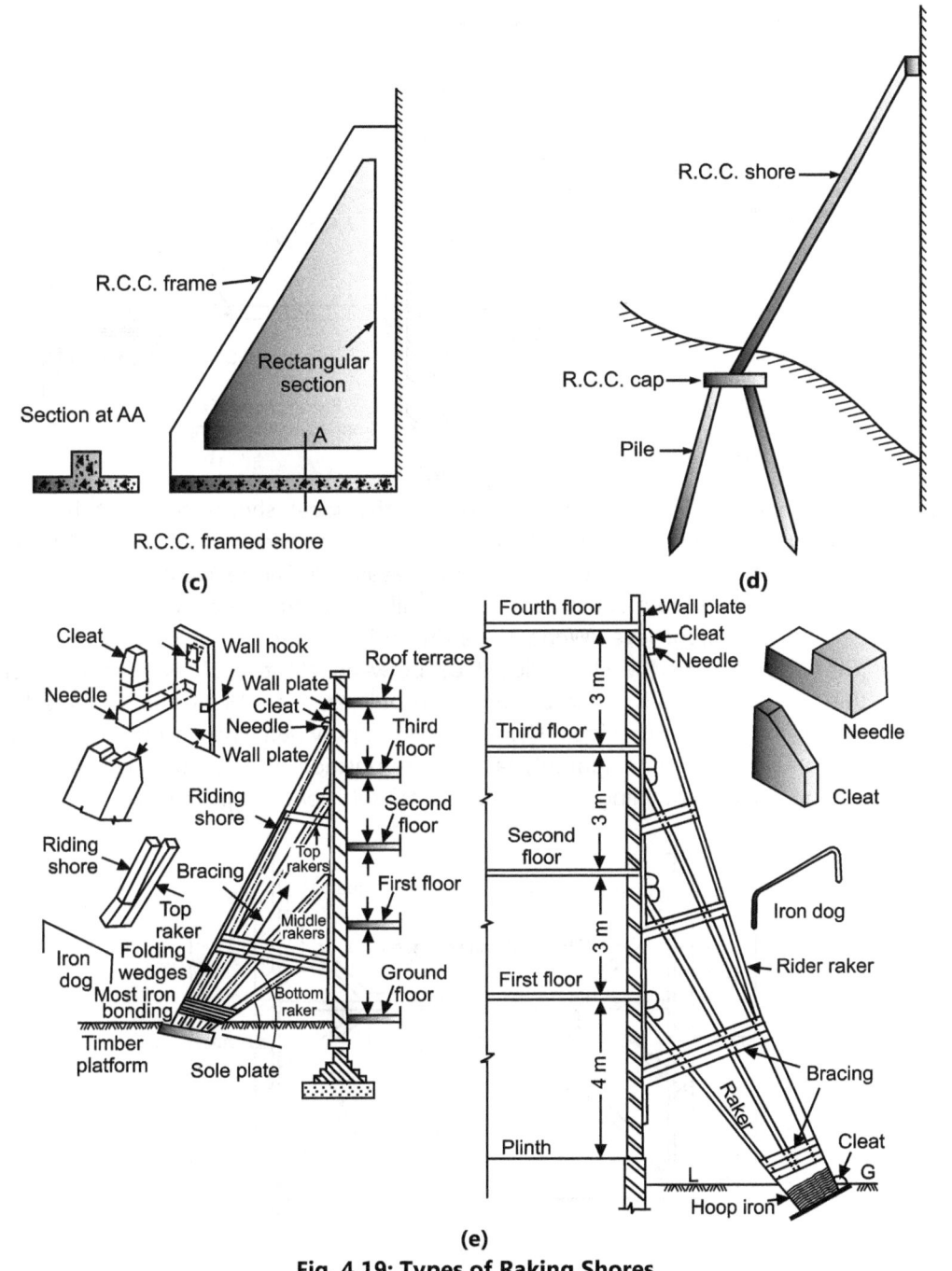

Fig. 4.19: Types of Raking Shores

[b] Flying Shores or Horizontal Shores (Ref. Fig. 4.5):

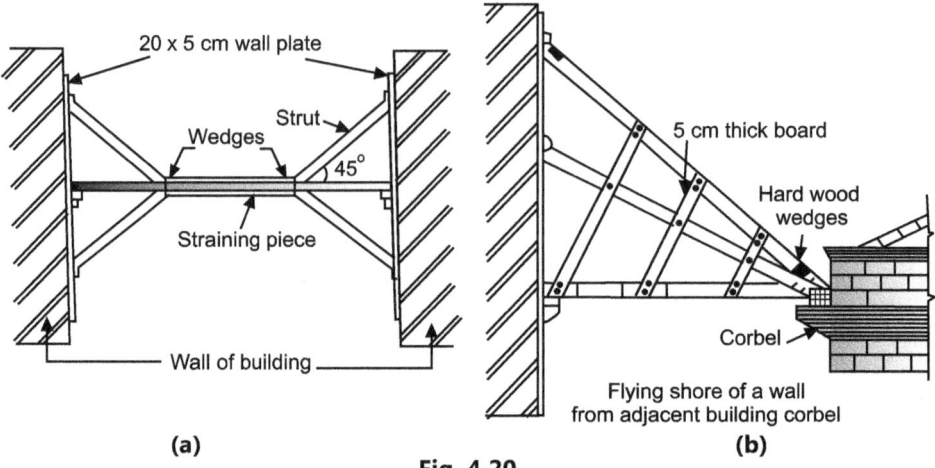

Fig. 4.20

Horizontal shores called as flying shores are the ideal shores to resist horizontal component of destabilising force. This type of shoring is provided when, parallel walls to provide support at a reasonable distance [< 10 m] is available. Centre line of horizontal shore and centre line of wall should meet at floor level. Similarly, centre line of strut, and centre line of wall should meet at floor level. Wedges are driven in between straining piece and strut. Angle of the inclination of the strut should be between 45° to 60°. When the distance between the two parallel walls is more than 10 m but less than 15 m, then double flying shore as shown in Fig. 4.20 is provided. Flying shores are provided when damaged building is being removed. Flying shores temporarily take up the position of dismantled building and is kept in position till new building is constructed to sufficient height to provide required stability.

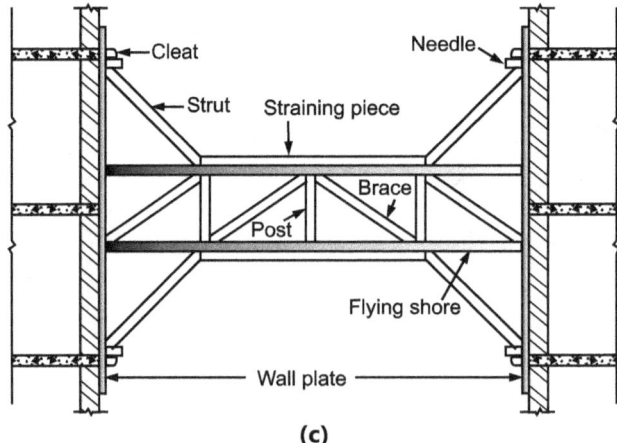

(c)
Fig. 4.20: Flying stores

[c] Vertical Shore or Dead Shore (Ref. Fig. 4.21):

This type of shoring is provided, when,

(i) It is required to strengthen or replace existing unsafe foundation.

(ii) To remove and rebuild a part of defective load bearing wall or

(iii) To provide larger doors, windows or openings in existing walls.

Comparatively, nature, quantity and location of forces acting are known in this type of shoring, than in case of raker shoring. As such, risk involved is comparatively less. Following steps are taken while providing the shoring:

(i) Those doors, windows and other opening floors and other parts of structure, which are likely to be effected by removal of defective wall or demolition of wall, are properly strutted or supported.

(ii) Small openings of size just enough to insert wooden beams or steel joists are made in wall above the portion of wall which is required to be removed.

(iii) Top and bottom portion of the opening is levelled and steel joist / wooden beam is inserted in the hole. If required, slightly wider wooden plank or steel plate is provided over top of the beam to distribute load evenly over large area.

(iv) The projected ends of beams are supported by heavy vertical strut called as dead shore. As shown in Fig. 4.21, head piece or sole plates are provided so that load is transferred on the dead shore correctly.

(v) Once again, whether all struts provided in all openings are properly fixed or not is checked and then defective portion is gradually removed.

(vi) Defective portion of wall/foundation is replaced properly.

(vii) Shoring is removed in the following sequence only.

    (a) First needle beams are removed.

    (b) Struts from windows, doors etc. are then removed.

    (c) Finally, struts of floors are removed.

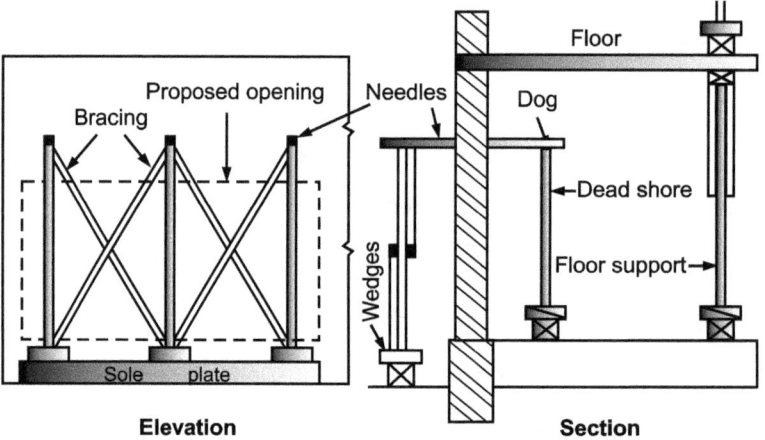

Fig. 4.21: Dead or vertical shores

Distinction between Scaffolding and Shoring:

(i) Both shoring and scaffolding are temporary structures, but comparatively shoring is required for a longer period than scaffolding.

(ii) Scaffolding is subjected to lesser loads viz. load of construction materials and workmen working on the platform, and nature of load can be estimated fairly accurately. In shoring it is not possible to precisely determine load acting on shore.

(iii) More care, skill and factor of safety is required for providing shoring than for providing scaffolding.

(iv) Prior permission/approval of local municipal bodies may be required while providing shoring, whereas no such prior approval is required in case of scaffolding.

(v) Scaffolding is intended to serve as work platform.

4.8 IRC Method of Design

Overview

Indian roads congress has specified the design procedures for flexible pavements based on CBR values. The Pavement designs given in the previous edition IRC:37-1984 were applicable to design traffic upto only 30 million standard axles (msa). The earlier code is empirical in nature which has limitations regarding applicability and extrapolation. This guidelines follows analytical designs and developed new set of designs up to 150 msa.

Scope

These guidelines will apply to design of flexible pavements for Expressway, National Highways, State Highways, Major District Roads, and other categories of roads. Flexible pavements are considered to include the pavements which have bituminous surfacing and granular base and sub-base courses conforming to IRC/ MOST standards. These guidelines apply to new pavements.

Design criteria

The flexible pavements has been modeled as a three layer structure and stresses and strains at critical locations have been computed using the linear elastic model. To give proper consideration to the aspects of performance, the following three types of pavement distress resulting from repeated (cyclic) application of traffic loads are considered:

1. Vertical compressive strain at the top of the sub-grade which can cause sub-grade deformation resulting in permanent deformation at the pavement surface.

2. Horizontal tensile strain or stress at the bottom of the bituminous layer which can cause fracture of the bituminous layer.

3. Pavement deformation within the bituminous layer.

While the permanent deformation within the bituminous layer can be controlled by meeting the mix design requirements, thickness of granular and bituminous layers are selected using the analytical design approach so that strains at the critical points are within the allowable limits. For calculating tensile strains at the bottom

Exercise

1. Define M20. Name the different methods of concrete mix design and explain the I.S. guidelines for the concrete mix design.
2. Explain the concept of mix design.
3. Enlist the basic data required for mix design.
4. What are the different factors that control quality of concrete?
5. Describe statistical quality control of concrete.
6. State the various steps in concrete mix design according to DOE method.
7. Explain the term 'Target strength' for mix design.
8. Define standard deviation for samples.
9. What would be the average strength of samples of concrete if desired characteristic strength is 20 N/mm² for standard deviation of 4.6 N/mm²?

(**Ans.** f_m = 27.59 N/mm²)

10. Explain factors affecting the choice of mix proportions.
11. Write in general step-by-step procedure for concrete mix-design.
12. What is concrete mix design? Enlist the various methods of mix design for low and medium strength of concrete.

■■■

Unit 5

NON-DESTRUCTIVE TESTING AND DETERIORATION OF CONCRETE

[A] NON-DESTRUCTIVE TESTING OF CONCRETE

5.1 Non-Destructive Testing

Non-Destructive Testing is powerful method for evaluating existing concrete structure with regard to their strength and durability apart from assessment and control of quality of harden concrete. It can also be used in the investigation of crack depth, micro cracks and progressive deterioration in existing concrete structure.

5.1.1 Schmidth's Rebound Hammer

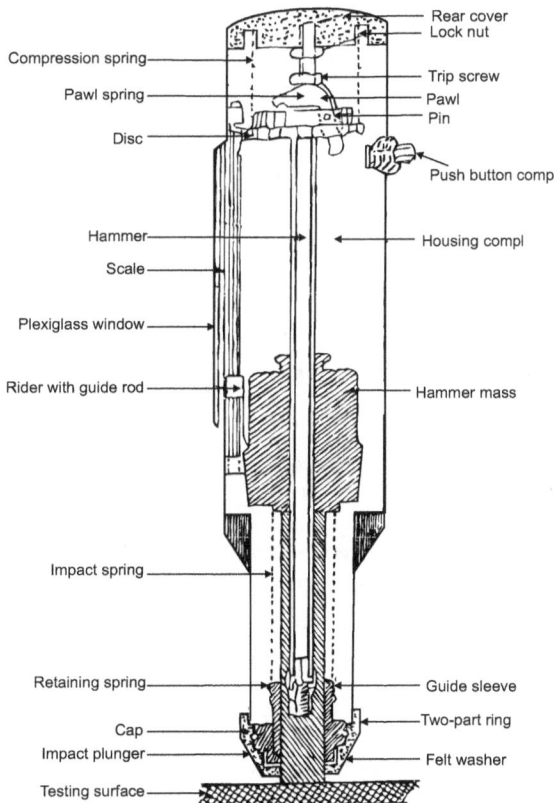

Fig. 5.1: Rebound Hammer

This test is also known as rebound hammer, impact hammers or sclerometer test. The test is based on the principle that the rebound of an elastic mass depends on the hardness of the surface against which the mass impinges. Fig. 5.1 shows the rebound hammer. The spring controlled hammer mass slides on a plunger within a tubular casing. The plunger retracts against a spring when pressed against the concrete surface, and this spring is automatically released when fully tensioned, causing the hammer mass to impact against the concrete through the plunger. When the spring controlled mass rebounds, it takes with it a rider which slides along a graduated scale and is visible through a small window in the side of casing on which the observation gives the rebound number. Then the calibration chart is used to relate the rebound number to compressive strength of concrete. The typical calibration chart is shown in Fig. 5.2. This test can be performed horizontally or vertically. The results obtained from rebound hammer test are affected by smoothness of surface, age of specimen, moisture condition of concrete, carbonation of concrete surface etc.

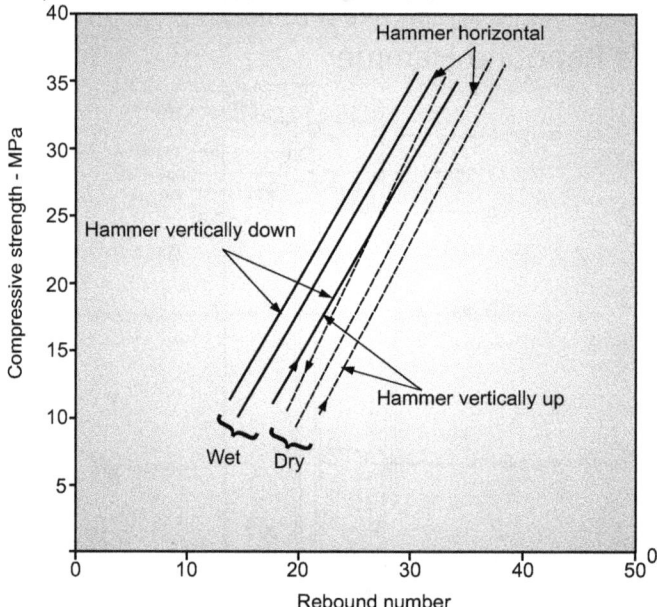

Fig. 5.2: Relationship Between Compressive Strength and Rebound Number with Hammer Horizontal and Vertical on a Dry and a Wet Surface of Concrete

5.1.2 Ultrasonic Pulse Velocity Method

This method involves the measurement of velocity of electrostatic pulses passing through concrete from a transmitting transducer to a receiving transducer. The pulse also can be generated by hammer blow. The pulse generator circuit consists of electronic circuit for generating pulses and a transducer for transmitting these electronic pulses into mechanical energy having frequency 15 to 50 kHz. The time of travel between initial onset and the reception of the pulse is measured electronically. A typical test circuit is shown in Fig. 5.3.

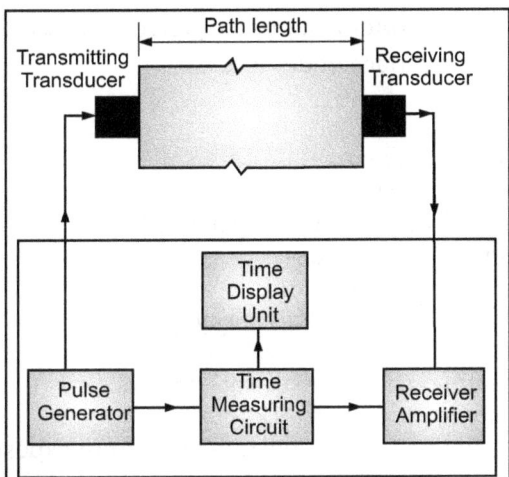

Fig. 5.3: Schematic of Ultrasonic Pulse Velocity Method

There are three ways of measuring the pulse velocity through concrete:
(1) Direct transmission.
(2) Indirect transmission.
(3) Surface transmission.

These are shown in Fig. 5.4.

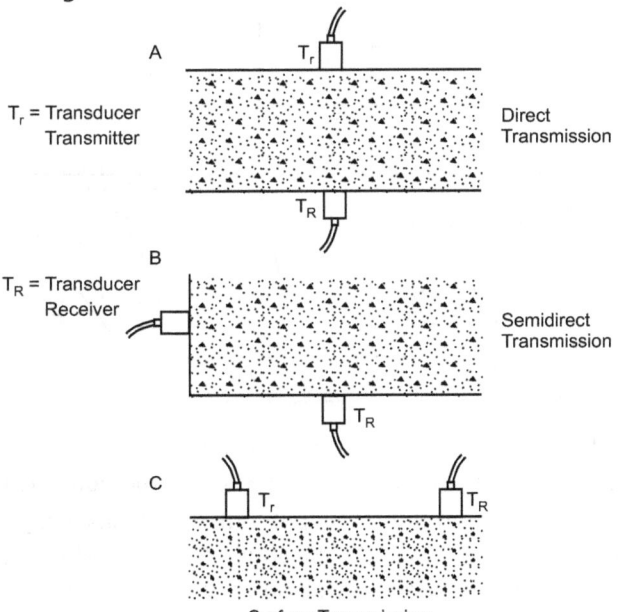

Fig. 5.4: Method of Measuring Pulse Velocity Through Concrete

Factors which affects the measurement of pulse velocity are as follows:
1. Smoothness of contact surface under test.
2. Influence of path length.
3. Temperature of concrete.
4. Moisture condition of concrete.
5. Presence of reinforcing steel.

The various applications of the pulse velocity methods are:
1. Establishing uniformity of concrete.
2. Establishing acceptance criteria.
3. Determination of pulse modulus of elasticity.
4. Estimation of strength of concrete.
5. Determination of setting characteristics of concrete.
6. Studies on durability of concrete (cracks etc.).
7. Measurement of deterioration of concrete due to fire exposure, mechanical, frost or chemical action.
8. Measurement of layer thickness.

5.1.3 Pull-out Test

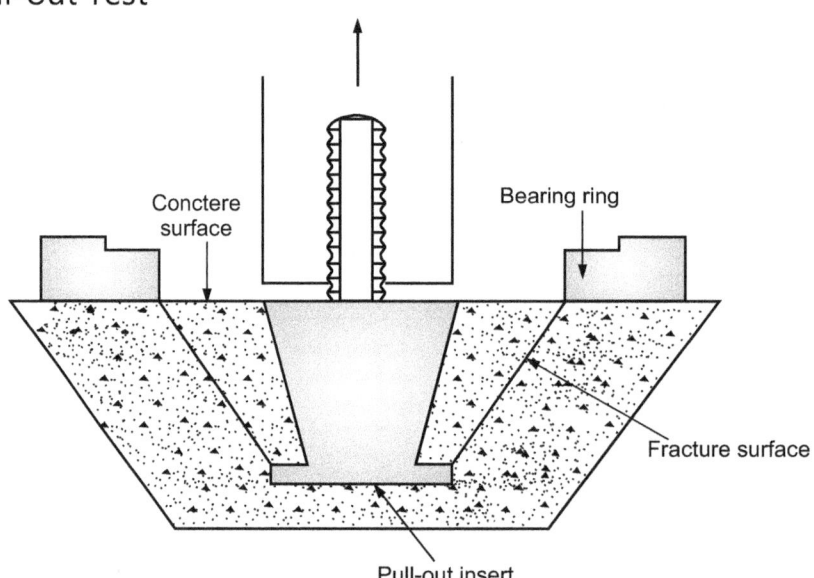

Fig. 5.5: Diagrammatic Representation of the Pull-out Test

This test measures the force required to pull out a previously cast in steel rod with an embedded enlarged end in the concrete. Stronger the concrete more will be the force required to pull out. The force required for pull out is related to the strength of concrete. The important feature of method is that the pull-out force and concrete strength is relatively unaffected by mix characteristics and curing history. Fig. 5.5 shows the pull-out test. The test can be performed either 'cast in method' or by 'drilled hole method'. In 'cast in method' the pull-out assembly is inserted into form work at the time of concreting the actual structural member. And in 'drilled hole method', hole is drilled into concrete and a wedge anchor bolt with expanding sleeve is tapped into the hole.

5.1.4 Impact Echo Test

An important limitation of ultrasonic tester is that it can only predict quality of concrete in general, but cannot give information about presence, if any, of micro porosity, voids, flaws or cracks. To bridge this gap, impact echo tester have been developed based on reflective wave technique. When a reflective wave is passed through a concrete member, presence of any micro defect is displayed on the monitor. Thus, this is a handy tool for an effective scanning of an interior concrete. Recent versions of this device are highly versatile.

Impact on the surface produces a disturbance that travels into the object along spherical wavefront. The waves are reflected by internal defect (difference in elastic constants and density) or external boundaries. When the reflected waves, or echoes, return to the surface, they produce displacement that are measured by a receiving transducer. Using time domain analysis, the time from the start of the impact to the arrival of the wave echo is measured, and the depth of reflecting interface can be determined, if the speed of wave is known. Following approximate relation can be used,

$$f = \frac{C_p}{2D}$$

where,
f = Frequency of wave
C_p = Speed of wave through the thickness of member
D = Depth of the reflecting interface.

The impact echo test has been successful in detecting a variety of defects, such as voids and honeycombed concrete in members, determination in bare and overlaid slabs, and voids in tendon ducts. The schematic of impact test is shown in Fig. 5.6.

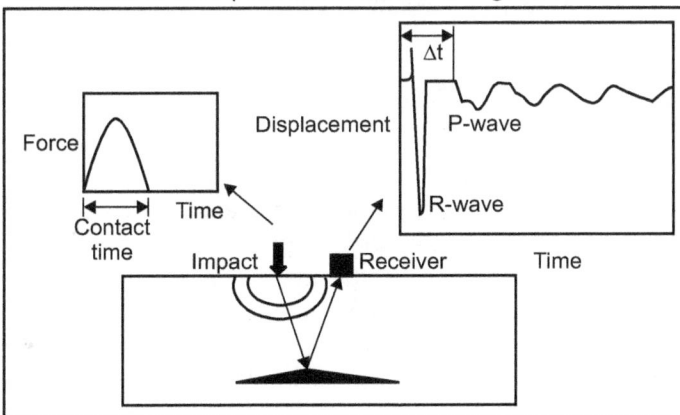

Fig. 5.6: Schematic of Test Using Impact to Generate Stress Waves

[B] DETERIORATION OF CONCRETE

5.2 Introduction

Though concrete is quite strong mechanically, it is highly susceptible to chemical attack and thus concrete structures get damaged and even fail unless some measures are adopted to counteract deterioration of concrete, and thereby increasing the durability of the concrete structures. The external (or environmental) agencies causing the loss of durability include weathering, attack by natural or industrial liquids and gases etc. Whereas, the internal agencies responsible for the absence of durability are harmful alkali-aggregate reactions, presence of sulphates and chlorides from the ingredients of concrete etc. In case of reinforced concrete the ingress of moisture or air may lead to the corrosion of steel and cracking and spalling of concrete cover. So the recommendations for making durable concrete usually envisage the limits for maximum water-cement ratio, thickness of cover, type of cement and the amounts of chlorides and sulphates in the concrete.

5.3 Permeability of Concrete

The flow of water through concrete is similar to flow through any porous body. The pores in cement paste consists of gel pores and capillary pores. Since the capillary pores are larger in size than gel pores, and the cement paste is 20 to 100 times more permeable than the gel itself, the permeability of cement paste is controlled by the capillary porosity of the paste. The permeability of cement paste also varies with the age of concrete or with hydration. With the age, permeability decreases because gel gradually fills the original water filled space. For the same water-cement ratio the permeability of paste with coarser cement particles is higher than those with finer cement. In general, the higher the strength of cement paste, the lower will be the permeability. A durable concrete should be relatively impervious.

5.3.1 Factors Affecting Permeability

The factors which affect the permeability of concrete are:
1. Cement and water.
2. Aggregate.
3. Curing.
4. Admixtures, and
5. Absorption and uniformity of concrete.

1. Cement and Water: The water-cement ratio and the consistency of concrete are inter-related. For pastes hydrated to the same degree, the permeability is lower the higher the cement content of the paste; that is the lower the water-cement ratio. Permeability decreases with the increase in the cement void ratio. For hand-rodded concrete the permeability increases when the water is reduced below that which will produce a slump of about 50 to 80 mm. With well cured concrete having the optimum quantity of mixing water, an increase of cement content above that in a 1 : 2 : 4 mix does not materially affect permeability. Finer the cement less is the permeability.

2. Aggregate: For a given water-cement ratio, greater the maximum size of aggregate, greater is the permeability. This is because of the relatively large voids. Well graded concrete reduces the permeability. Fig. 5.7 shows the effect of size of aggregate on permeability.

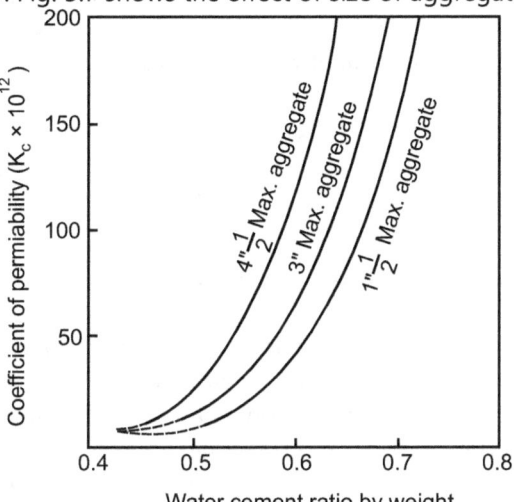

Fig. 5.7: Effect of Size of Aggregate on Permeability

3. Curing: Continued hydration of the cement results in the reduction in the size of voids which decreases the permeability. Water-tightness increases with curing. Well and undistributed curing decreases the permeability of concrete. Fig. 5.8 shows effect of curing period on permeability.

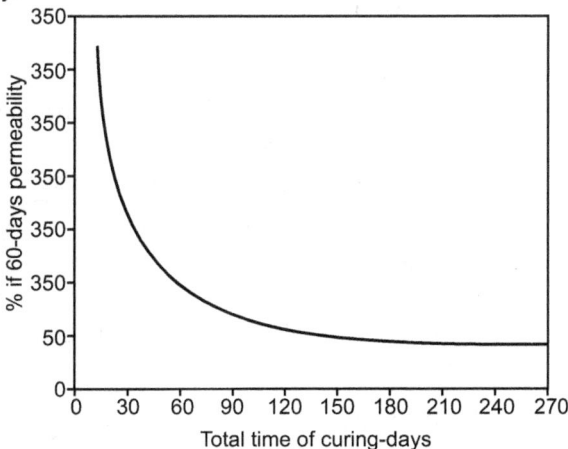

Fig. 5.8: Effect of Curing Period on Permeability

4. Admixtures: Any admixtures used to improve the water tightness of the concrete reduce the permeability. This is true for lean mix. In general, the use of extra-cement will be more effective than the use of other water-proofing admixtures. Sometimes the surface treatments reduce the leakage through porous concrete. Air-entraining agent does not affect the permeability appreciably.

5. Absorption and Uniformity of Concrete: Absorption is a physical process by which concrete draws water into its pores and capillaries. The absorption depends upon the structure of the concrete. The permeability is very sensitive to the structure of the concrete. Non-homogeneity affects the permeability. The defects in the concrete due to the cracks in the structure, void spaces due to separation or honeycombing increases the absorptions. To decrease the permeability. The mix should be workable so that segregation is avoided. But care is to be taken to see that the excess water and laitance do not accumulate at the surfaces of fresh concrete mass.

5.3.2 Measurement of Permeability In the Laboratory

The permeability of concrete can be measured in the laboratory by a simple test, but the results are mainly comparative. To determine the permeability under pressure, the inflow method or the outflow method may be used. In either case a cylindrical specimen is sealed at its curved surface inside a suitable metal container, so that water under pressure may be applied to the top flat surface only. Compressed air is often used to apply the pressure, but care must be taken to prevent air from being absorbed in the water, otherwise some of the air may be released under the reduced pressure inside the specimen and thus decrease the rate of flow. The quantity of water flowing through a given thickness of concrete in a given time is measured and the permeability is expressed as a coefficient of permeability which can be determined from the relation:

$$\frac{Q}{A} = K_c \cdot \frac{H}{L}$$

where,
Q = Rate of flow in cm^3/second.
A = The cross-sectional area of the sample in cm^2.
H = Drop in hydraulic head through the sample in cm.
L = Thickness of the sample in cm.
K_c = Coefficient of permeability in cm/sec.

5.3.3 The Permeability can be Reduced by

(i) Using adequate cement content.
(ii) Using lowest possible water-cement ratio.
(iii) Adopting proper compaction methods using full compaction.
(iv) Proper curing of concrete.

5.4 Durability of Concrete

A durable concrete is one which can withstand the conditions for which it has been designed, without deterioration over a period of years. Durability of concrete depends on its resistance to deterioration and the environment in which it is placed. Usually the concrete is durable, however, lack of durability may be due to the following factors:

(i) Use of inferior quality material.
(ii) Improper compaction and curing.
(iii) Improper cover to reinforcement.
(iv) Improper design and detailing.

The use of unsound cement may cause disintegration due to volume changes as some chemical actions are delayed. The unsound aggregates may react with atmospheric gases or may show alkali aggregate reactions with cement. The resistance of concrete to weathering, chemical attack, abrasion, frost and fire depends largely upon its quality and constituent materials.

Improper compaction and curing produces permeable concrete which may give an access to water which deteriorates the reinforcement and reduces the load carrying capacity of the member.

The other factors which make the concrete permeable are use of low cement content and high water-cement ratio. With strong, dense aggregates, a suitable low permeability can be achieved by having a sufficient low water-cement ratio, by ensuring as thorough compaction of concrete as possible and by ensuring sufficient hydration of cement through proper curing methods. By reducing the permeability of concrete, durability can be increased. The permeability can be reduced by using adequate cement content, using lowest-possible water-cement ratio, adopting proper compaction methods ensuring fall compaction, and proper curing of concrete.

The concrete cover to main reinforcement in any R.C.C. member is very important. Improper cover reduces bond and gives an access to water which corrods the reinforcement. Also if the concrete is exposed to severe exposure of chemical attack etc. the concrete cover should be increased.

The designing and detailing practice may be also sometimes responsible for disintegration of concrete. The crack width of concrete should not be more than 0.3 mm for normal structures. Based on this value; the reinforcement spacing etc. are recommended in IS : 456.

5.5 Chemical Attack

The resistance of concrete to attack by chemical agents is less than other forms of attack. The common forms of chemical attack are the leaching out of cement, and the action of sulphates, sea water and acidic water. The resistance of concrete varies with the types of cement and the resistance increases in the following order:

(a) Ordinary and rapid hardening portland cement.
(b) Low heat portland cement.
(c) Sulphate resisting cement.
(d) Super sulphate cement, and
(e) Alumina cement.

In hydraulic structures, water may leak through cracks or through areas of porous concrete. The water passing through the concrete dissolves some of the readily soluble calcium hydroxide and other solids and may cause serious disintegration of the concrete.

5.5.1 Sulphate Attack

The sulphates of sodium, magnesium and calcium are present in alkali soils and waters. These sulphates react chemically with the hydrated lime and hydrated calcium aluminate in the cement paste to form calcium sulphate and calcium sulphoaluminate. These reactions result in the expansion and disruption of the concrete. The deposition of sulphate crystals in the pores of the concrete tends to disintegrate the concrete. Alkali waters entering concrete may evapourate and deposit their salts. The growing crystals resulting from alternate wetting and drying may eventually fill the pores and develop pressures sufficient to disrupt the concrete. Resistance to disintegration is more in dense, impervious concrete having low water-cement ratio and containing entrained air.

The vulnerability of concrete to sulphate attack can be reduced by the use of low C_3A content cement. Use of pozzolans increases the resistance to sulphate attack. High pressure steam curing improves the resistance of concrete to sulphate attack. Addition of calcium chloride reduces the resistance to sulphate attack, whatever may be the type of cement used.

The resistance of concrete to sulphate attack can be tested by storing the specimens in a solution of sodium or magnesium sulphate or in a mixture of the two.

5.5.2 Chlorides Attack

Chloride exists in concrete as both bound and free ions, but only free chlorides directly affect the concrete. Chlorides may present in the concrete from several different sources. For example, soluble chlorides may be introduced in fresh concrete by the use of aggregates containing chlorides. Some cement may also contain small amount of chlorides. Chlorides may also enter the concrete from the environment. But the chloride ions in the concrete should be limited to its critical value to control the corrosion of reinforcement. Following table 5.1 gives the quantitative risk of concrete based on chloride content.

Table 5.1

Chloride content by mass cement (%)	Probability of corrosion
< 0.4	Low
0.4 – 1.0	Medium
> 1.0	High

Also, IS : 456-2000 has prescribed the limit of total amount of chloride in concrete (mass %) by mass of cement. However, for prestressed concrete the total amount of chloride ions in concrete should be limited to 0.06 per cent.

5.5.3 Acid Attack

Concrete structures are used in storing the liquids, some of which are harmful to the concrete. In industrial plants, concrete floors come in contact with liquids which damage the floor. Also, SO_2, CO_2 and other acid fumes present in the atmosphere affect concrete. Sewerage water also very slowly causes deterioration of concrete.

Acids first react with free lime of concrete forming calcium salts and later on attack the hydrosilicates and hydroaluminates forming the corresponding calcium salts, whose solubility will govern the extent of deterioration caused to the concrete. It is clear from Fig. 5.9, the hydrochloric acid corrodes the concrete to a greater extent in comparison to the sulphuric acid at low concentrations because H_2SO_4 forms a less soluble $CaSO_4$ on reacting with lime of concrete, which seals the pores of concrete for further permeation and offers resistance to acid corrosion. But at higher concentrations of H_2SO_4, the concrete strength is reduced due to accumulation of $CaSO_4$ in the pores.

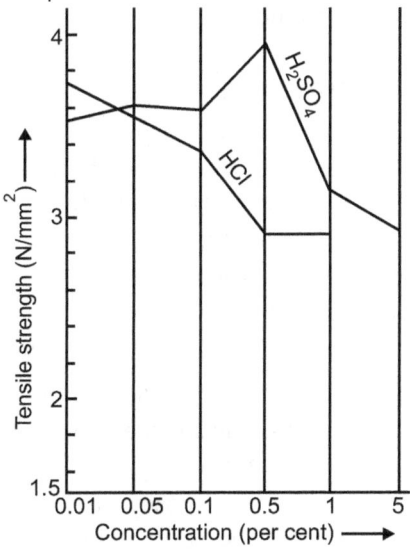

Fig. 5.9: Deterioration of Concrete Due to Acid Attack

5.5.4 Attack by Sea Water

Concrete in a sea water may suffer due to attack of dissolved chemicals on the product of hydration, crystalization of salts within the concrete under conditions of alternate wetting and drying, frost actions, mechanical attrition and impact by waves and corrosion of reinforcement embedded in it.

As discussed in the sulphate attack that magnesium sulphate reacts with free calcium hydroxide in set portland cement to form calcium sulphate and magnesium hydroxide. Magnesium sulphate reacts with hydrated calcium aluminate to form calcium sulpho-aluminate. These have been assumed to be the actions primarily responsible for the chemical attack of concrete by sea water.

It is assumed that concrete is not 100% impervious. The water that percolates into the concrete causes corrosion of steel. The product of corrosion being higher volume than the material they replace, exert pressure which results in lack of durability to reinforced concrete. Sea water holds certain quantity of sand and silt particularly in the shallow end. The velocity of wave actions causes abrasion of concrete. The impact and the mechanical force of wave action also contribute to the lack of durability of concrete. Effect of sea water is more severe on reinforced concrete than on plain concrete because of corrosion of reinforcement.

The resistance of concrete to sea water attack can be improved by:
(a) Using impervious and dense concrete. The rich concrete with low water-cement ratio makes the concrete impervious.
(b) Provision of adequate cover (generally 50 mm to 80 mm) of reinforced concrete.
(c) Adding to partial replacement of cement by pozzolana.
(d) Using high pressure steam curing.

5.6 Carbonation of Concrete

Now-a-days, concrete carbonation has been increased on account of increase in levels of environmental pollutants. Carbonation occurs in concrete because the calcium is attacked by CO_2 of the air and gets converted to calcium carbonate. Cement pastes contains 25-50% weight of calcium hydroxide, which means that the pH of fresh cement is at least 12.5. The pH of a full carbonated paste is about 7. The concrete will be carbonated if CO_2 from air or from water enters the concrete according to

$$Ca(OH)_2 + CO_2 \rightarrow CaCO_3 + H_2O$$

When $Ca(OH)_2$ is removed from the paste hydrated CSH will liberate CaO which will also carbonate. The chemical reaction starts at the surface and gradually goes within the concrete mass and is measured as depth of carbonation.

The rate of carbonation depends upon porosity, moisture content, quality of concrete, strength and environmental conditions. The carbonation process requires the presence of water because CO_2 dissolves in water forming H_2CO_3. If the cement is too dry (RH < 40%), CO_2 cannot dissolve and no carbonation occurs. If on the other hand, it is too wet (RH > 90%), CO_2 cannot enter the concrete and the carbonation will not occur. Optimum condition for carbonation occurs at RH 50% (in the range of 40 to 90%).

Carbonation of concrete improves the various characteristics of ordinary concrete as reduces the porosity, specific surface of cement paste and permeability, ultimately increases the resistance to sulphate attack. Normal carbonation results in a decrease of the porosity of non-reinforced concrete. However, it is disadvantage in reinforced concrete as pH of carbonated concrete drops to about 7, this value is below the passivation of threshold of steel.

Carbonation may be recognized in the field by the presence of a discoloured zone in the surface of the concrete. Carbonation can be visualized by using phenolphthalein.

The phenomenon of carbonation results for the chemical reaction of the lime in the concrete with CO_2 from the air to form $CaCO_3$. This reduces the alkalinity of the concrete. This chemical reaction starts at the surface and gradually goes within the concrete mass and is generally measured either in terms of depth of carbonate or in terms of colour changes.

The carbonation depth test is carried out in closed location to note the disinfection effect of carbonation on surface strength. This test is based on the principle of chemical reaction of the concrete surface to a phenolphthalein based straining agent. As the carbonation has its effect on pH of concrete, the change in colour indicates the extend of carbonation. This test is suitable for in service evaluation. For this, the test equipment comprises of a driller, container containing phenolphthalein based straining agent with a longer sprayer.

This test is conducted by drilling a hole in the surface to different depths upto cover concrete. Then spraying the phenolphthalein based spraying agent in the hole and observing the colour changes. This turns to pink colour when concrete is alkaline (pH above 8.3) but remains colourless when the concrete is fully carbonated. This method is reliable and fast method according to the concrete in any environment. It is independent of size, grade and location of R.C.C. member.

The result of carbonation test depends upon the environment conditions, change in the environment condition will affect the result. The following table 5.2 gives the carbonation depths for various grade of concrete based on some accelerated studies.

Table 5.2

Estimated 20 years carbonation depths for different grades of concrete		
Sr. No.	**Estimated 20 years depth (mm)**	**28 days compressive strength (N/mm^2)**
1	6	58.00
2	14	41.50
3	22	31.50
4	33	21.00

From above table, it is clear that the carbonation depths are less in high strength of concrete than in low strength concrete, all other parameters remaining the same.

5.7 Corrosion of Reinforcement

Concrete normally provides a high degree of protection against corrosion to steel reinforcement. This is because concrete inherently provides a highly alkaline environment for the steel which protects the steel against corrosion. In addition, concrete of low water-cement ratio and well cured has a low permeability which minimizes penetration of corrosion. If the concrete is of suitable quality, then corrosion of steel can be prevented, provided the structure is properly designed for the intended environmental exposure. The first evidence of corrosion is brown staining of the concrete around the embedded steel. This brown staining results from corrosion of steel without cracking of concrete. Sometimes, cracking of concrete occurs shortly because the corrosion products of steel (an iron oxide or rust) has a volume twice as much as that of metallic iron from which it is formed. The forces generated by this expansive process can far exceed the tensile strength of concrete with resulting cracking. Steel corrosion not only cause distress but may also cause structural failure resulting from the reduced cross-section and hence reduced tensile force capacity of the steel.

Steel corrosion can take place by several mechanisms but indirect oxidation of steel in concrete is believed to be the main cause of corrosion distress in concrete. This type of corrosion is termed *electrochemical corrosion*.

5.7.1 Mechanism of Electro-Chemical Corrosion

The metals have a tendency to oxidize to a metal ion in an aqueous solution of normal ionic activity at standard temperature. The ionization of metal i.e. oxidation of metal at the anode is often referred to as the primary stage of the corrosion reaction called *anodic reaction* and can be represented by

$$Fe \rightarrow Fe^{++} + 2e$$

This reaction results in the anodic region of the metal to have an excess of electrons. Therefore, to maintain equilibrium of electric charges an equivalent quantity of hydrogen is plated out at adjacent surfaces of the metal. This thin film of hydrogen around the cathode exhibits further progress of corrosion reaction, unless the hydrogen film is removed in some manner. The destruction of hydrogen film may take by oxygen depolarisation at the cathode or by evolution of hydrogen as a gas. These processes called *cathodic reactions* are usually represented by:

$$\frac{1}{2} O_2 + H_2O + 2e \rightarrow 2\,OH^-; \text{ or}$$

$$2H^+ + 2e^- \rightarrow H_2$$

These cathodic reactions which are often called the secondary reactions control the rate of corrosion of the structural steel. This chemical reactions are depicted in Fig. 5.10. Therefore, any environmental condition which influences these reaction will influence the rate of corrosion. Since cathodic depolarisation is dependent on the concentration of dissolved oxygen next to the metal, it is influenced by the degree of aeration, temperature, salt concentration etc. The secondary reactions permit the primary reaction to proceed with the accumulation of ferrous ion in the solution which in the presence of water and oxygen are oxidised and precipitated as rust.

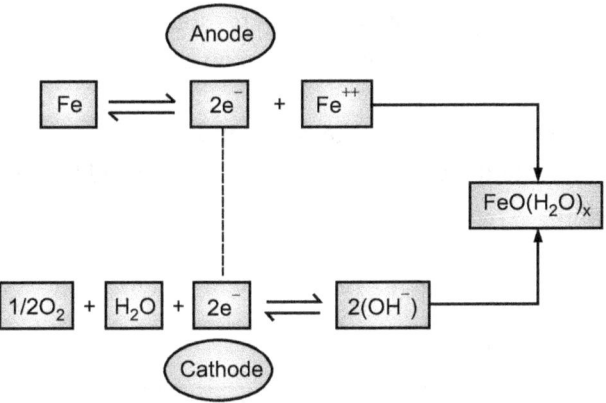

(a) Chemical reaction at anodic and cathodic area

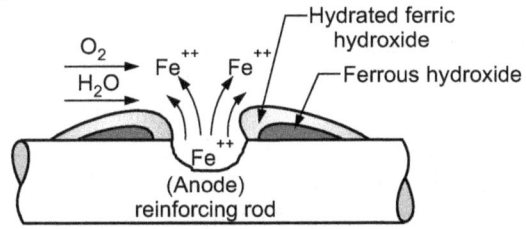

(b) Formation of rust at anodic region

Fig. 5.10: Chemical Reaction Resulting into The Formation Of Rust

However, two stages of oxidation may exist depending upon the availability of oxygen. The products of first stages namely ferrous hydroxide is more soluble than the second stage product i.e. hydrated ferric hydroxide. The first is formed directly at the metal surface and is converted to the latter at a little distance away from the surface where it is in contact with more oxygen as shown in Fig. 5.10.

The structure and composition of the rust varies considerably with the conditions prevailing during its formation and the structure of rust plays an important role in the subsequent corrosion process, for example, if the rust layer is hard, dry and fairly adherent to the metal surface, it may retard corrosion by forming a protective coating. On the other hand, if the rust layer is spongy and readily detachable, it will absorb oxygen and moisture from the surrounding media and consequently add to further corrosion.

The following methods are adopted to prevent the reinforcement from corrosion:

(a) Using adequate concrete cover. It is necessary to ensure that minimum required cover has been provided to all elements everywhere.

(b) Corrosion inhibitators are used as additives in concrete.

(c) Surface sealants are used on the surface of concrete (Silane, epoxy or methyl mithacrylate).

(d) Reinforcements are coated with corrosion resistant material.
(e) Cathodic protection (Powerful method to stop corrosion in salt contaminated bridge decks).

The reinforcement coating include the following:
(a) Cement slurry coating (adopted on sites by using skilled labours).
(b) Polymer coating.
(c) Galvanised coating.
(d) Fusion bonded epoxy coating.

Exercise

1. List various destructive and non-destructive tests to be conducted on hardened concrete.
2. (a) State and explain the factors affecting the permeability of concrete.
   (b) How the permeability of concrete is measured in the laboratory ?
   (c) How the permeability of concrete can be reduced ?
3. (a) What do you mean by Carbonation of Concrete ?
   (b) How carbonation of concrete can be determined ?
   (c) Explain in detail corrosion of reinforcement.
4. Write a note on :
   (i) Pull-out test
   (ii) Pulse velocity method
   (iii) Non-destructive testing on concrete.
   (iv) Permeability of concrete.
   (v) Durability of concrete.
   (vi) Sulphate attack on concrete.
   (vii) Acid attack on concrete.
   (viii) Attack by sea water.

CONCRETE TECHNOLOGY (SE - NMU)   UNIVERSITY QUESTION PAPER

University Question Paper
March 2015

Time : Three Hours   **Max. Marks: 80**

Instructions to Candidates:
1. *Do not write anything on question paper except Seat No.*
2. *Graph or diagram should be drawn with the black ink pen being used for writing paper or black HB pencil.*
3. *Students should note, no supplement will be provided.*
4. *Neat diagrams must be drawn wherever necessary.*
5. *Figures to the right indicate full marks.*

UNIT I

1. (a) Describe the manufacture of Portland cement. In what way does it differ from rapid hardening element. **[08]**

    (b) (i) Explain the term grading of aggregate. Explain its effect on properties of concrete. **[04]**

        (ii) Write a short note on compressive strength of cement. **[04]**

    (c) What do you mean by alkali aggregate reaction? State the factors promoting alkali aggregate reaction. What are the measures of controlling alkali aggregate reaction. **[08]**

UNIT II

2. (a) What is the importance of compaction of concrete? What are the different methods of compaction. **[08]**

    (b) Explain the difference between bleeding and segregation and state measures to be taken to avoid each. **[08]**

    (c) Write short notes on: **[08]**
        (i) Under water concreting
        (ii) Methods of batching

UNIT III

3. (a) (i) What are the advantages of light weight concrete? **[04]**

        (ii) What is polymer concrete? Write its application in concrete world? **[04]**

    (b) What is high performance concrete? Explain the role of course aggregate, paste characteristics and interfacial bond between them in high performance concrete. **[08]**

(c) (i) Write a short note on 'Ferro cement'. [04]

(ii) Write a short note on 'Pumping of concreting'. [04]

UNIT IV

4. (a) Explain the terms, target mean strength and characteristics compressive strength in case of concrete mix design. State the relationship and factor affecting it. [08]

(b) Define M.20 Name the different methods of concrete mix design and explain the I.S. guidelines for concrete mix design. [08]

(c) (i) Explain factors affecting the choice of mix proportions. [04]

(ii) Enlist the basic data required for mix design. [04]

UNIT V

5. (a) Write a short note on: [08]

(i) Pull out test.

(ii) Non destructive testing on concrete.

(b) (i) What the symptoms of distress of concrete? [04]

(ii) Now distress of concrete can be diagnosed? [04]

(c) (i) Write a short note on "Carbonation of concrete'? [04]

(ii) State the types and causes of cracks in concrete. [04]

■■■

www.ingramcontent.com/pod-product-compliance
Lightning Source LLC
Chambersburg PA
CBHW081918170426
43200CB00014B/2760